GIBLIN'S PLATOON
THE TRIALS AND TRIUMPHS OF THE ECONOMIST
IN AUSTRALIAN PUBLIC LIFE

GIBLIN'S PLATOON
THE TRIALS AND TRIUMPHS OF THE ECONOMIST IN AUSTRALIAN PUBLIC LIFE

WILLIAM COLEMAN   SELWYN CORNISH   ALF HAGGER

E PRESS

Published by ANU E Press
The Australian National University
Canberra ACT 0200, Australia
Email: anuepress@anu.edu.au
Web: http://epress.anu.edu.au

National Library of Australia
Cataloguing-in-Publication entry

Coleman, William, 1959- .

Giblin's platoon: the trials and triumph of the economist in Australian public life.

Bibliography.
Includes index.
ISBN 9 20942491 1.
ISBN 9 20942505 5 (online).

1. Economists - Australia. I. Cornish, Selwyn. II. Hagger, A. J. (Alfred James). III. Title.

330.994

All rights reserved. No part of this publication may be reproduced, stored in a retrieval system or transmitted in any form or by any means, electronic, mechanical, photocopying or otherwise, without the prior permission of the publisher.

Indexed by Robin Ward.
Cover design by Brendon McKinley.
Cover image: *Professor Lyndhurst F. Giblin* © Estate of William Dobell. Licensed by Viscopy, Sydney, 2006.

This edition © 2006 ANU E Press - reprinted with corrections October 2006

L. F. Giblin 1872–1951

J. B. Brigden 1887–1950

D. B. Copland 1894–1970

Roland Wilson 1904–1996

'The civilisation of a country may be judged from its statistics.'
    L. F. Giblin

'Australian history is, of course, largely economic history.'
    D. B. Copland

'Economists are heretics.'
    J. B. Brigden

'A man of stature and personality can hardly be said to die.'
    Roland Wilson

Table of Contents

Preface:	ix
Acknowledgements:	xi
List of abbreviations:	xiii
Note on archival sources:	xv
1. Tasmanian genesis:	1
2. Building:	31
3. Gold and capital:	45
4. Economic science and political power:	59
5. Giblin and Keynes:	85
6. The Great Depression and the battle for inflation:	107
7. Open letters and private correspondence:	131
8. The seven-pointed star:	149
9. In war and peace:	175
10. The last ridge:	207
References	239
Index	255

List of Figures

1.1. Giblin (bearded), among 'The Elect', on his return from British Columbia 12
1.2. Captain Giblin, still with 'socialist beard' 17
1.3. Eilean Giblin (second from left) with Australian suffragettes, Rome 1923 20
2.1. Wilson about to depart for Oxford 43
4.1. Copland dazzles in Melbourne 62
4.2. 'The Brigden Condition' 81
4.3. The impact of a tariff under the Brigden assumption 81
4.4. 'The Sidgwick Assumption' 82
4.5. The impact of a tariff under the Sidgwick Assumption 83
4.6. The Minimum Population for a Tariff to be Wage Improving 84
7.1. Giblin with young friends 146
8.1. Giblin at his desk 166
8.2. Brigden at his desk 167
8.3. Copland at his desk 168
8.4. Wilson at his desk 169
8.5. One of 1.7 million pamphlets issued to win public favour for the ill-starred National Insurance scheme 172
9.1. Brigden (left), as Secretary of Munitions sharing a platform with R. G. Menzies 180
9.2. Wilson at the time of the United Nations San Francisco conference 204
10.1. Copland (centre) in charge at the Australian National University. 219
10.2. Copland and Medley (at left) as friends on the Council of the Australian National University 220
10.3. The Dobell Giblin was expecting 234

List of Tables

5.1. Multiplier concepts from c. 1930 94
8.1. Giblin's taxation comparisons 155
8.2. Comparison of grants recommended by the Commonwealth Grants Commission with grants implied by a *per capita* schema, $m, 2005-06 158

Preface

This book tells the story of four men – L. F. Giblin, J. B. Brigden, D. B. Copland and Roland Wilson – who, in 1920s Tasmania, formed a personal and intellectual bond that was to prove a pivot of economic thought, policy-making and institution-building in mid-century Australia.

The book seeks to supply in words the group photograph that, sadly, seems not to exist. In our book, as in the hypothetical wished-for photograph, L. F. Giblin stands firmly at the centre, glaring at the observer, the focus of our attention, implicitly commanding the following of the others. Copland stands loyally, close by his right hand; Brigden is at his left, a bit further away, as if seeking a little space; and Wilson stands between Brigden and Giblin, directly contemplating the onlooker with a cool, sceptical expression.

Our photograph does not seek to glamorise or sentimentalise: it allows a stark light to fall on any unattractive surface. But it does allow the subjects to arrange themselves, so that they reveal what they chose, even if they did not realise they were revealing it.

The photograph has an arresting background; one that explains why it has been taken at all. For the story told here is larger than that of the four lives. It is the story of the advent of the economist in Australian public life. A more extensive telling of this tale would involve others, including E. O. G. Shann, L. G. Melville and H. C. Coombs. But these persons either leave early, or join late. It is our four who lead the advance, endure reversals, and finally consolidate the position.

This arrival of the economist was a pregnant development in Australian history. It has been deplored, celebrated and mythified. But less often understood. It stands outside the three foci of Australian history-writing: material history (exploration, technology, and business), political history and social history (overwhelmingly, labour history) and cultural history. Our story cuts across all of these – labour history especially – but has at its core a report of intellectual achievements, which were strong enough to anticipate and stimulate the leading currents in economic thinking across the world.

We are, then, providing a piece of Australian intellectual history that has not been properly valued. In doing this we are paying a tribute to one of the central themes of Giblin and his platoon: that Australia was more than it seemed, to its inhabitants and foreigners alike. And, if this truth were realised, could be still more than it was.

William Coleman
Selwyn Cornish
Alf Hagger

Acknowledgements

We gratefully acknowledge the donors of the generous financial assistance to the costs of research which made this book possible.

- The Reserve Bank of Australia
- The College of Business and Economics of the Australian National University
- The School of Economics of the Australian National University
- The University of Tasmania

We would also like to express our debt to several persons.

Professor Michael Roe was actively consulted throughout the research of the book, and attentively read the entire manuscript. Ian Castles gave us the benefit of his marvellous knowledge of detail and documentary sources, and, as guardian of the Roland Wilson Archives, kindly put these at our disposal.

We also thank Marjorie Harper for participation in a workshop on part of the manuscript, and for granting us access to some documents of which she is custodian; and Peter Karmel and Cristina Marcuzza for presenting to and participating in other workshops on the manuscript.

We also thank Paul Samuelson for his permission to use some correspondence, Craufurd Goodwin for drawing our attention to some interesting Bloomsbury connections, Kaye Fenton for preparing a meticulous and near-exhaustive bibliography of the four at the beginning of our research, and Frank Hytten for his hospitality and memories.

We give our special thanks to Lady Joyce Wilson for providing us, and giving us permission to use, the several photographs of Sir Roland Wilson.

And we thank John Ancher for his assistance with the archives of The Hutchins School, and Rosalind Moad for her assistance with the archives of Wycombe Abbey School.

We also thank the staff of:

- the Australian National University Archives
- the Bank of England Archives
- the King's College Library Archives
- the London School of Economics Archives
- the National Library of Australia Manuscript Collection
- the Reserve Bank of Australia Archives
- the Archives of Tasmania
- the University of Melbourne Archives
- the University of Tasmania Archives

List of abbreviations

Individuals

LFG Lyndhurst Falkiner Giblin
DBC Douglas Berry Copland
JBB James Bristock Brigden
RW Roland Wilson
AWF Arthur William Fadden
EMG Edith M. Giblin
HCC Herbet Cole (Nugget) Coombs
HSN Harold Sprent Nicholas
JAL Joseph Aloysius Lyons
JMK John Maynard Keynes
JR John Reynolds
KHB Kenneth H. Bailey
LGM Leslie Galfreid Melville
PS Percy Spender
RGC Richard Gardiner Casey
RGM Robert Gordon Menzies
RK Raymond Kershaw
WKH William Keith Hancock

Newspapers, organisations, books

ABC Australian Broadcasting Corporation
CWJMK The Collected Writings of John Maynard Keynes
NZDB New Zealand Dictionary of Biography
SMH Sydney Morning Herald

Archives and records

ANUA Australian National University Archives
AWM Australian War Memorial
DAFTHP Department of Foreign Affairs and Trade Historical Publications
FUL Ingamells Collection, Flinders University Library
JCPML John Curtin Prime Ministerial Library

KCLA Keynes Papers, King's College Library Archives

LSE Cannan Papers, London School of Economics Archives

NAA National Archives of Australia

NLA Manuscript Collection, National Library of Australia

PRO Public Records Office

RBA Papers of Governors and Senior Personnel, records in the custody of the Reserve Bank of Australia Archives

RWA Roland Wilson Archives

UMA Faculty of Commerce and Economics Papers, University of Melbourne Archives

Note on archival sources

The archival abbreviations noted above are used in the text to refer to items drawn from these collections.

Any archival reference will begin with the abbreviation of the archives, followed by an abbreviation of the 'creator' of the collection of papers being referred to. So,
NLA JAL
indicates an item which is part of the Joseph Aloysius Lyons papers in the Manuscript Collection of the National Library of Australia. If the author of the item referred to is not the 'creator' of the collection in which it is held, then the initials of the author are appended. For example,
NLA JAL:LFG
denotes an item authored by Lyndhurst Falkiner Giblin which is part of the Joseph Aloysius Lyons papers in the Manuscript Collection of the National Library of Australia.

Where only one collection in an archive is used, the abbreviation for the 'creator' of the collection is dropped. So, for example, as only the Keynes collection of the King's College Library Archives is used
KCLA LFG
denotes an item authored by Lyndhurst Falkiner Giblin which is part of the Keynes collection of the King's College Library Archives.

1. Tasmanian genesis

'It started – as always, with him – in Tasmania'
Roland Wilson

Giblin

3.00 pm, 2 March 1951, Hobart. The cremation of Lyndhurst Falkiner Giblin. This is a ceremony without Christian rites. Instead of a priest – Giblin could not abide a 'parson' at his funeral – a Norwegian economist friend gives the homily. The god-fearing relatives of the Giblin clan glower from the benches. From the gramophone sounds a Bach Fugue treasured by Giblin. His brother reads from Tennyson's *Ulysses*,

> I cannot rest from travel …
> Beyond the utmost bound of human thought

Thus passes the mortal frame of L. F. Giblin, one of Australia's great originals. Warrior, sage, and peacemaker; explorer, politician and poetaster; rationalist, stoic and mystery – the strange hero of an unexpected tale.

The Australia that Giblin departed in 1951 was much changed from the one he entered on 29 November 1872. Until the end of that year all news of the outside world still came to Australia by ship. Truganini lived in Macquarie Street, Hobart. Convicts guarded by Red Coats still laboured in nearby Port Arthur. No child was required to attend school in any part of Australia. The continent was a brood of six jealous colonies. Midday was differently observed in Hobart, Melbourne and Sydney; dozens of different bank notes circulated; and six miniature colonial armies and navies kept guard against indistinct threats.

By the time of Giblin's death a single federal government had by design, expedience and rude hammering been forged from the colonies, and now contentedly assumed all the prerogatives of sovereign power. On a rabbit-ridden, treeless plain a national capital had been raised. A national university endowed. A central bank created. And economics – which at the time of Giblin's birth had been a matter of words (speeches, and volumes) – had now become a matter of numbers (statistics, 'multipliers'); people (students, professors, chief economists); and institutions (departments, bureaus, treasuries). A discipline had been spawned and its senior members took an eminent place in the counsels of the newly created state. That discipline was thick with Giblin's former students, present colleagues, and protégés. This was his bequest.

Giblin's inheritance will help us to understand his bequest.

In 1827 Giblin's great-grandfather, Robert Wilkins Giblin, had arrived in Hobart Town on the *Sir Charles Forbes* in the company of his eight children and 73 female convicts. Robert Wilkins stepped ashore a ruined man. The school he had run in England had failed in the banking crash of 1825. He was starting again, the hard way. He would do what he did his entire life: teach. Within a few weeks he had opened a school that promised 'frequent lectures on Astronomy, the mechanical powers, hydraulics, pneumatics, electricity, chemistry, etc., etc.'. A surer means of income was found when Lt-Gov. Arthur made him principal of the new Kings Orphan School, a school created by the benevolent patronage of the Governor. Another outlet of Giblin's energies was the new Hobart Mechanics Institute, also patronised by Arthur. Giblin taught with 'success'.[1]

What we see in the great-grandfather are three poles of attraction in his great grandson: science, education, and youth. A fourth pole – public service in public life – only becomes apparent in later generations. Robert Wilkins's son, Thomas, fathered Edward Owen Giblin (1849–95), who fought in miniature the battle for sanitation undertaken by Edwin Chadwick in London in the preceding generation. When Edward Owen was appointed Health Officer to Hobart Town, the Hobart Rivulet was a sewer – both literally and officially. And the prevailing system of cesspits spelt typhoid and diphtheria. Edward Owen recommended the prohibition of cesspits to the City Council and the introduction of night soil removal and sewers. The Alderman resisted. The Alderman yielded. The *Public Health (Hobart) Act* of 1884 phased out cesspits. Edward Owen could later report that, in one particular row of 15 tenements where typhoid had appeared regularly, it was now 'banished'.

Edward Owen also maintained a busy medical practice. It is presumably out of a debt to Edward Owen in some matter of life and limb that a Hobart schoolmaster decided in 1884 to christen his youngest son, Edward Owen Giblin Shann (1884-1935). Fifty years later, when Australia struggled for breath in the Depression, Edward Owen Giblin Shann and L. F. Giblin were invested with an equal trust to advise on the relief of the economy. This is how one of the most renowned economists of the 1930s Australia bore, as an unlikely middle name, the surname of the most renown.[2]

---

[1] This is the judgement of Mowle (1943). It is not the judgement of all. At Newtown a committee of Giblin's determined adversaries composed an indictment against him, and stretched themselves to include the charge that Giblin had allowed his pupils to gather wood alone, and thereby be exposed to communication with convicts. Giblin was, however, also charged with striking a boy 'six times right and left with his doubled fist about the head and face' (Robson 1983, p. 283). Giblin had no effective reply to this accusation. He was dismissed in 1832. The family's interpretation of these events is provided in W.W. Giblin (1945).

[2] Shann and Giblin were to work together, notably in preparing the 'Premiers' Plan', but they were not close. Shann in Giblin's view was 'too much of a clever talker'. In 1935 Giblin blandly wrote to

Robert Wilkins Giblin had also fathered a William Giblin. His son William Robert Giblin (1840–87) became Attorney-general, Treasurer, Premier, Chief-justice of Tasmania – and father of Lyndhurst Falkiner Giblin.[3] This son was christened 'Lyndhurst', in an unexpected – even eccentric – tribute to the Lord Chancellor of the Wellington and Peel governments, Lord Lyndhurst.[4] The 'Falkiner' commemorated William Robert's mother who died shortly after William Robert's birth.

From the beginning of his adult life William Robert had been 'dedicated to the moral and social elevation of the underprivileged'. He was president and founder of the Hobart Working Men's Club. He promoted football leagues to fight larrikinism and vandalism. He taught in the Sunday School. He won the goodwill of Hobart, and with that, won a seat in the House of Assembly. He became Premier for a total of 67 months in two periods between 1878–84 and provided the first spell of stable government the colony had enjoyed. As Premier he was beyond the call of any single interest and drew talent wherever he could find it (including one of the architects of Federation, Andrew Inglis Clark). A 'liberal by conviction, in sympathy with [the] English advanced Liberal Party' (Walker 1976, p. 8), William Robert broadened the franchise and restrained expenditure. His horizons were expansive for an introverted colony and he pressed the merit of annexing Papua on an indifferent Tasmanian public. London's disapproval of this project prompted the formation of the Federal Council of 1883 – one

---

his wife, Eilean, 'You heard of course of Shann's death – I forget if I commented on it. The reports were rather obscure, but it seems pretty certain that he killed himself – threw himself from the window' (RBA LFG 3 July 1935). In the same letter, Giblin spends some emotion on the death of one of his student peers at Cambridge, William Harrison Moore (1867–1935), the diplomat and constitutional lawyer who had a major role in shaping the Statute of Westminster.

[3] William Robert Giblin's first son was William Leslie Giblin (1867–1901), who died in the service of US Army Medical Corps. The third son, Alan Vincent, followed his father's career in law. He served in the Boer War and it is said that it is his likeness that features in the Boer War Memorial Statue in Hobart.

[4] A son of an American artist, Lord Lyndhurst was a wrangler at Cambridge, who first came to public notice in 1817 in defending the would-be revolutionist 'Dr' James Watson from charges of high treason. Lyndhurst, at that point, was a republican, even 'jacobin', but, as a result of his trial performance the Tories discovered his merit, and apparently soon after, he theirs. He was awarded a series of legal positions by Tory governments, and keenly defended all their reactionary measures. He combined this with a strenuous support of the admission of Jews into parliament and the rights of women. In his eighties Lyndhurst occupied himself with kite flying and translating the Greek Fathers on the topic of divorce. Perhaps one may detect in this choice an attraction to the eccentric that was conspicuous in his son, but not otherwise manifested in the father's sturdy self-presentation.

landmark in the journey to Federation – and Giblin represented Tasmania. Alfred Deakin, in retrospect, judged Giblin as 'too big for the colony'.[5]

With his brilliant intellect, elevated character, and public standing, William Robert Giblin must have been an extraordinary – perhaps overwhelming – example to the young Lyndhurst.[6]

But Giblin's father and forefathers also unwittingly endowed Giblin with one pole of disapproval – formal religion. Robert Wilkins was a godly man. And he raised in his sons the same consciousness. One witness of Thomas Giblin's household in the 1870s recalled: 'Religious instruction was strictly observed by family prayers every morning, at which the whole family and staff attended, and regular attendance at Church twice every Sunday' (Giblin 1945). Thomas's brother William was a deacon in the Congregational church. William's son, William Robert, once won £10 for a poem on the conversion of St Paul 'in a well contested competition', and was active in the affairs in the same faith as his father. Those were confident days in the history of Australian Congregationalism, a denomination founded in Tasmania in 1823, and by now extended to all colonies, claiming James Fairfax (of the *Sydney Morning Herald*) amongst its brethren. This Australian Congregationalism was robustly evangelical, scriptural and proud of its affinity with the obstinate Puritan dissidents of earlier centuries.

Befitting his upbringing, Giblin 'knew his Bible well' (Earp 1960);[7] there are numerous biblical allusions in the writings of Giblin. But almost all of them are ironical. Raised a Bible-Christian, Giblin became at some point a sceptic, a scoffer, an atheist. There seems to have been no particular occasion for this drastic transition. Certainly, he was not personally made for Puritanism – enjoyment came too easily to him. Late in life he recalled from his childhood a tiny act of moral rebellion. At a public banquet held at his home and presided over by his father: 'we [Giblin children] lurked in the background and devoured countless jellies, and after the cousins had withdrawn I shocked the virtuous cousins by

---

[5] The climax of William Robert's career was his 90-minute address to the House of Assembly in 1884 recommending the House's assent to a Federation Resolution. It reads well today. One witness recorded: 'It had to my mind the tone of the speech of an English Cabinet Minister, in the House of Commons, than the sort one is accustomed to from Australian politicians, even the most eminent' (Walker 1976, p. 2).

[6] Not to mention William Robert's apple orcharding, strenuous physical exertion and love of poetry, all perennials in his son's life.

[7] Giblin once passed judgement on the Book of Judges (8: 4–8), where Gideon is instructed to choose every man that 'lappeth of the water with his tongue as a dog lappeth'. 'Men do not, in fact, lap with their tongues, as dogs lap, in any circumstances' (Giblin in Copland 1960, p. 143).

draining the wine cups, some of them left half full'.[8] He chided his sister: 'From what little I understand of Christianity I should say that the spirit that prefers reading the bible to giving innocent enjoyment to children is not Christian' (RBA LFG 18 June 1892).

In the larger picture, Congregationalism was to go into a general decline during Giblin's lifetime. And Giblin found in the mainstream of Protestantism nothing more satisfactory.[9] More generally, historians of religion have stressed that around the time of Giblin's birth in 1872, 'God died'. Giblin was one particle of the surge of 'liberalism and modernism' and *fin-de-siecle* 'paganism'. His rebellion against formal religion was an important element in his anti-Victorianism.

But Giblin's spiritual education left one deep imprint: the ethic of selflessness. It was said of him that, although 'he hated religion', 'there was no one more "christian" in his outlook than he was ... He was always ready to help and never asked for a reward' (Hytten 1951). It was this ethic that prompted him once to expostulate: 'The ego, the distempered devil of the self ... There is the enemy' (Giblin in Copland 1960, p. 129). It was the ethic that incited him to hail George Borrow – of *The Bible in Spain* – 'as a kindred spirit' (Earp 1960, p.15). It was the same ethic that left Giblin 'happy' when his sister announced her intention to be a missionary.[10]

If Giblin's spiritual education had left an imprint, Giblin's secular education was also pressed. Colonial Tasmania – contrary to common presumption – excelled in humane inquiry, and prospered as a consequence of its official connections in that regard. Dr Thomas Arnold of Rugby school fame had, at the solicitation of his friend the Governor, Sir John Franklin, taken pains from afar to nurture the seed of education in the infant society. Franklin himself founded the Scientific Society, whose journal *Tasmanian Journal of Natural Science* was of 'astonishing competence' (Serle 1973). In 1844, Franklin's vice-regal successor founded the Royal Society of Tasmania, the oldest Royal Society outside Great Britain. The

---

[8] Would his virtuous father also have been shocked? Another lifelong memory hints at a difference in temperament between father and son. Giblin had been climbing bull-oak trees at Browns River for birds' nests. 'I had made up an apocryphal story, which I thought very funny, depending upon a confusion of 'Bull-oak' and 'bloke', which Father received very coldly. (The chilly reception must have made a deep impression)' (RBA LFG 11 November 1948).

[9] 'If you can keep up the idea of calm reverence in an English church then you and I are made different. There are beautiful things in abundance of course. But never, not even at the Abbey, where conditions are most favourable, have I sat through it without being jarred in half-a dozen places; most of all by the general sinkage of all meaning before the exigencies of the music, and the miserable affected tones of the parson.' (RBA LFG 20 September 1892).

[10] Giblin in his old age held that Puritanism 'did something for people that was fine and big and you want to be able to appreciate it'.

arts also prospered. John Glover experienced a reinvigorated artistic impulse upon his arrival in Tasmania and benefited from the development in Hobart of 'an appreciative group of patrons of painting executed for the pleasure of local residents'. The Hobart Mechanics Institute, the oldest in Australia, gave lectures, entitled 'Perception of the Beautiful'. 'A tiny cultural elite was gathering and recognizing itself' (Serle 1973, p. 14).

The Tasmanian cultural elite sought a worthy education for its sons and found it in one of Franklin's posthumous but enduring bequests, the Hutchins School, which became the pre-eminent institution of education in Tasmania. Lynd was conspicuously bright – 'far cleverer' his father believed, than Lyndhurst's elder brother, who was to win a scholarship to Oxford.[11] Shortly before finally succumbing to heart disease at the age of 46, William Robert spoke of his own lack of education as his greatest regret in life. William Robert would not allow Lynd to be deprived of its benefit.

Giblin attended Hutchins between 1881 and 1889. He won all the prizes. He was Exhibitioner, Dry Scholar, and the sole 'Associate of Arts First Class'.[12] One other distinction won there proved of lifelong significance. In 1860 Tasmania's Council of Education had instituted an annual examination in imitation of the new 'local examinations' of Cambridge and Oxford. The best two candidates were awarded £200 per annum for four years to enable their attendance at a British university. In 1889 Giblin won.

Giblin enrolled in the University of London in 1890. Science was his focus. He studied Physics, Zoology and Comparative Anatomy, Mathematics, and Applied Mathematics and Mechanics. In the battle between Classics and Moderns, Giblin was evidently on the side of the Moderns. Within the university, intellectual leadership was centred in the driven, brilliant and somewhat eccentric figure of Karl Pearson[13] (or Carl Pearson as he was until a sojourn in Germany prompted him to germanicise his name). Pearson was just about to complete *The grammar of science* and coin the term 'standard deviation'. He was also a follower of the eugenic principles of his mentor Francis Galton and was committed to the idea

---

[11] In 1887 a future Vice-Chancellor of the University of Tasmania recorded in his diary: 'I see a good deal of Lyndhurst (Giblin) now. He certainly is a clever boy – and remarkably advanced for his age. He is now in my Bible class, and often surprises me by his grasp of things, which one would hardly expect a boy of 14 to have any ideas about' (Walker 1976, p. 46).

[12] In 1933 Giblin wrote to Hutchins school to oppose the erection of a school chapel (RBA LFG 27 October 1933). A little later he was to tell the headmaster of Geelong Grammar, Sir James Darling, that he was irritated by the school's Anglican Service. To his amusement Darling replied: 'Well all I can see is for you to come and be school chaplain. I don't mind what your religion is' (RBA LFG 4 April 1935).

[13] Giblin was invited to attend Pearson's funeral service in 1936.

that procreation should utilise superior stock, and superior stock were largely determined by physique. Giblin studied under the direction of Pearson and these eugenic principles lingered in Giblin's mind.[14]

After three years Giblin left the University of London without a degree and entered Kings College, Cambridge. What occasioned this move is unknown. Perhaps the good offices of Pearson, a Kingsman, assisted him.

At King's Giblin was happy. Many years later he composed an affectionate memoir: 'A Day at Cambridge. Lent Term, King's College, 189-'. It is a description of a busy round of simple pleasures: his favourite beer, launching a row boat on the Cam among the snow flakes, singing in a college where 'every second man had his piano'.[15] It is almost cosy.

He later traced his acquisition of his musical tastes back to King's.[16] But the life of the mind is almost absent from this memoir. He reports attending a lecture by 'a very distinguished mathematician but the worst lecturer in the world'. The impression is that the high points are fellowship, not thought. The excellence Giblin pursued was physical. Six feet tall and weighing 14 stone (Earp 1960), Giblin was a star on the rugby football field. He played for Kings, the University XV, and then became a 'famous International' playing for England. But he left Cambridge with second class honours.[17]

In considering his record at Cambridge the issue that comes to mind is the lost opportunity for the future economist. In the 1890s Cambridge was the foremost centre in the world for the theoretical study of economics. A Moral Sciences Tripos (that is, a social sciences degree) had been established since 1851, and reformed in 1889. A chair had existed since 1828 and was now filled by Alfred

---

[14] It is significant that an early issue of the *Economic Record* includes a savage and absurd eugenicist plea by the first teacher of economics at the University of Tasmania, Jethro Brown. He declares: 'Rational selection may supplement the operation of natural selection. I do not mean to suggest that a scientist should go around with an axe and a bath, smashing half the men and drowning half the women. Such loose measures might attain good results. But that sort of thing is not done in polite society' (Brown 1927). Polite society could, however, make a medical certificate of 'fitness to marry' a compulsory prerequisite for marriage and arrange 'the segregation or sterilisation of obviously defective types'. The fact that Brown also recommends a 'living wage' and 'child endowment' (as means of encouraging the fit to breed) is a reminder that eugenics was a thing of hope for 'progressives' of the period.

[15] Giblin records his dissatisfaction at the beef served at King's. He explains its poor quality by the fact that rural tenants of King's were allowed to pay their rent in kind, rather than cash. 'Under these circumstances it was to be expected that the College would get what the market rejected'.

[16] His musical tastes were 'romantic': the later Beethoven, Brahms, Sibelius.

[17] Or, more properly, 'Senior Optime'. Giblin took his BA in 1896. He waited until 1928 to convert it to an MA.

Marshall, who was rolling out courses on production, distribution, free trade and protection. There was a demand for students with the capacity for analytical thought. And Marshall was glad for 'postgraduates' (such as Giblin was) to take the Moral Sciences Tripos. J. N. Keynes, the father of J. M. Keynes, was one such postgraduate who did.

But Giblin did not take the Moral Sciences Tripos, and he did not come to the attention of Marshall.

Cambridge did, nevertheless, bestow on Giblin one prize of an intellectual character: an entrée into one of most powerful cultural coteries of the 20th century - Bloomsbury. But the initial connection was not through any acquaintances at King's, or even Cambridge.[18] Instead, it came through a circuitous route beginning with a London literary figure who never attended Cambridge, E. V. Lucas (1868–1938). An essayist and *Punch* humorist, Lucas attended the University of London in Giblin's last year, and presumably here their lifelong friendship was formed. Lucas also presumably introduced Giblin to his collaborator Edward Garnett (1868–1937), who was to become another of Giblin's friends. A few years older than Giblin, Garnett had already established himself in London as a thoroughly modern *auteur* of socialism, Fabianism, Nietzscheianism. On the lookout for any new creative spirit, Garnett and Lucas had become the 'agents', patrons, editors and friends of Henry Lawson, then struggling in London, and whom Garnett felt was a 'scandalously neglected' talent. Another neglected talent was Dostoevsky, whom Garnett, with his wife Constance, largely introduced to the English reading public.

Edward and Constance had a son, David, or 'Bunny', later to loom large in the lives of Duncan Grant and Vanessa Bell. Born in 1892, the infant David 'loved' Giblin, whose visits were encouraged by distant family connections. Garnett recalled a walking party of 1897 composed of his parents, aunts and uncles, Prince Kropotkin – Constance was a dedicated supporter of Russian revolutionaries – and Giblin. Giblin 'sat listening silently to my mother's exposition of Russian politics and revolutionary aims' sipping a mug of strong

---

[18] During Giblin's residence the only figure at King's with any connections with Bloomsbury was G. Lowes Dickinson, who Giblin later counted as a friend. A classicist and historian, Dickinson is most remembered today for his apologia for homosexuality. 'For those who like young men ...', wrote Dickinson, 'Cambridge, especially King's, is ideal'. Throughout his life Giblin did, literally, like young men. The extent to which he liked them in the more specific Dickinsonian sense is little more than conjecture. The hale spirit of Giblin's memoir of Cambridge is a world removed from the tremulous and incensed atmosphere of Dickinson's *Autobiography*. But the milieu in which he moved at Cambridge was largely homosexual. As he told his wife forty years later :'Most of my old acquaintance in Cambridge – James, Macauley, Dickinson etc. were rather monastic and only politely interested in women' (RBA LFG 29 June 1932).

Westerham ale. 'There was a strength and repose about Giblin, even as a young man, which set one immediately at rest. Hurry of any sort and the urgent petty occupations of daily life were in his presence, revealed as unnecessary and futile. There was any amount of time for things that mattered …' (Garnett 1953, p. 33).[19]

Twenty years later, in 1917, it was Giblin's friendship with the adult Bunny, oiled by the reassuring fact of Giblin's King's College education, that was to prise open the door to Bloomsbury. But in 1897 all Cambridge had left Giblin with were warm memories and a second class honours degree. What to do now? An excursion abroad would have been a not atypical graduate's answer. And a typical choice in the 1890s might be Heidelberg, Athens, or even India. Giblin chose otherwise. On July 14 1897 the *Excelsior* docked in San Francisco, and unloaded $500 000 of gold. The rumours of a fabulous gold reef in Canada's northern extremities had suddenly been proved true. The Klondike gold rush was on and 100 000 men from across the world rushed to Canada to fight their way to the most distant reaches of British Columbia. Giblin was among them. He told five-year-old Bunny that he would bring him back four golden chairs.

He was accompanied to Canada by an Australian-born fellow student and fellow spirit, Martin Grainger (1874–1941). Grainger, declared Giblin, 'is one of the most remarkable people I have met' (RBA LFG 11 April 1896). He had secured the First in mathematics at Cambridge that had eluded Giblin, but was leaving the opportunity of academic preferment for the rigours of the wilderness, and this choice remained unrevised throughout life.[20]

The pair reached Canada on a cattle boat; 'an experience which gives those who undergo it a fairly close acquaintance with many things not learned in books'. Once there Giblin did not find gold, and perhaps never much sought to.[21] He did, however, seek to find survivors. In their search for wealth, many miners had been reduced to total destitution. The Canadian 'North Country' where they

---

[19] Garnett notes that Giblin was reading *Beavis: The story of a boy* 'with profound attention for the fourth time'. This novel of the nature mystic Richard Jefferies is a 'celebration of the vigour and freedom of a childhood spent in the countryside' (S. M. Coleman, 'The Life and Work of Richard Jefferies', http://www.arthur-ransome.org/ar/literary/bevis.htm). Years later Giblin was to tell his sister Edith that 'copies of Bevis are in continued flow through my hands' (RBA LFG 9 April 1934).

[20] It is recorded that Giblin breached protocol on the occasion of his being presented to King George VI; he did not wear gloves. It is also recorded that Grainger, too, breached convention when he was presented to the same King. He wore moccasins.

[21] His fellow Kingsman F.R. Earp stated that Giblin and Grainger 'bought a concession on which there was certainly gold, but most of the money went on the purchase but not enough on the machinery to work it, so their funds were exhausted and the concession lapsed before it paid' (Earp 1960, p. 17).

sought riches is cruel and relentless country. Devil's Gorge, Hell's Gate, Rapid of the Drowned: these are its features. Of the thousands who set out for the Klondike by the overland route beginning at Edmonton, only 20 per cent finished the journey. Not one of the 4000 horses they took with them did. And in winter the countryside was almost totally impassable. The sporadic supply trails of summer ceased. To survive was to kill whatever was still living: moose, wolf, porcupine, squirrel. And if you did not – by inexperience, exhaustion, or folly – you died. In early spring of 1899, in a tale worthy of King Croesus, gold miners along the banks of the Dease and Liard rivers were snowed in, trapped and starving. The government of British Columbia dispatched a rescue party, with Giblin second in command. Travelling by dog teams, the rescue party successfully negotiated frozen lakes, located the survivors and provided an ambulance for those too weak to walk. On the return journey, with Giblin now in command, their food supplies gave out. A moose hunt preserved them from dearth and disaster.

Giblin's adventures in the Yukon bring out in bold profile several of his characteristics. It highlighted his aptitude for leadership – not an *ambition* for leadership – but simply a capacity for it.

His adventures also brought out his willingness to undertake selfless acts, which complemented his leadership. And they brought out the satisfaction he felt as a result of defying physical misery. Or, perhaps more truthfully, his satisfaction from defying it more better than could any other. 'The temperature was a brisk 38° below zero but Grainger and Giblin seemed to enjoy such temperatures'. Indeed, 'there were occasions when they deliberately went out in the coldest weather to prove to themselves that they could take the worst' (Camsell 1960, p. 25). One morning Giblin arrived at base with the cheerful report that overnight the temperature had dropped to -52° (= -47° C).

In the Yukon Giblin also received the education provided by hardship. On one occasion later in life Giblin announced that 'to be any good, an economist ought to have been hungry in his youth' (Hytten 1971, p. 53). This is surely an unreliable test – most of the best economists would have failed it. But Giblin honestly passed it.

Finally, the Yukon allowed the young Giblin to boldly articulate his self-definition. He was Viking. At Cambridge he had become engrossed by the Icelandic saga, *Burnt Njal*. It was 'as good as the Iliad'. He visited Iceland (Reynolds c. 1951) and appears to have learnt the language and translated parts of its literature.

The Icelandic sagas are myths without mystical mist. They are chronicles of bargains and combat. They tell of Hallgerda ('fair of face and tall of growth', but evil at heart) and, as her counterpart, the good, if sexless, Unna. They celebrate Gunnar: hardy, fearless, hot in battle, but ardent for peace. 'In all the long series of quarrels that are thrust upon him', commented Giblin in a public lecture on the sagas, 'through all the onslaughts that are made and ambushes set, there is only one occasion where he is not ready to make peace' (Giblin [1923] 1960). And Gunnar is wise. He was set apart from those men beholden by 'swift certainty as to what they wanted and how to get it'. Gunnar was given to 'care and anxious thought', 'a persistent struggle to see mankind through, knowing they would lose the last fight'.

Giblin's passage of youth in the frontier country of Canada afforded a tangible fulfilment of his northman fantasy. It so happened that several of the remote outposts of the Hudson Bay Company were supplied by means of row boats. Giblin, with Grainger, successfully presented himself as an oarsman to the company. He now had his own long boat. A hollowed spruce tree was his vessel. A single spruce tree was his huge oar.

At the conclusion of several months oarsmanship, he extended his mariner fantasy even further by training as a seaman. But this disappointed him. The steamship had removed the elements of nature he so loved from seafaring.

But at the same time Giblin had decided against Canada.

> This country is not a bad one to knock about in; the North particularly, but it has no conscience and that gets on one's nerves after a time … it's when they pretend to be a community, the absence of any common feeling or idea becomes glaring. The majority confess a most brazen dollars and cents criterion of every question, and the most decent minority are cynics. And political morality in the narrower sense is as shameful I believe, as the worst that the [United] States can show, with the absence of any bills and success to palliate it. I believe Australia is better; that it has a touch of conscience and glimmerings of an idea; at least there is a chance of it, without the juggernaut of American material success to crush and the charybides of English immobility to engulf. (RBA LFG February 1903).

He sailed from Vancouver to Port Phillip, where he piloted his vessel through dangerous waters. In Hobart he returned to his true vocation, and became a foundation master in the King's School, a breakaway school from Hutchins. It was, perhaps, a financial crisis at the school that set him roving again. He returned to London through Java, where he fell in again with Martin Grainger, and together they pursued a new interest: Ju-Jitsu.

The 'gentle art' of Ju-Jitsu had left the Japanese countryside with the dissolution of the samurai and had spread to Japanese towns in search of custom, and from there to the world beyond. Europe received its first exposure to Ju-Jitsu in 1899, when the 18-year-old Yukio Tani arrived in England to entertain musical halls audiences by challenging all comers. A minor craze ensued, with even Conan

Figure 1.1. Giblin (bearded), among 'The Elect', on his return from British Columbia

Source: RBA PN002639

Doyle having Holmes practising his own anglicised version. Tani established a 'Japanese School of Ju-Jitsu' in London in association with Giblin and Grainger. 'They had fitted up a gymnasium in the basement of a house in Gordon Square, where they gave lessons and held exhibitions. At the latter, Giblin sometimes took the part of the heavy man who could be thrown and reduced to helplessness by a Japanese half of his weight' (Garnett 1953, p. 111).

Giblin and Grainger edited the guide, *The game of Ju-Jitsu. For the use of schools and colleges*. It is more than a manual: it is a piece of advocacy. Ju-Jitsu, say the authors, furnishes health – 'not the timid health that is content to avoid sickness, but the health that is alive and rampant'. Its special merit, however, is as a sport. Cricket, football and rowing require space unavailable to the 'town-bred boy'. Ju-Jitsu demands 'little space and no complicated apparatus' and is 'possible in the middle of town, indoors or out, by gaslight or daylight'. Boxing could claim the same but, although boxing is an 'admirable game', the interest in Ju-Jitsu is more demanding and intense: 'it stands to boxing as chess to draughts'. And 'hard hitting' knocks you about more than you like. With Ju-Jitsu, 'Man to man as God made you (usually with the addition of a jacket), you may fight it out to the inevitable finish; defeat when it comes is absolute, and the beaten man rises without strain or bruise ready to try gain. This is the peculiar glory of it' (Giblin in Miyaki and Tano 1906).

But however financially successful the judo partnership may have been, it could not withstand other criteria. Grainger wished to marry. And so Giblin took to sea once again.[22] As a consequence of a treaty of the imperial powers, the Solomon Islands had recently become open to economic exploitation. Lord Stanmore of the Pacific Islands Company engaged Giblin to further the company's coconut interests in the islands. 'So I swotted up agriculture, and then chartering a little steamer, I spent three months in the Solomons sailing around the coast line and examining the country and its possibilities' (*Table Talk*, 30 April 1931).[23] A virulent local fever forced him to leave.

He returned to Hobart, planted an apple orchard that he was to keep all his life, and began a career. His career was to be political. He joined the newly formed Liberal Democratic League. The aim of this party was to win the balance of power in Tasmania between the two larger parties – the Anti-Socialist Party and the Labor Party – and thereby 'force drastic financial reform' on the state's shaky finances. 'We urgently need more population, more revenue and less capital

---

[22] To smooth his marriage, Grainger decided to write a novel to pay off his creditors. Giblin was acquainted with another literary sea rover, Joseph Conrad. In February 1904 he records: 'Met Conrad in Kensington Gardens and talked for a while about his new book' (quoted in Copland 1960, p. 142). The 'new book' is presumably *Romance*. Or perhaps *Nostromo*, then still being written.

[23] Or was it a 'pearl trading venture'? (Garnett 1953, p. 111).

expenditure', Giblin declared. This was perhaps an electorally unpalatable nostrum by itself. But whatever modest chance Giblin had of election, he threw away with his stance on defence. At one public meeting during the 1909 election campaign it was moved that Australia should donate a Dreadnought to the Royal Navy, although at that time the Royal Australian Navy did not yet exist and Australian naval defence consisted of paying a Royal Navy squadron to base itself in Australia. Giblin moved an amendment suggesting that Australia give first priority to its own defence of its own waters. It is recorded that Giblin had some difficulty in finding a seconder amongst the 'uproar and yells from the audience inviting him to sit down' (Green 1960, p. 30).

The Liberal–Democrat League failed. The Anti-Socialists won a majority in the 1909 election; the League secured just one seat out of 30, and only 9.7 per cent of the overall vote. In the seat he was contesting, Giblin received just 5 per cent.

The Liberal–Democrat League vanished and its members attached themselves to either the Anti-Socialists or the Australian Labor Party. Giblin immediately chose the Labor Party.[24] A fruitful but difficult association had begun, one that was to bring him into close contact with future leading political personalities – including J. A. Lyons and John Curtin.

Why did he join the Labor Party? To join the conservatives was impossible. There was nothing 'Tory' about Giblin. But joining the ALP was possible. He sympathised with the working-class movement; the Tasmanian Labor Party had been founded in the same Working Men's Club that his father had founded. He had, of course, worked as a lumberjack, sailor, teamster, boatman and cook. On a more programmatic level he had on his return to Tasmania founded an 'informal discussion group' of socialists, whose activities included sports meetings, picnics, lectures on current affairs and socialist doctrine. Its members included J. A. Lyons and John Curtin's future father-in-law, Abraham Needham, and presumably on occasions John Curtin himself, who Giblin would surely have met on Curtin's various visits to the island at that time.

It was in these years before the First World War that Giblin sported a 'flowing Socialist beard' (Reynolds c. 1951),[25] and declared himself a socialist virtually from birth. The meaning of 'socialist' was conveniently indefinite. His own conception of this doctrine allowed him to support private finance of infrastructure development: 'as good labour men, even as good socialists we cannot do better than support' it. (Green 1959. See also Robson 1983, vol. 1, p. 295). As a consequence, 'His socialism, though never his intelligence, was always

---

[24] More correctly, the Workers Political League, as the Labor Party was styled in Tasmania until 1918.

[25] The beard survived until his entraining for France in 1916. The King's Regulations put an end to it.

open to question' (Davis 1975, p. 415). But this questioning did not necessarily isolate him from the most powerful elements in the party; in 1910 an attempt to incorporate a 'socialisation objective' into Labor's constitution was defeated. Labor instead pledged itself to 'the cultivation of an Australian sentiment, the maintenance of a White Australia and the development in Australia of an enlightened and self-reliant community', all issues Giblin distinctly supported.

Giblin managed to avoid a 'probation period' that certain Labor stalwarts wished to impose on him. A more enduring difficulty in his new political association lay in Giblin's distance from the 'industrial wing' of the Labor Party.[26] Giblin sympathised with the working-class movement. He was soon to provide advice on the 1910 Tasmanian *Factories Act* and the *Wages Board Act,* that put a minimum on some wage rates, and a maximum of 48 hours on the working week, at a time when waitresses in Hobart 'coffee palaces' were working up to 84 hours a week (Robson 1983, vol. 2, p. 233). But, like his father, he took a 'missionary' attitude to the working class. They were to be 'raised', not rallied to. And his aspirations were far wider, more social than economic. In 1911 Giblin declared the party did not need men only concerned with wages.

In summary, Giblin was a typical 'left-liberal' of the pre-1914 world. He favoured equality, and opposed hierarchy and mere convention. This made him 'left'. But he was committed to the prerogative of the individual over the prerogative of the collective. This made him 'liberal'. The key figure in this mindset was J. S. Mill. A representative figure was Alfred Wallace, the evolutionist and land nationaliser, who had links to founding figures in the Tasmanian labour movement (Coleman 2001a). Giblin was deciding his political affiliation during a time when Australia laboured under a strict two-party system, with no centre party savouring of Mill, and the defining political axis was simply supporting – or opposing – the new insurgent Labor Party. Giblin could only support.

He became active in Labor Party deliberations. He pressed for the staged nationalisation of land; voluntary voting; proportional representation;[27] uniform divorce laws; an increased number of states. He also proposed a motion for the

---

[26] At the time of his joining the Labor Party, Giblin's distance from the industrial wing was no problem – there was no 'industrial wing' in Tasmania. There were no trade union delegates at the party conference until 1912. There was not even a Trades and Labour Council in Tasmania until 1909. The stock mythology of the Labor Party's foundation – of strikers and black stumps – does not capture the reality in Tasmania. There the 'industrial wing' was created by the 'political wing', rather than the other way around.

[27] Giblin was 'thoroughly immersed' in proportional representation, and a member of the Select Committee of 1915 that ushered the new electoral scheme into Tasmania (Green 1956, p. 78). At the end of his life Giblin was a member of another official inquiry into the vexed issue of proportional representation.

'prevention of the marriage of Asiatics and Europeans and the marriage of idiots'.[28] We might see here the influence of eugenic doctrine. But his motion was also consistent with the outlook of the ALP of the time. In the same year, 1912, the Fisher Labor Government introduced the maternity allowance, but the legislation debarred 'asiatic' mothers from receiving it.[29]

The *Westralian Worker* reported that Giblin's 'sabre [was] the keenest and most pointed at the conference' (*Westralian Worker* 9 February 1912).[30] In the Tasmanian election of January 1913 he successfully stood as a Labor Party candidate, topping the list of ALP candidates in the federal seat of Denison (Bennett and Bennett 1986), and became an advisor to the Treasurer J. A. Lyons in the subsequent minority Labor Government.

Giblin's promising political trajectory was unbalanced by the arrival of the First World War. Giblin was not one of those who raced excitedly to the colours. It was, he said, a 'bloody war'. In any case, a broken wrist from a bicycle accident had left him at the time a not very useful warrior. But with its mend, and with the maximum age for enlistment raised to 45, he volunteered in the Australian Imperial Force (AIF).

What can be said about his war experience? That he was lucky to emerge alive; that he 'should' have been killed; and that some his dearest friends had little expectation of his surviving.

What does his war experience reveal? Largely what the Yukon had already revealed, but in still more vivid hue. Above all a fulfilment achieved in being 'in action', in both the broad and narrow senses. Giblin was 43 years old when he volunteered, older than 98 per cent of the recruits to the AIF. From 1909 he had served in the Army Intelligence Corps as a 'citizen soldier'.[31] An honourable and useful staff position would have been available. But he enlisted in an ordinary line unit: the 40th battalion, raised under the auspices of the Tasmanian Government, and manned and officered solely by Tasmanians.

---

[28] See pp. 32–4, 'Proceedings of ALP Hobart January 1912' (JCPML 00653/151/21). The motion was rejected on Fisher's urging.

[29] Giblin put a low value on the maternity allowance. In the 1926 Royal Commission on National Insurance this exchange took place over the impact of the allowance on infant mortality:

Giblin : I should say the figures undoubtedly show that, judging from the mortality position and the diseases of the puerperal state with mothers, the maternity allowance has not been successful.

Senator McDougall : Then in your opinion, it has not been of economic value to the nation.

Giblin : It may have helped the doctors.

[30] JCPML 00653/150/5.

[31] Giblin had been judged as 'officer material' several years before by the military authorities (Barrett 1979).

Figure 1.2. Captain Giblin, still with 'socialist beard'

Source: RBA PN002638

He was first severely wounded on 15 April 1917 near Armentieres (Green 1960). At the field hospital he genially entreated the authorities to send him back to the front, rather than to medical care in England. The medical officer turned out to be one of his former fellow students from Cambridge, and granted his request. A few weeks later, in the battle of Messines of June 1917, he was awarded a Military Cross for leading his men 'with great determination to the assault, reaching his objective through intensive artillery and machine gun fire'. In the assault he was severely wounded a second time, and dispatched to England.

In this island sanctuary, Giblin pursued other areas of life. Bunny Garnett was now 25, a conscientious objector, and required by law to contribute to the war effort through agricultural labour. To conform with this requirement, he and a fellow objector (and one-time lover) Duncan Grant were now sharing the Sussex farmhouse 'Charleston' with Vanessa Bell in their own version of a *ménage-a-trois*. Giblin 'full of warmth and friendliness' came during his convalescence to visit Garnett 'to reassure himself that I [Garnett] was not having too bad a time as a conscientious objector!'.

> He was very large, with close cropped hair, rugged features, tanned to pale mahogany, very slow in speech, and untidy in unbuttoned tunic and badly wound puttees. (Garnett 1953).

But how might these Bloomsbury lilies of the field react to the sudden appearance of this unknown bronzed warrior? 'Confronted by Vanessa ... with a sure instinct, he began to speak of his old friends at Cambridge, Lowes Dickinson, Wedd and Clapham'.[32]

There may have been another motive for Giblin's visit. John Maynard Keynes often frequented the Charleston household, which he had originally organised. Giblin, Garnett recalled, 'wanted to know all that we could tell' about Keynes whom he 'had heard about'. Giblin and Garnett dined and parted. 'Giblin's future did not seem likely to be a long one'.

Giblin returned to take part in the Battle of Passchendaele, a battle that illustrates, even more sombrely than the Somme, the vision of the War as being a matter of lives being squandered for a few miles. A village by the name of Passchendaele was to be taken, and 310 000 Allied casualties obtained it. Giblin's unit was thrown into the maelstrom, and at the end of battle he was the most senior surviving commander of the 40th battalion's 10th brigade. 'Of the Battalion there were only about a hundred left out of the six hundred who went into action eight days earlier. These men with Giblin at their head had reached the lowest

---

[32] J. H. Clapham (1873-1946) was an eminent economic historian, and close friend of Giblin at Cambridge. Nathanial Wedd (1864-1940) was an influential fellow at King's College, and ally of his fellow 'Apostle' Lowes Dickinson.

depths of misery by the time they had arrived at the area of sodden shell-holes allotted to them. Giblin moved about them, quietly talking to the exhausted ones, and seeing that they had hot food and drink' (Green 1960).

The costs of battle encouraged attempts to clarify the purpose of the struggle. In October 1917 Giblin wrote to his Tasmanian Labor colleague James Ogden to argue that war aims should have no imperialistic dimension; that revolutionary Russia should receive a sympathetic treatment; and that Australia should place German New Guinea under international control (Lake 1975, p. 117). The winter and the subsequent spring of 1917, saw the nadir of morale among the Allied forces. Early in 1918 Giblin told the woman he would marry that the trial of Bertrand Russell for pacifism was 'incredible'.[33]

Three weeks leave in the summer of 1918 was devoted to Venus rather than Mars. Gunnar had found his Unna. On 29 July 1918 he married, in a registry office, Eilean Burton, 33 years old and 12 years his junior. They shared unorthodoxy. She had distinct artistic connections and was given to 'unconventional dress'. She was a carpenter, who made some of her own furniture. Educated at Wycombe Abbey School – housed in a magnificent mansion in 160 acres of grounds – she had devoted several years to social work in the East End of London. She considered herself a socialist and a feminist. At the marriage ceremony there was, on her plea, no wedding ring.[34] They are both recorded as living at Spencer Road, East Mosely, London.[35] Two 'eccentrics' had found each other, and remained constant, despite the impositions their unusual personalities made on each other. One acquaintance of the pair has judged that 'She was as likeable as he was. They were a fine couple with a narcissistic devotion to each other'.[36]

During their honeymoon, Giblin with Eilean, visited Charleston a second time. And this time he caught Keynes.

---

[33] Russell had studied at Trinity College, Cambridge (1890–94), and remained a lecturer until 1901. Giblin had a role in Russell's tour of Australia in 1950.

[34] To be more exact: she would not have a ring if Lyndhurst did not have a ring. On their arrival in Hobart in 1919 Lyndhurst's mother was distressed by the ringless finger, and Eilean relented.

[35] Family legend relates that 'Eilean's and Lynd's marriage was very "sudden" to say the least'. But they had met before. In one account she arrived in Tasmania in 1913 intending to be a shearer's cook, and was directed to Lyndhurst at Seven Mile Beach. In another account their meeting is both more fortuitous and more foreseeable. 'Some years before 1914 Eilean had some job in Hobart, and she never could stand many foolish folk and their chatter. Eilean then used to go off on her own at weekends and camp in some wild part of Tasmania. There she met a bloke who also got bored with silly people and their idle talk, and he also used to get away alone and go camping. And that was that' (RBA, letter of K. M. Burton to Desmond Giblin).

[36] James Cumes PKT Mailing List Archive 27 November 2000.

Figure 1.3. Eilean Giblin (second from left) with Australian suffragettes, Rome 1923

Source: nla pic-vin 3279316

> I remember that we talked about his 'Gold' article in the *Economic Journal* in 1914 though at the time I was not even on the outer fringes of economic learning. (Giblin 1946).

Within days he was returned to the front to be part of the final advances of the summer of 1918. On 8 August 1943 he was to recall:

> On this day 25 years ago the Australians and the Canadians made their great push which was the beginning of the end of the last war. I came back from leave (in England) that day and met the swarms of prisoners trailing back as I went to join my unit – on new ground, not pocked marked by shell holes or belted with barbed wire. It seemed a new world.

On 9 August he wrote to his bride: 'Just back in time for this push. It has been wonderful. We are in 6 miles' (NLA LFG 9 August 1918). He added that 'Fritz generally appears to be clearing out', and there had been 'very few casualties'. One of the few was himself. In a night attack in the battle of Bapaume of August 1918 Giblin was seriously wounded for a third time.[37] On the arrival of the Armistice he was convalescing in England.

In two years Giblin had been promoted to the rank of Major, awarded with both a Military Cross and a Distinguished Service Order (a decoration superior to the Military Cross) and had been 'Mentioned in Dispatches'. It was an illustrious record. But this military man was anti-militarist. He opposed conscription. He was, in a loose sense, a pacifist, desolated by the waste of war and disgusted by its misrepresentation as anything other than a grim necessity. In 1934 he publicly protested at the Governor of Victoria appearing in military uniform.

> We are pledged to outlaw war, and we require the King's representative to dress as an outlaw. We ... are still suffering the dire effects of the last war. Yet when we are out to give a people's welcome to the King's representative ... we are in effect not only lauding warfare, as the lordliest life on earth but painting it with the outworn colours of gay and gallant chivalry. (Quoted in Copland 1960, p. 130).

To Giblin war was the colour of dust.[38] Gunnar now put aside his helm, sword and bill and sought peaceful employment.

---

[37] This would cause him considerable discomfort. It is characteristic that he attributed this mostly to the anaesthetic.

[38] Giblin's aversion to merely 'artistic truth' left him aloof from some pacifist literature. '*All quiet on the Western front* is selling well here' he told Eilean in 1929. 'There's no doubt about its merits but I doubt its truth as a normal picture – which the notices of it seem to suggest. The frequency of mangled bodies seen in great detail is very much overdone; the general tone is suitable enough for an occasional day or two when everything went wrong; but it is difficult to believe that German morale could have stood the continued strain that the book presents' (RBA LFG 12 July 1929).

He was 46. His father – Treasurer, Premier, Acting Governor, and Chief Justice – had died at that age, and on the afternoon of his funeral Hobart had largely closed to show its respect (Walker 1976, p. 39). Giblin had achieved little in public life by this time. To fulfil his aspirations the obvious remedy would be to revive the career as Labor parliamentarian that had been interrupted fewer than three years earlier. But the party had changed in that short time. It had split and radicalised. The prosecution of the war had been used to drive the Labor party into opposition seats. Their adversaries had claimed the war and army for themselves and the ALP seemed ready to concede both. At their 1918 conference the party had adopted the proposition that the war had been caused by capitalism. Major Giblin DSO, MC might not have cut amongst the delegates quite the figure a 'war hero' might have been expected to.[39]

Another consideration was the novel experience of the ALP's annihilating defeat in the federal elections 1917. 'This marked the end of the first era in labour history during which its [the ALP] support grew in leaps and bounds, when its opponents had to sink their differences, adopt its methods and match its program, and when it seemed set to become the natural party of government. In the next twenty-five years Labor would hold office at the national level once, for twenty-sixth months' (Hirst 1999, p. 76).

Finally, might the example of Keynes have suggested a new way of advancing what Giblin thought important? Keynes the economist, public servant and 'public intellectual' had made a greater splash than most politicians. This kind of public life also presented itself to Giblin. Giblin had previously advised Sir Neil Lewis, Premier of Tasmania. Lewis was now Treasurer in the Nationalist Government of Tasmania, and he wanted Giblin as the new Statistician of Tasmania.[40]

Brigden

While Major Giblin DSO, MC was recuperating in England, one Private Brigden was also recovering from a severe gunshot wound. The similarity ceases there.

James Bristock Brigden's youth contrasts strongly with Giblin's. Giblin was Cambridge-educated; a Premier's son; a star of international rugby meets. Brigden was the son of a tram conductor. A primary education was his sole schooling. Sport was an indulgence he could not manage.

He was born 20 July 1887 in Maldon, a Victorian goldrush town that once boasted 60 hotels and three theatres, but whose seam of luck was fully exhausted by the

---

[39] It is worth noting that two of Giblin's senior peers in the Tasmanian ALP were to leave it not long after. James Ogden was expelled from the Labor Party, joined the Nationalists, and later the UAP. Lyons defected from the ALP to the UAP in 1931.

[40] The last ALP conference Giblin appears to have attended was October 1919. Giblin took up his duties as Statistician soon thereafter, which would have precluded any more political activities.

time of James's appearance. Restless and intelligent, Brigden left this small opportunityless town, but lacking skills he drifted. He became a cabin boy; the *SS Wilcannia* took him to London where he found himself 'stranded in the east end of London in a bad winter, as one of the unemployed' (JBB to DBC 26 September 1922).[41] He suffered 'a good deal of hardship' (Hytten 1971).

'Somewhat embittered' by this experience, on his return to Australia he became one of the founders of the new Shop Assistants Union.[42] After hearing Ramsay MacDonald speak in Melbourne in 1906, he devoted himself to 'active participation in the vigorous political life of the time and to intensive reading in political and economic subjects'. He became a participant in Labor Party activities and a delegate to the State Conference of the Victorian Political Labor Council in 1914 and 1915.[43] But his ideological affiliation was to 'radicalism' rather than 'socialism'. Like Giblin he was drawn to equality, but not to the collective. Hope lay in the development of the individual potential and virtues – including ethical sensibilities – regardless of social background (Whitwell 1986, p. 76). He could have been described as a wage-earning 'bourgeois radical'.

In order to 'get way from wage earning' he began poultry farming, although without leaving Labor politics.[44] He subsequently entered the ice business and witnessed the monthly price-fixing meeting of the relevant combine, the Melbourne Ice Traders Association, who were themselves injured by the monopoly prices the ice manufacturers charged. Brigden became an enthusiastic advocate of the (unsuccessful) 1911 referendum to give the Commonwealth Parliament power to nationalise any industry considered a monopoly. He also supported the unsuccessful 1913 referendum to extend Commonwealth powers to industrial relations.

After a disastrous fire destroyed his business, he turned to 'political journalism' as his 'enduring ambition'. Little came of the ambition apart from a few contributions to *Labor Call* (the organ of the Political Labor Council of Victoria). At the outbreak of war he was living with his parents, and 'driving a team of horses around Melbourne' (Hytten 1971).

---

[41] Copy of the letter in the possession of the authors.

[42] The minutes of a meeting of the Shop Assistants Union of Victoria on 30 December 1907 record Brigden as a member of the committee. On 28 April 1908 he tendered his resignation from the union on the grounds that he was no longer 'in the trade'.

[43] According to one obituary (probably written by Colin Clark), it was during this time that Brigden 'apparently' had contact with Giblin, presumably at Labor conferences. ('J. B. Brigden', *Economic News*, December 1950)

[44] Not surprisingly, Brigden opposed in 1915 an attempt to exclude employers from membership of the Labor Party (*Labor Call* 4 March 1915).

It was a world war that shook society's circumstances and presumptions sufficiently to loose Brigden from their constriction.

Brigden enlisted in the 29th Battalion in October 1915. This enlistment raises an interesting query. Not long before Sarajevo, Brigden had dismissed in print the struggle between the Entente and the Central Powers as no more than a British attempt to preserve a privileged position in world trade against a German resolve to break this 'monopoly' by force. Adopting the voice of some future historian chronicling events of the world war that already seemed inevitable, Brigden wrote: 'And because Austrian success was intolerable, Russia intervened. Because Russia attacked, Germany fought. Because Germany fought, France also. Because German success would be dangerous to her interests. Each for himself, His Trade, His Markets, His Profits, His Vested Interests, His Country, Right or Wrong' (*Labor Call*, 7 January 1912). Selfish capitalism, he believed, was the source of war and conflict.

Neither would Brigden have had any illusions about the conditions of battle. The Australian War Memorial writes of the recruits to the 29th battalion: 'Having enlisted as part of the recruitment drive that followed the landing at Gallipoli, and having seen the casualty lists, these were men who had offered themselves in full knowledge of their potential fate'.

But the first year of the war saw broad solidarity in favour of the war. The Labor Party supported the war. The union press also supported it. So did the *Bulletin*. It appears that something like a remarkable 60 per cent of Australian males between 25 and 29-years-old volunteered.[45]

Some years later Bridgen reflected on how joining up seemed to have changed his course of life for the better:

> Up to the war I hadn't much luck, rather the contrary ... but since some strange benefactor of a Bosche ... sent a piece of German lead through me I haven't been able to stop it. (Quoted in Roe 1991).

In August 1916 a less welcome piece of German lead had killed his younger brother, David, 19-years-old.[46] James Brigden's own fortunate 'benefaction' came on 23 March 1917. The 29th battalion had occupied the village of Baumetz in the wake of the German withdrawal to the Hindenburg line. At 4.30 am a German artillery barrage portended a counterattack. Brigden found himself on the crest of a sunken road with his comrades facing an advancing enemy

---

[45] 589 947 men offered themselves for military service (Beaumont 2001, p. 110), and 21 per cent of AIF recruits were aged 25–29, the age bracket that Brigden fell in. The 1911 census counted 200 000 males aged 25–29. Twenty-one per cent of 589 947 approximately equals 60 per cent of 200 000.

[46] David Brigden was one of 11 000 Australian casualties suffered in an unsuccessful attempt to storm Mouquet Farm.

encirclement. The Germans broke through the rear and reached the village. A message escaped from the embattled village: the '29th has been cut to pieces' (Austin 1997). In fact, the battalion had survived. And so had Brigden. But a gunshot wound had 'entered his chest and terminated his active career'.

By 'the merest fluke in the drafting of stretcher cases at an English port' Brigden spent his long convalescence in a hospital in Oxford. One of the volunteer assistants there was a Mrs Edwin Cannan, wife of the eminent economist Professor Edwin Cannan. Impressed by the 'slant of his conversation and occasional writing', Professor Cannan became a patron. So did another Goliath of Oxonian political economy, and another of Brigden's eminent hospital visitors, Professor F. Y. Edgeworth. Edgeworth became, in Brigden's words, one of his 'academic foster parents' (Brigden 1926), who (like Cannan) gave him personal tuition.[47] Brigden later recalled that he 'owed greatly' to the theorist.

Brigden guessed that they had welcomed him as a 'raw non-public school man in Oxford'. Brigden undervalued himself and his mentors. His value to them went much further than his being 'non-public school'. The fluent, economical and orderly prose of this novice would have impressed any teacher. His sincerity and kindness would win many audiences over his life. And, perhaps, the fact that he was obviously a frustrated talent appealed to their sense of patronage.

Brigden 'became and remained an enthusiastic Cannanite'. Cannan's anomalous mixture of doctrinal conservatism and doctrinal criticism seems to have been a powerful example to the young Brigden. A similar example was provided by Edgeworth, an exponent of neoclassical economics, who (in Brigden's words) 'no heterodoxy could shock' (Brigden 1926).

With the assistance of the dons, a Soldier's Scholarship and Army leave, Brigden was admitted to Oriel College, Oxford, and obtained a diploma in political science, subsequently converted to a BA by a further year of study in law.

Oxford did not diminish his identification as a 'Radical' in politics. He attended a Labour Party rally of 12 000 people at the Albert Hall in London and appears to have gained the acquaintance of certain leading British Labour figures, including the pacifistically inclined Arthur Henderson, who had resigned his cabinet post in 1917 over Britain's refusal to negotiate with Germany. 'I spent the day of the famous 1918 election in his constituency, and his opponent romped home – with an effigy of the Kaiser hanging from the gallows of his motor car' (Brigden 1924).

Brigden's interests – reform, learning and labour – found an intersection in the Workers' Education Association, which he joined 'at once' in Oxford, and this

---

[47] Brigden took Edgeworth's courses on 'Currency and Banking', and 'Public Finance'. His Diploma in Economics is filled out with courses on government and law.

was to become a critical move for Brigden. In the short-term it would supply an income that was now especially needful: he had recently married Dorothy James, of Ide Hill, in the church of that picturesque village sitting at the highest point of Kent. It was perhaps with the assistance of Henry Clay of New College, whose experience in WEA classes had formed the basis of his incessantly reprinted text book, that secured for Brigden the appointment he needed. He would be the WEA Lecturer in the 'industrial areas' of Sheffield. It was presumably through this appointment that Brigden came to the attention of the founder and General Secretary of the WEA, Albert Mansbridge, a man who had already developed a keen interest in Australia.

Mansbridge had toured Australia in 1913, and from his memoirs it is clear that this was one of the great events of his life (Mansbridge 1920, pp. 47–50). In 138 speeches – to universities, trade halls, and employers' federations – in Wollongong, Ballarat, Broken Hill, Newcastle, Castlemaine, Geelong, Albany, and Kalgoorlie – Mansbridge and his wife fired enthusiasm for his schemes and won ample moral and financial support. The Workers Education Association in Australia bloomed, and its ties with its English parent were thick. One Antipodean bud lay in Tasmania. There the WEA was offering courses ranging over Economics, Psychology, Literature and Social Reconstruction, and in almost every settlement that could claim a town hall: Hobart, Launceston, Burnie, Deloraine, Gormanstown, Devonport, Ulverstone, Zeehan, Strahan, and the forlorn and bizarre mining outpost of Queenstown.

In 1921 a vacancy became available for a WEA lecturer in Queenstown, and Brigden applied.

Copland

The son of a premier; the son of a bootmaker. The third member of the four, Douglas Berry Copland, was a child neither of the urban elite nor the provincial proletariat. He was the offspring of hardy and thriving Scottish pioneers on the Canterbury Plain in New Zealand.

Copland was born on 24 February 1894 to Presbyterian Scottish immigrants, Alex and Annie Copland. Their homestead had 50 draught horses and 16 children. Douglas was the 13th.

His background left its imprint. Throughout his life he boasted he could do most farming jobs. And all his life he was to be a pioneer, sowing and raising in barren land where no one had ventured before. And there remained something 'Scottish' about him – nimble and active, conscious of a pound, eager for self-improvement and education.

But his background could be no more than a background, as Copland's severe asthma was traced to an allergy to horses, and consequently husbandry was disqualified as an occupation. At the same time he felt insufficiently 'pious' for the Ministry: solemnity was never characteristic of this man who 'loved a joke', especially shaggy dog stories. Perhaps teaching, then? He completed two years at Christchurch Teachers' Training College before enrolling in Canterbury College, part of the University of New Zealand. There he displayed the desire to occupy centre stage that was to become characteristic of him. He was an active member of the Christian Union; he was on the Student Association Executive; and was recognised as a Life Saver.

Two circumstances pushed him from the still waters of teacher-traineedom into more vigorous currents. Firstly, he came to the notice of Professor (Sir) James Hight (1870-1958), the leading figure of New Zealand academia in the first half of the twentieth century. A scholar, teacher and institution builder, Hight was endowed with remarkable confidence and vision. Born in New Zealand, and only making his first visit to Europe at the age of almost 60, he never assigned himself a junior status, and confidently believed that he was part of an international mission to uphold and cultivate a universal civilisation. 'It would be only a little fanciful to say that he held Richelieu and Mazarin barely less significant for New Zealand than the Maori seafarers and Edward Gibbon Wakefield' (NZDB). Encyclopedic in reach, multi-disciplinary in method, he lectured and published on the Maori Wars, law, and geography. He did not neglect economics. He had striven to create a Bachelor of Commerce at the university early in the 1900s. In 1909 he appointed himself to the newly created chair of history and economics. He was an inspiration, model and mentor to Douglas. It was he who insisted – almost compelled – Douglas to switch from mathematics to economics (Copland 1950).

The second circumstance was the world conflagration which ignited in Douglas's 20th year. Several of his brothers were serving in the New Zealand Expeditionary Force, and his immediate younger brother, Robert Davie, was killed in action in 1916. Indeed, 42 per cent of men of 'military age' served in the NZEF.[48] Douglas Berry Copland also sought to enrol but was rejected as medically unfit due to a lesion in his heart muscle. This setback 'greatly unsettled' him – he was never able to meet his thwarted will with equanimity. He found distraction by busying himself with a Census. But the war's ramifications would yet seek him out.

On the other side of the Tasman Sea, the war was straining emotions, and this was telling on the University of Tasmania. One Herbert Heaton had been recently appointed Lecturer in History and Economics thanks to the patronage of Albert Mansbridge (the post required lecturing and tutoring WEA classes). In August 1915 Heaton had 'provoked an outburst in the press and the parliament' when it was reported he had said that, as both the Allies and the Germans had

---

[48] http://www.mch.govt.nz/heritage/nzww1.html

presumably committed atrocities, a draw would be the best outcome of the war (Davis 1990, p. 70). Although Giblin sided with him, Heaton resigned from his post at the University of Tasmania in late 1916. The University of Tasmania advertised for a successor; the advertisement was pinned up on the noticeboard of Canterbury College.

> I came in and saw this advertisement and I wasn't, well I was interested but I never thought for one moment of applying for it. But Doctor Hight came into the room where I was getting my gown to give my lecture and asked if I had seen this. And I told him that I had and in the discussion I explained that I didn't think I was up to the level to apply ... And he persuaded me to apply. (Copland 1968).

Wilson

Wilson was 10 years younger than Copland, 17 years younger than Brigden and more than 30 years younger than Giblin. His short life previous to his meeting the other members of platoon requires little elaboration.

He was born on 7 April 1904 at Ulverstone, a settlement of 1129 people living in 219 dwellings in north-western Tasmania. His father was a builder of limited formal education, but possessed of 'an intelligent and inquisitive mind, and a sharp, if sardonic sense of humour' (Cornish 2002, p. 8). Roland was the second son of five boys.

At the age of 14, with the First World War sustaining the Edwardian enthusiasm for 'boy soldiers', he was inducted into junior military cadets, weighing just 25 kilograms. His slight build and short height were to remain a 'defining feature'. One later acquaintance recalled: 'My first impression, of course, as everybody's was of his diminutive stature' (Stone 1997, p. 5). The other members of the Platoon were tall: both Giblin and Brigden were six-footers. Roland Wilson in adulthood was scarcely five feet two inches tall (Cornish 2002 p. 7).

His stature did not prevent his success on the playing field. And his success there did not preclude even more in the schoolroom. Nominally Protestant, Wilson's formal education began at Ulverstone's convent school – the same which Giblin's political peer J. A. Lyons had attended. The boy was quick, and he won a bursary in the newly founded Devonport High School. In 1921 he gained the highest marks in Economics, Book-keeping, Geography and French, a feat which carried with it prizes in those four subjects. He also excelled in the state as a whole such that he was awarded the 'William Robert Giblin Scholarship', established in memory of Lyndhurst's father. Wilson was about to come to the attention of Lyndhurst.

*

The First World War had been a social *super nova* that had blown apart old bonds, and scattered surviving materials. Four such fragments had been randomly thrown into proximity and were about to converge through the power of intellectual gravitation.

2. Building

'The world is old, and we are new.'
L. F. Giblin

In the years between 1919 and 1924, four men – Giblin, Copland, Brigden and Wilson – formed a bond at the University of Tasmania that was to endure until death. Together, in that short span, they made Tasmania one of the more interesting centres of economic inquiry anywhere in the world. The theory of the Multiplier received its earliest discussion there. The modern theory of the impact of protection on real wages was distinctly anticipated. One of the first investigations of the Quantity Theory to go beyond enumerating price levels and money supplies was also undertaken there. This seeming Ultima Thule of economic thought became, for a while, an Edinburgh of the South.

And the four gave Tasmania more than a simply vigorous seat of economics. Contemporary observers recorded the exhilarating stimulus these four men provided a then depressed, defensive and introverted society. And, yet, Tasmania also gave to them. Tasmania – it may be said – gave them her problems. In the 1920s Tasmania the issue of growth and decline was blatant. In the first third of the twentieth century, her population grew by only 0.7 per cent per annum compared with 1.6 per cent per annum of Australia as a whole. Tasmania also gave them her isolation. In 1920s there was no telephone link to mainland Australia, [1] no airlink to the mainland, and no sea link from the state's capital to the mainland. A journey to Melbourne from Hobart required a rail journey of almost six hours to Launceston, followed by a passage across the uncalm seas of a strait sevenfold as broad as the English Channel. [2] It is worth pondering the intellectual energy created by 'stranding' a small group of congenial and inquiring persons. Giblin, Copland and Brigden were thrown on their own, fairly considerable, resources.

Finally, Tasmania gave them the fruits of the struggle of a colonial meritocracy to reform, advance, and enlighten their community; a full endowment of institutions to air and analyse its problems. With a population of 200 000 people Tasmania could claim two houses of parliament, the longest experience of 'responsible government' of any Australian state, [3] a governor, an 'ambassador'

---

[1] There was to be no telephone connection until 1936, when the (then) largest coaxial telephone cable in the world was laid across Bass Strait.

[2] An illustration of the impediments of moving to and from Tasmania is that in 1919 Copland was absent from the University on account of the difficulties experienced 'in securing a passage to Tasmania' (Dunn and Pratt 1990, p17).

[3] Formally since 1854: one year longer than New South Wales.

to England in the form of a High Commissioner, a Statistician, a Royal Society, and Rhodes Scholarships. And it had a university.

Ideas of a university

Copland arrived in Tasmania to find a university existing in painful miniature. The University of Tasmania had been born of a conflict between the visionary aspirations of Tasmania's cultural elite and the colony's slender material resources. A youthful Giblin had once witnessed his father's friend Inglis Clarke holding forth John Henry Newman's *Idea of university* as the appropriate model for the island university. The *Idea of the university,* Tasmania's institution could not be. Nevertheless, in the face of significant opposition, the friends of higher learning successfully founded the University of Tasmania in 1890. [4]

In keeping with the straitened economic circumstances of the times, the University's entire academic staff initially consisted of three people. And to pursue the economy further, all three were appointed at the lecturer level: this was a university without professors. And the three were not 'fellows'; the University deemed them to be 'servants' in status, and the University chose to use that language to describe its scholars for the next 30 years. There was some growth over that period, but when Copland arrived it could still be described as minuscule. In 1918 the total number of students in the university was 85. The total teaching staff in 1925 was 19.

Economics had been examined since 1893. The very first reading list for 'political economy' was solid and modern: Mill, Jevons, and Marshall's utterly up-to-the minute text, the *Principles of economics*. But this vigorous start was followed by 25 years of drift until the arrival of Copland in 1917. The newly appointed Lecturer in History and Economics was disappointed to find '… an extensive course in history but in economics there was only … one subject, political economy as it was called' (Copland 1968, p. 7). Copland decided that this situation could not be tolerated, and he set about changing it with the enormous drive that was to characterise his subsequent professional career.

Within months of his arrival in Tasmania in 1917 Copland had arranged a conference between the University's Extension Board, professional accounting bodies and the Registrar of the University, and in August 1917, Copland proposed the establishment of a four-year Bachelor of Commerce degree. The parliament promised £500; the Hobart Chamber of Commerce promised another £500. After more than a year's delay the University Council finally agreed in December 1918 to establish Copland's commerce degree. The fee for the new degree was to be about £25 and 4s – about four months of average earnings, and inexpensive in

---

[4] Queensland, with more than twice the population of Tasmania in 1890, was not to establish her university for another 20 years.

the values of the day.[5] The subjects were to include: Economic Geography; Economics I and II; Currency and Banking; and Statistical Method. Graduates duly followed, with Myrtle Reid-McIlvrey admitted to the BCom in 1924.

Copland's attention then turned to the establishment of a new faculty – the Faculty of Commerce – to administer the new qualification. This took very little time: the Faculty became a legal entity in April 1919 with Copland as its first Dean.

In creating a degree with no almost staff, Copland assumed an enormous load. It appears that he was, incredibly, responsible for 20 courses over a single year. This was incredible, and slightly crazy. Something had been set incorrectly in Copland's mental mechanism. He was a cauldron in which fires burnt too fiercely. This uncontrolled furnace eventually produced calamity. He collapsed in Melbourne during an academic visit.[6] He spent three months recuperating. There were to be more collapses.

But it was this same heat that shattered walls, and forced a path for him through almost all obstacles. He was propelled; he would never rest and never be entirely content. In 1920 the Council offered to pay him £500 per annum at a time when lecturers were sometimes rewarded with £200 per annum. But this flattering offer did not bring any self-satisfaction. 'I am prepared to accept the proposal of the Council', he coolly replied.[7] He was painfully jealous of any preferment his colleagues might enjoy;[8] and was spurred by a well-developed sense of his own worth. All four university colleges in New Zealand had professors of economics. Why should he not be a professor of economics? The day after his 26th birthday he wrote to Council proposing that a Chair in Economics be created.

It is at this point Copland's career intersects with Giblin's.

In December 1919 Giblin had been appointed to the post of Statistician to the Government of Tasmania. This appointment was more than it seemed. It carried the duty of advising the Tasmanian Government on financial and economic

---

[5] The fee of the new commerce degree compares favourably to the £40 (per annum) that Robert Wilkins Giblin charged almost a century before for enrolment in the New Town Academy.

[6] This collapse appears to have taken place in June 1921. In August he was still on sick leave (Dunn and Pratt 1990, p. 27). The *Westralian Worker* also reported a 'nervous break down' in Perth in November 1921.

[7] Copland was 'a difficult man to work with' (Hytten 1971). Another colleague judged: 'He liked being the boss' (Reddaway quoted in Millmow 2003).

[8] See, for example, Copland's evident anguish at a member of his department receiving an appointment to inquire into state high schools (Dunn and Pratt 1990, p. 31).

matters – perhaps the first such position in Australia.[9] Giblin was also taking the place of an eminent preceding occupant: R. M. Johnston (1844-1918) who, as Statistician between 1882 and 1918, had made a significant contribution to the techniques for national income accounting, and had pioneered the argument that Tasmania suffered from 'disabilities' imposed by Federation. Johnston had also been a political economist: mathematical in his method, and conservative in his conclusions. Thus with this appointment Giblin was well positioned to speak with some weight of the worthiness of Copland's proposal for the Chair of Economics.

At about the same time Giblin was elected to the University Council and soon became a member of the faction that wielded power in the University – 'The Block'. Giblin was the person to have on side for any decision, especially of a financial nature. Giblin quickly decided that Copland's case for his appointment was worthy.

Thus an alliance between Copland and Giblin formed that was to stay fast until death. It was not, however, a symmetrical, or equal, alliance. Copland was twenty-six years old; Giblin was forty-seven. Copland's relationship with Giblin has been described by Tom Fitzgerald as 'ungrudgingly, filial'.[10] Copland said as much himself. 'Perhaps I know better than any of the economists of that day what it meant to come under his parental care' (Copland 1960, p. 4).

Copland revered Giblin. But Giblin did not revere Copland. Copland recorded, accurately, that he was 'young and inexperienced in academic affairs' when he first met Giblin, and that the older man was 'never failing to deliver a reproof' to the younger one 'where he thought it was needed' (Copland 1960, p. 4). There was also a wider, more psychological gulf. Copland was restless, Giblin calm. Copland was obvious; Giblin was, in his own description, 'reticent'. Giblin had a sense of life's ironies that the literal Copland never possessed.[11] Copland was in the words of one warm admirer, 'a simple man' (Downing 1971). Giblin was mysterious.

Yet Giblin was 'a man of great sympathy and understanding'. And Giblin was quick to recognise an ample talent and keen to 'kick it along' (Wilson 1984). Giblin piloted the fragile raft of Copland's reform through the extensive reefs of the University. It was Giblin who, within a few weeks of the proposal,

---

[9] In 1924 the Tasmanian Statistical Office was merged with the Commonwealth Bureau of Census and Statistics, and Giblin transferred to the Commonwealth service as Deputy Commonwealth Statistician for Tasmania, while retaining his function of advisor to the Tasmanian Government on economic matters.

[10] JCPML 0653/068/20/6/6.

[11] Giblin once admitted that he could not resist 'baiting' Copland. Montague Norman was another whom Giblin confessed he could not resist 'baiting'.

submitted to the University Council on March 1920 a memorandum supporting Copland's case. It was Giblin who successfully moved at Council that a Chair (combined with the Workers' Education Association [WEA] position of Director of Tutorial Classes) should be established. It was, undoubtedly, Giblin who, as a member of the Standing Committee considering applications, persuaded the Committee to recommend Copland to Council. The Council offered him the appointment on 21 December 1920, and Copland became the first Professor of Economics in the University of Tasmania, still not yet twenty-seven years old.[12]

The alliance between Giblin and Copland continued during their dealings with the WEA responsibilities associated with the new Chair. Copland was firmly committed to the Association. The WEA expressed the predominant spirit of early post-war years. As he later recalled, his fellow movement members 'were greatly influenced by the rising school of progressive thought on social problems … we read *The New Statesman*, *The New Age* and the *Manchester Guardian Weekly* rather more than the *Economist*' (Copland 1952, p. 31). And by allying itself with 'progressive thought' the Association promised to capture for economics rising members of the labour movement 'who might, and often did, become ministers in State cabinets'.

Under Copland's stewardship the WEA in Tasmania had grown from two branches in 1917 to nine branches in 1920. Staffing this expansion was a challenge, and there existed a vacancy in the West Coast branch. At the Council meeting of March 1921 Giblin reported that the British WEA had recommended one of their staff, J. B. Brigden, for the appointment.

The Peaks of Lyell

By July 1921 Brigden had arrived in Tasmania to take up duty in what was surely the hardest of hardship posts in academia: an evening class teacher in Queenstown, a lonely mining settlement 260 kilometres west of Hobart, nestled in a mountainous wilderness rising to 4000 feet.

Queenstown was not then 30 years old. It was spawned at the time Giblin was in the Klondike, when a 'Copper Rush' in western Tasmania sent thousands to Mount Lyell, and the Hobart stock exchange remained opened throughout the night to cope with the excitement.

In its subsequent history, 1.3 million tons of copper ore was torn from the 'peaks of Lyell', and crushed and incinerated in the smelters at its foot. In the valley below grew Queenstown 'hewn out of dark-swamp forest' (Blainey 1954, p. 92).

---

[12] Copland has not been the youngest person to claim a professorial appointment in Australia. Enoch Powell was 25 when appointed Professor of Greek at Sydney University.

The town stood in the path of the Roaring 40s. It was visited by tornadoes, and it rained 300 days a year.

The natural climate was further despoiled by man. The extraction of the copper required sulphur; the 'brimstone' of the Bible.

> Sulphur was the curse of Mt Lyell. When the big company smelted its pyrite in ten or eleven furnaces Queenstown found its climate changing. In still weather sulphers from the smelters thickened into pea soupers, choked Queenstown, and blanketed the valley. For days on end men working in the flux quarries on the hills above the town basked in winter sun, and looked down on the creamy waste of cotton wool in the valley. Men who set out with hurricane lamps for the smelters in the morning were sometimes found miles away in the evening. Sulphur was in every breath of air; even tobacco lost its taste. (Blainey 1954, p. 99).

Sulphur deadened the sense of smell, and thereby dulled the sense of taste. It corroded buildings and power lines. It washed into the Queen River, and reportedly left it the most polluted waterway in the Southern Hemisphere. It acidified the vapour borne by the clouds, and the poisoned rain burnt away the vegetation in torrential downpours.

Whatever wood was left was felled to feed the furnaces. Perhaps three million tons of wood were cut between 1896 and 1926. At its peak, 20 acres of forest per week were consumed to stoke the fires. By 1900 Mt Owen – once carpeted in forest – had been stripped totally bare of leaf, blade and stem. It was now a looming presence of red and black rock, variously compared with a cemetery, a desert, a battlefield, hell with the fires gone out.

And for such an existence, there were only meagre material compensations. The end of the First World War spelt a slide in the price of copper. By 1921 it stood at only $US279 per ton compared with $US644 at the 1917 peak. The company proposed a 20 per cent cut in pay. Half the workforce were dismissed. Closure loomed. So did an all-out strike.

Into this environment Brigden arrived, resolved to spread the sweetness and light of economic reason. One result was *The economics of Lyell*, published in May 1922 under Copland's patronage, and intended to provide his West Coast WEA students with a 'textbook'. The issue that this publication grapples with was the creation of wealth and its distribution – both acute matters in Queenstown. In order to engage with the issue of distribution Brigden produced, in appendices, an estimate of Australia's national income, the first since those of Timothy Coghlan of 1886. Brigden's method was simple if not crude: he extrapolated across the entire workforce the *per capita* value added through industry that had been recorded by a 1915 census. He thereby obtained a figure £377m for Australia's total income in 1915, an estimate that compares decently with the later 'authoritative' estimate of £377m (Butlin 1962). Brigden then sought to break this total down into profit and wage shares. He made a rough estimate of the annual rate of return which the owners of this wealth might have achieved, then applied his rate-of-return estimate to a figure for the stock of wealth produced by the Census of Wealth carried out for 1915. In this way he arrived at a figure of £130m for aggregate income from ownership of property in 1915, and so (residually) £247m for income from work (the second component).

'This was no great beginning after Coghlan's achievements': so writes the historian of Australian national income accounting of Brigden's effort (Butlin 1962, p. 38). Perhaps beginnings are frequently 'not great'. Brigden's simple exercise is nevertheless important because it represents the first attempt to educate the public in the concept of national income, and the relative size of the wage and profit shares into which it is divided. [13] This was an educational exercise that Brigden, Copland and Giblin were to deploy repeatedly, especially during the Great Depression.

The appointment at Queenstown, therefore, brought Brigden his first publication in economics. But would Dorothy Brigden have been adequately consoled? The contrast with Ide Hill would have been fierce. Possibilities of escape must have been steadily pondered. They may have seemed frighteningly narrow.

But in 1922 there arrived an opportune death. William Pitt Cobbett was the eminent and irascible foundation Professor of Law at the University of Sydney and renowned scholar of international law. On his retirement he moved to Hobart, where he died in 1919. In his will he directed that a trust fund of £5000 be established to advance economic inquiry. How came this strange gratuity to economic research? It appears that William Pitt Cobbett was a kinsman to another, much better-known Cobbett: William Cobbett (1763–1835) journalist, stirrer, reactionary, radical and hammer of political economy. It is tempting to ask if William Pitt Cobbett's difficult brilliance may have owed something – by either inheritance or example – to William Cobbett. These are speculations. What is fact is that, in 1883, William Pitt Cobbett's father published a new edition of William Cobbett's enduring piece of reportage, *Rural rides during the years 1821–1832: with economical and political observations,* spiced with rants against Ricardo and 'Scotch feelosofers'.

---

[13] Brigden's foray into national income accounting was soon to be eclipsed by J.A. Sutcliffe's *The national dividend of 1926*. 'This is an amazing book' wrote Giblin. 'Never, I should think has such a feast of the most difficult economic and statistical conclusions been packed into a modest 70 pages. We have the national income, not for one poor year, but for every year from 1911 right down to 1924–25, computed in two ways, giving remarkably harmonious results' (Giblin 1927b).

It is through Pitt Cobbett's esteem for the economist-hating William Cobbett that Brigden managed to join the University proper, and transfer to Hobart as the new Pitt Cobbet Lecturer in Economics.

A 'man's man' of broad and true scholarship

Copland was organising his final recruit to Giblin's Platoon. As the student who had come second in the state in the matriculation examination, and as winner of the William Robert Giblin Scholarship, Roland Wilson had come to Copland's attention. Copland came up to Ulverstone to seek an interview with Roland's father, a builder. University was not what the father, or son, had envisaged.

> I didn't even know what a university was in those days, and I'm not too sure whether many other people did either. (Wilson 1984).

Wilson was coaxed into completing a single year of the new Bachelor of Commerce degree in the University of Tasmania.

It was 'all a bit strange', Wilson recalled 60 years later. The majority of lectures took place between 5 pm and 9 pm. He was the sole full-time student. And the interest of almost all other students was strictly vocational, save for his classmate, Keith Isles, with whom he later did battle in the *Economic Record*. [14] But there were compensations. Copland was an 'exceptionally good teacher' (Hytten 1971). Copland brought his own strong sense of aspiration into the classroom. He would scatter Latin tags, in the face of the mute incomprehension of students. A favourite that he would leave his students was: *Cras ingens, interabimus aequor* – 'Tomorrow, again the unknown seas'. As one former student recalls:

> Physically, Douglas Copland was not easily overlooked. His frame was tall and broad-shouldered, his figure lean and athletic until middle age, thick and bulky thereafter. His face was somewhat heavy, given mobility by a curious and attractive lightness in the eyes and genial expression of bonhomie ... He had an ebullient personality and an unusual booming rasping voice (probably the product of asthma and elocution lessons) ... These were assets for a public speaker. Audiences were seldom indifferent. (Harper 1984).

Wilson was also not indifferent to Brigden, who taught Wilson Economics II in 1923, and whose lectures Wilson assiduously typed out. Between the dry, laconic, sometimes 'acid tongued' Wilson, and the poetic, discursive, ever-courteous Brigden, there grew a rapport that might not have been anticipated. Brigden seemed to pluck in Wilson a string that gave a deeper, fuller tone than his commonly sharp, astringent notes.

---

[14] Keith Isles (1902–77), economist, and Vice-Chancellor of the University of Tasmania during the latter part of the Orr affair.

The year before meeting Brigden, Wilson first encountered Giblin, in a different and more unexpected way. Wilson recalled the ocassion in his 1976 Giblin Memorial Lecture:

> While I was a student at this University my second-year essay on inheritance laws and taxation led him to seek personal acquaintance with the obscure author. A hand-written note invited me to lunch – which turned out to be poached eggs in a Murray Street café. It was followed by the suggestion that I should draft a bill on the subject of my essay for submission to the Tasmanian Parliament – a proposal which left me completely flabbergasted – and then by a visit to the Royal Tennis Court where I was introduced to the mysteries of one of the games at which he so excelled. (Wilson 1976, p. 308). [15]

Giblin persuaded Wilson to do another year's study: 'He began actively to encourage my studies'. In a later year of his degree, Giblin appointed him Secretary of the State Disabilities Committee, 'So I had six months of very good apprenticeship with him looking over my shoulder'. Giblin later explained to Keynes, 'We talk one another's language more than most, and I am greatly attached to him' (KCLA LFG 15 May 1943). A 'warm friendship' that would last 30 years had begun.

Giblin's patronage of Wilson was to occasion a pivotal incident of Giblin's difficult relationship with Tasmanian society at large in the 1920s. John Reynolds (1901–85), [16] a youthful contemporary in the 1920s, has provided the background in a memoir entitled, 'L. F. Giblin: A plea for an adequate biography and Tasmanian incidents' (Reynolds c. 1951).

> The post-war generation in Hobart was as mentally adrift and unadjusted as elsewhere throughout the world. The high hopes of brighter new worlds as preached by the starry-eyed patriots, which had taken fathers and elder brothers to Gallipoli and Flanders, did not eventuate. Old pre-war Hobart, and Tasmania for that matter, seemed by 1921 to be slipping back into the outlook of the depression years of the eighteen nineties. The old exclusive social sets … still set the fashion in thinking; deference was paid to them by the University, and religious and other bodies.

---

[15] 'I dared not tell him at that time that I had been compelled to take his invitation down to his office to have his crabbed script decyphered by one of his clerks. Years later in Canberra, I idly asked one day about the circumstances in which he was shot through the hand, this being the commonly accepted explanation for his peculiar hand-writing. His somewhat icy reply was that he had never been shot through the hand, and why did I ask? I did not pursue the subject' (Wilson 1976, p. 308).

[16] The father of Henry Reynolds.

It was into this gloomy atmosphere that Giblin appeared like a brilliant meteor.[17]

> For those with eyes, he gave new horizons, quite literally. He encouraged travel abroad, when a presumption reigned that this pleasure was reserved for the rich. He encouraged Tasmanians to discover their own state. He never ceased to talk about the attractions of the Tasmanian mountains and the unique character of the island's geology, flora, and fauna. To demonstrate his beliefs, he led many expeditions into the then 'unknown' country west of Mt Wellington …

In 1926 Giblin became probably the first man, and almost certainly the first white man, to defy the 'absolutely foul weather conditions and intense exposure' and successfully scale Mt Anne (1425 metres).[18] 'His simple talks to plain folk about these feats had a great deal to do with the formation of the now flourishing walking, mountaineering and skiing clubs' (Reynolds c. 1951).

It only further tickled Giblin's admirers, and grated his adversaries, that Giblin deported himself 'eccentrically'. Five years before Bunny Austin, the Davis Cup champion, had refused the traditional tennis attire of cricket flannels, and had asked his tailor to create some shorts, Giblin had already adopted shorts for the summer of 1928. When the Governor required all attendees of Royal Society of Tasmania meetings to wear dinner jackets, Giblin arrived late, in a battered slouch hat and haversack, 'went right up the front, sat down just opposite the Governor and cocked one hobnailed boot almost in his face' (Hytten 1971, p. 53).

Giblin's capacity to shock also took more serious forms. In 1925 at the formal dinner to commemorate the centenary of the separation of Van Dieman's Land from New South Wales, he expressed a preference for a Soviet form of government for the island.

Giblin, in other words, was a 'progressive'. 'It is impossible within the limits of this article' wrote Reynolds 'to recall all his battles with prejudice and stupidity'.

One battle involved his youngest protégé, Roland Wilson. As Wilson later recalled, Giblin had 'eventually persuaded a very reluctant young man to seek an opportunity for overseas study'. But where lay that opportunity? The Tasmanian Scholarship that had borne Giblin to Cambridge had been abolished.

---

[17] 'It was in Tasmania during his middle age (1919–29) that Giblin exercised a wide influence upon his generation, and this phase will provide a biographer with deeply interesting, if illusive, material'.

[18] Giblin did not succeed on the first attempt. In 1920, 1921 and 1922 Giblin and his brother Allen led three expeditions of exploration in the Weld River Valley in south-western Tasmania. Their 1921 attempt to reach Mt Anne was forced back 'having taken three and a half days to penetrate 18 miles through horizontal scrub' (Wilson 2001).

The one path to overseas study was the Rhodes Scholarship. But here stood an obstacle. 'Since the inception of the scheme of the Rhodes Scholarships candidates had come exclusively from private secondary schools which enjoyed the doubtful patronage of the "Right People"' (Reynolds c. 1951). Wilson came from a State school, and Giblin was very much not of the 'Right' people.

But Giblin ran the Scholarship selection committee, and with Copland and Brigden called into battle, the committee chose Wilson.[19] His success was vehemently resented: it was 'unthinkable' that a Rhodes Scholar could come from a state high school, and have studied economics but not Latin. A display of indignation was organised. A 'Member of the University Senate' complained anonymously in the Hobart *Mercury*:

> The local selection committee made the choice of the wrong type of man to be our Rhodes Scholar for 1925 ... The Rhodes Trust discourages the candidature of students specializing merely in a science or a commerce course, but requires a 'man's man' of broad and true scholarship.

The Hobart *Mercury* itself pronounced in its editorial of 19 March 1925:

> Rhodes 'knew that the business mind which is only a business mind, or the scientific mind which is only the scientific mind, is not the highest type of mind or the type necessary for a true statesman or leader of men ... Philosophy, literature, history, science, economics – that is the order by rank.

The controversy discouraged Wilson. He was tempted to relinquish the award, and accept in its stead a position as factotum to the directors of the local Cadbury concern. The urgings of Copland and Giblin braced him to ignore the contempt of the *Mercury*. As a result Giblin became a 'target of abuse'.[20]

The *contretemps* over the 1925 Tasmanian Rhodes Scholarship underlines Giblin's struggle against an introverted and excluding Tasmanian elite. But it may also be one symbol of the arrival of the economist in Australian public life. An economist had won the Rhodes Scholarship.

---

[19] Copland wrote to the Committee of Rhodes Scholars: 'Mr Brigden supports me in this high appreciation of Wilson's work. We are both of the opinion that Mr Wilson has exceptional qualifications ... We do not expect to find such a talent among our students for some time' (UMA DBC 2 December 1924).

[20] 'Major Giblin, like his hero Shaw, thrives on criticism and publicity. Indeed, those who do not like him – and they are not a few – say that he deliberately courts it' (*Weekly Courier*, 29 February 2004). Giblin was never a member of the Tasmania Club. He probably would never have been admitted, and would never have wanted to be.

Wilson was soon to be a student at Oriel, Brigden's old college. But before he had even left, he had been introduced to Oxford. A debating team from the University of Oxford was touring Australia, and the University of Tasmania's team had accepted their challenge. Brigden – the witness, presumably, of many debates in the trades hall and the University Union – wrote a long letter of gentle advice to the home team's speaker, Roland Wilson. The First Speaker, Brigden advised, should justify their contentions on pragmatic grounds, as pragmatic grounds are always the most persuasive. Only the Second Speaker should resort to principles. 'Whatever you do don't cram for the debate. You should have finished with all those textbooks and things which I gave you … Above all be careful to have no weak points. The great fault in debating is to include too many arguments, the weaker of which your opponents sieze upon.' Brigden appended a three-page speech by way of suggestion. 'Our little University will, I am sure, come well out of it. They may, you know, be holding us cheaply' (NLA JBB 3 May 1925).

Wilson went into battle against two luminaries of 1920s Oxford. The Oxfordians' first speaker was Christopher Hollis, a one-time President of the Oxford Union, later an editor of the *Tablet*, an author of a long study of the Tichborne Claimant, and a close friend of Roy Harrod.[21]

Wilson was affirming 'That the principle of compulsory industrial arbitration on the part of the State be approved'. The University library was crowded. The debate 'most entertaining'. The Oxfordians advanced 'an easy flow of words and ready wit'. Wilson replied in a 'telling manner' (*Mercury* 6 May 1925). The negative won.

---

[21] The Tichborne Claimant was Arthur Orton, a butcher from Wagga Wagga, who persuaded many who should have known better that he was Sir Roger Tichborne, the missing heir to the title and estates of the Tichborne family.

Figure 2.1. Wilson about to depart for Oxford

3. Gold and capital

> 'Wilson ... is surely my star pupil'
> *D. B. Copland*

As Wilson was preparing to leave Australia to study, Copland was readying himself for the same purpose. Copland might have borne a professorial title, but he also had several resemblances to the raw research student packing for Oxford. Like Wilson, he was young: only thirty-one years old. Like Wilson, he was an antipodean who had never left Australasia. Like Wilson, he wanted to undertake 'further study', and had been considering undertaking a doctorate at the London School of Economics (Hodgart 1975, p. 4). Copland may have had the dignity and income of a Chair, but his psychology was still that of a youthful direction seeker. This chapter, then, is the story of two young Australians making their voyage of discovery in the wider world.

Unlike Giblin or Brigden, the two were travelling the world in time of peace, rather than war. But the dislocation of the war, and the attempts to surmount and efface it, were to leave a strong impression on their 'further study'. On the eve of their journeys, on 28 April 1925, Winston Churchill, as Chancellor of the Exchequer, made an announcement of general significance for the world, and of a more professional significance for the two travelling scholars. In an effort to re-establish peacetime normality the gold standard would be restored with immediate effect, and the gold value of a pound sterling fixed.[1] This decision has been confidently judged to be damaging to Britain's economy, and has been (more speculatively) blamed for the Wall Street boom and the subsequent crash that was to demolish all hopes for the old financial order. Such attempts of Churchill to make good the impact of the war were to preoccupy the thoughts of all four in the 1920s.

Their thinking left marks on economic doctrine – especially on the linkage of capital inflow, the terms of trade, and the real exchange rate – long after the effects of the First World War had been submerged. In the 1970s the linkages traced out by Wilson and the others took on a renewed life as key elements in the analysis of the 'Dutch Disease' and the 'Gregory Thesis'.

America via England

When Wilson arrived in Oriel College towards the end of 1925, economics was stirring at Oxford. An 'honours school' in Politics, Philosophy and Economics had been created in 1920, and 'the almost irresistible rise of economics in PPE'

---

[1] Keynes told Copland that, in being consulted by the Chancellor, he had realised that 'Churchill did not grasp the intricacies of the gold situation and the exchanges' (UMA DBC 16 June 1925).

had commenced. The old subject of Political Economy had been renamed, and Modern Statistical Methods were being taught. Roy Harrod was lecturing on Money, Banking and Currency, and International Economics. One future Nobel Laureate, James E. Meade, was a fellow student of Wilson's at Oriel, although still a disciple of Major Douglas, and still absorbed in classical studies.[2] Wilson bought Keynes' *Tract on monetary reform*.

Oxford rewarded Wilson. He won the Beit Prize in Colonial History with an essay entitled 'Social and economic experiments in Queensland'. He began the dissertation proposed by Cannan, 'The import of capital', spent long days in the Royal Colonial Institute and the British Museum accumulating data, and successfully submitted his DPhil in October 1929.

But Wilson was not entirely content with Oxford. His tutor at Oriel was inexperienced and 'knew nothing about the subject I was interested in'. And there were deficiencies in physical as well as human capital. 'I couldn't find a calculating machine in Oxford, they looked horrified at me when I asked' (Wilson 1984). Wilson was offered some seven-figure logbooks instead. In 1920s Oxford, it was all done by pencil.

And he had discovered America. In 1926, as a member of a student debating group assembled under the auspices of the English Speaking Union, he visited 38 universities in six weeks. He felt he was 'treated as royalty'. This was the beginning of a lifelong attraction to the United States.

He successfully applied for a 'Commonwealth Fund Scholarship'[3] to study in the United States. The University of Chicago seemed to be the right place to go. The physical capital was impressive. 'The first compulsory thing when I hit Chicago was to be driven over to the Commerce School and instructed how to work a few calculating machines. The facilities in Chicago were quite excellent for the day. They had a marvellous machine [that did] six figures by six figures by pushing a button and tot up the total for you' (Wilson 1984). And here was an intensity lacking at Oxford; in addition to final examinations, he faced quarterly examinations in subjects with such inhospitable titles as Economic Theory. There were new fangled topics: Industrial Organisation and Relations, presumably taught by a professor he was to befriend, Paul Douglas,[4] best recalled today for bestowing his name to the Cobb-Douglas production function. But, above all, there taught at Chicago Jacob Viner, who had just published

---

[2] Another (unlikely) Rhodes Scholar studying PPE in those years was P. R. Stephensen, the littérateur of 1930s Australian literary nationalism. J. C. Eccles, the 1963 Nobel Laureate in Medicine, was the 1925 Rhodes Scholar from Victoria.

[3] In other words, the Harkness Scholarship, that had been established in 1918 by the widow of Stephen P. Harkness, a partner of John D. Rockefeller.

[4] A liberal Democrat Senator 1949–67.

Canada's balance of international indebtedness, 'which was very much on the same sort of lines I was working on'.

Viner was not easily impressed by would-be scholars. One former student of his, James Buchanan, recalled many years later that Viner felt it his 'sacred duty' to annihilate his students' confidence. But Viner held Wilson to be 'one of the two or three best students I have ever encountered' (quoted in Cornish 2002, p. 14). [5] Wilson was awarded a PhD for his topic, 'Capital movements and their economic consequences', which Viner in his *Studies in International Trade* commended as 'a distinct advance over previous attempts'.

Wilson was never a scholar in the closet. One acquaintance recalls his first meeting with him:

> [I] had never met anyone quite like him. With his (almost perpetual) cigarette in one hand, a Scotch (or was it an Australian beer?) in the other, he was delivering himself of the most outlandish stories of whatever Conference he and the Treasurer had just been attending – all in that slightly husky, even graveley voice which so well befitted the lapidary comments he was making. (Stone 1997, p. 5).

Yet Wilson was not truly gregarious. He was uninterested in the nuzzling fellowship of the herd. He was drawn to a particular species of sociality – competitive sociality. This was often physical – tennis, table tennis, skating, billiards. But if he found little reward in simple familiarity and companionability, he was still capable of intimacy. He wrote regularly to his family '[his letters] are deeply personal and record the exceptionally close family relationship enjoyed by Wilson, especially with his father' (Cornish 2002, p. 15). [6] In Denver he met Valeska Thompson, an American, who was to follow him back to Chicago. They married in June 1930.

England via America

Copland had been seeking leave to study abroad before Wilson had been persuaded to complete even a single year of the BCom. His 'zest for study of contemporary developments in economic theory overseas was unsurpassed in Australia' (Tom Fitzgerald). [7] His mentor, James Hight, did not visit Europe until he was fifty-seven years old. But Copland was not to wait: he had won a Laura Spelman Rockefeller Memorial Fellowship, another blessing of oil money to higher learning, and that was to take him to the United States and Europe.

---

[5] Viner also noted that Wilson 'has an unusual degree of intellectual maturity for a person of his age'.

[6] Wilson's 'abiding fascination' with the motor car is first observed here (Cornish 2002, p. 15).

[7] JCPML 00653/068/12/43/1.

He departed Sydney 8 April 1925, and crossed the American continent bearing an impressive diary of appointments. On 29 May he conferred with Herbert Hoover, then the driving Secretary of a reinvigorated United States Department of Commerce. Copland judged the meeting a success. There was a sympathy about their aims. Hoover was zealous for efficiency and rationality. He favoured a 'scientific tariff uninfluenced by political considerations'. Copland approved. 'There is a little of the politician but a good deal of the statesman ... He gave a very decidedly favourable opinion to economists, and economics as a science' (UMA DBC 29 May 1925).

He then visited the newly founded Duke University in North Carolina and dined with the anthropologist Bronislaw Malinowski, also visiting the United States on a Laura Spelman Fellowship. Malinowski told Copland he had recently 'dined with two negroes at [the adjacent town of] Durham – this is probably the only time it had been done there' (UMA DBC 1 June 1925). [8]

From New York he embarked for Europe. A few days after his arrival in London, he lunched with John Maynard Keynes and Lydia at Gordon Square (19 June 1925). He was not taken with Lydia: 'no doubt she is a good dancer, but she looked very plain and her small figure did not suggest much capacity'. She was a 'spoilt prima donna'. Keynes was also a little disappointing. 'Keynes is not as tall as I thought and rather more effeminate'. [9] But they spoke 'pleasantly' for three hours. Keynes contended that Churchill's worst error was not to restore the gold value of the pound, but to restore it at the old rate instead of a lower rate. Keynes said Classical economics 'had rather worked itself out', and that he was writing 'a serious treatise on money'. This was the first knowledge to Copland of a book that was to loom in his policy analysis of the Great Depression, Keynes' *Treatise on money*.

Copland was more unmistakably impressed by Joseph Alois Schumpeter, whom he met in Germany in the following month. [10] Schumpeter complained to Copland that Germany had 'still too many so-called economists who are not at all advanced thinkers', and welcomed the possibility of Australian students undertaking doctorates in Germany. 'He had [the] idea that Japan and Australia were enemies and thought it very curious that Australia and Japan should be allies in war,

---

[8] An anthropologist would be especially sensitive to the taboos enveloping eating. The taboos of race and dining in the United States of the 1940s are delicately traced by Gunnar Myrdal (1944).

[9] It was a rare occasion for persons to be disappointed in Keynes' height. Known as 'lanky' at school, he was allegedly six foot six.

[10] While visiting Kiel, Copland observed German officers singing an anthem of the defunct German Empire. With his characteristic political nose he noted: 'It was significant that the hall porter sat through the song while the officers and their ladies rose' (UMA 4 July 1925).

but also very chivalrous of Australia to enter the war on behalf of England' (UMA DBC 4 July 1925).

Tracts on monetary reform

The most urgent business of post-war economists was to understand and correct the disequilibrium in international economic relations in the post-war world. Churchill's announcement of 28 April 1925 was the most salient manifestation of an impulse to reinstate the financial normality that had been swept away by the First World War. Before 1914 virtually the whole world – with China the main exception – adhered to the gold standard, a system that sought to make gold the essence of anything reckoned as money, thus reducing the various national currencies to merely measures of certain amounts of gold. In an age of imperial rivalry, gold was the world's financial emperor who brooked no borders.

The gold standard was destroyed in 1914. All of the belligerent nations (save the United States) discarded the gold standard and experienced rapid inflations. At the close of the war, Germany, Austria and Russia plunged into hyperinflation that annihilated traditional parities.[11] The end of the war also brought reparations, which applied new pressures to exchange rates. Some feared that the burden of reparations on the defeated powers would depreciate their exchange rates, as the defeated countries, in order to pay for reparations, sought to capture export markets by cheapening their exports.

Australia, too, effectively left the gold standard with war. Australian currency had been fixed to gold since the establishment of the Sydney Mint in 1855. With war the gold standard became a fiction, the note issue expanded, and in the six-year period following 1913–14 consumer prices rose by 60 per cent. With both the Australian pound and sterling separated from the gold standard, the rate of the exchange between the two pounds became variable. By 1924 the Australian pound had deviated from pound sterling by four per cent, a small deviation but the largest in 70 years, and the deviation scandalised many.

In seeking to understand this monetary instability, the four economists could draw on two opposing tendencies in monetary thought: one of which might be called 'neo-quantity theorising', and the other 'post-quantity theorising'.

Principal among neo-quantity theorists was Brigden's patron, Edwin Cannan, and to a lesser degree, Irving Fisher. Fisher had popularised the Quantity Theory in a so-called 'equation of exchange':

---

[11] Schumpeter had been part of the Austrian Government in 1919. He put to Copland that 'inflation at that time was an absolute necessity, socially everything had broken down and to refuse more currency would have brought revolution'.

$$MV = PT$$

where the symbol, M stood for the stock of money, V for the number of times M was turned over in the year (the velocity of circulation), P the price of a basket of goods during the year, and T the volume of trade over the year.

The Quantity Theory of Cannan and Fisher was logically distinct from the gold standard. But as quantity theorists wanted the money supply limited, and as the gold supply *was* limited, the notion of 'making money gold' was appealing. Therefore neo-quantity theorists favoured a restoration of the link with gold, although some (like Fisher) preferred the link to be a variable one. In Australia the neo-quantity theorists were in control of the newly instituted Notes Issue Board which controlled the quantity of Australian currency, and they applied a regime of monetary restriction from which they expected a restoration of the link to gold (Coleman 2001b).

The alternative to the Quantity Theory might be called 'post-quantity theorising', the leading articulator of which was Keynes in his *Tract on monetary reform*. This alternative accepted that the Quantity Theory bore truth, but maintained that the truth it bore was incomplete, conditional, even potentially misleading. They attached a significance to 'credit' and bank lending, which the Quantity Theory never had. To the 'post-quantity theorists', the question of the relation between money and prices, which had seemed closed with the Napoleonic Wars, was again an open one.

In this contest the four did as they usually did – cordially receive the modern innovation, while expressing respect for the past. None of the four took an extreme position. None of the four had a sharply defined doctrinal position.

Brigden, in a paper he submitted to the *Economic Journal*, took up a theoretical position imbued with the spirit of compromise. 'The growing liquidity of ownership makes it more impossible to draw a line between promises to pay money on demand at some future date, and even other property rights virtually convertible into money at will' (Brigden 1923, p. 22). Therefore, he concluded cautiously, 'the quantity theory is somewhat attenuated'. He expressed his vision of this attenuation with a metaphor seemingly deliberately modelled on Tycho Brahe's own attempt at compromise between Copernicus and Ptolemy. Whereas the classical view placed money at the centre of the solar system, with trade and banking orbiting about it, the new thinking would place trade at the centre, and would have money and banking doing the orbiting. Brigden would demote money, but not quite so radically: trade is the sun and money the orbiting planet – to this extent Brigden was the revolutionary Copernican. But banking itself was not a distinct planet charting its own course, but merely money's moon.[12]

---

[12] The paper was not accepted. Brigden later dismissed it as 'too academic'.

The contribution of the remaining three was not to affirm any strong theoretical proposition, but to give a measure of welcome to the tendencies of modern policy, and to investigate the alternatives empirically.

Copland's contribution was a novel investigation of the relation between the outburst of inflation and monetary expansion that Australia had experienced since 1914. His main concern was to determine whether the Quantity relationship held between money and prices. He began by using a wide range of Australian economic data to calculate estimates of M, V and T for 1901–17. He then computed the magnitude of $(V/T)M$ for 1901–17. If the 'equation of exchange' had held in Australia over the 1901–17 period, this computed magnitude should also have been the P series. So having produced the P series which would have been observed if the 'equation of exchange' had applied, he then compared it with the P series that was actually observed. His judgement was that the two P series – the hypothetical and the actual – displayed close agreement. This being so, he felt justified in concluding that 'The equation of exchange may be regarded as true for Australia' (Copland 1920, p. 505).

The exercise was an elementary one by later standards, but Copland maintained that it was entirely original: the hypothetical P series which he had generated was, he said 'the first of its kind known to the writer'. And he seems to have been correct. The level of empirical investigation of the Quantity Theory still consisted of comparing percentage changes in actual M and actual P. [13] It was not until the mid-1920s that Holbrook Working initiated the calculation of coefficients of correlation between M and P (Working 1923).

The confirmation of Copland's contribution was its acceptance – in no ordinary way - for publication in the *Economic Journal* by its editor, J. M. Keynes. Keynes wrote: 'I am much obliged to you for sending me your masterly article on 'Currency and prices in Australia', and I gladly accept it for the *Economic Journal*. You have clearly taken great pains in the investigation, and the results are of high general interest.' [14]

Copland did not see his vindication of the Quantity Theory as vindicating the policy of a gold standard. As Copland claimed: 'Modern theorists base their work on this distrust ['of any standard based upon a commodity like gold'], and one of the principal aims of monetary theory in recent years has been to devise a means of escape from the gold standard' (Copland 1920). At most, Copland and

---

[13] See, for example, the effort by the senior academic figure in British economics, J. S. Nicholson (1917).

[14] Keynes' quote in Copland's application for the Sidney Myer Chair of Commerce at the University of Melbourne, (UMA 11 July 1924).

Giblin [15] would grant a benevolent nod to a flexible gold standard of the type favoured by Fisher – in this scheme, the gold value of money would be fixed by government, but its gold value would be periodically revised by government.

Copland himself did not fight the war against the gold standard. But as editor of the *Economic Record* he gave room to his old Tasmanian pupil Keith Isles to launch a Quantity Theory critique of the gold standard from Caius College, Cambridge (Isles 1931).

Isles began with the contention that the gold standard had been adopted in Australia with little or no consideration of its suitability to local circumstances. It was, regrettably, not suitable, as it left the money supply vulnerable to balance of trade shocks, since the world would use money balances in times of export booms to pay for Australian exports (and, conversely, Australia would use part of her money balances to pay for imports in times of import booms). Compounding the difficulty, the banking system spread throughout the economy (both secondary and primary) the impact of disturbances to the foreign exchange reserves, caused by such fluctuations in exports of primary products. An increase in sterling balances in London (due perhaps to improved wool prices) would induce banks to increase lending in Australia. As a consequence, 'Rapid expansions and contractions in credit' are the concomitant of the gold standard. 'Monetary policy should be designed to prevent them [= reverberations of disturbances of primary products], but Australian monetary policy actually promotes them'.

In the next issue of the *Economic Record*, Isles' paper was criticised by his old classmate from Economics II, Roland Wilson (Wilson 1931a). His studies since the two last met had prepared Wilson well to give Isles a lesson in careful empirical inquiry. He showed that a correlation Isles had prized – that between 'net increase in banking funds abroad' and the 'excess of deposits over securities' – was an accounting tautology. As for the hypothesised dependence of advances upon the excess of deposits over advances, Wilson showed the correlation between the two was *negative*. But Wilson was more interested in truth, than in proving Isles wrong. He also demonstrated, in support of Isles, a correlation of 0.44 of excess advances with prices.

Isles replied in the next volume of the *Economic Record* (Isles 1932). He conceded some errors. He perhaps need not have been so modest. In the last pages of his reply he noted the 'considerable sympathy' between a plotting of the annual rate of change in prices in Australia between 1913 and 1930, and the plotting of the (inverted) unemployment rate. Isles had stumbled on the Phillips Curve.

---

[15] Footnote 1 reads: 'The writer wishes to acknowledge his great indebtedness to Mr. L. F. Giblin, Government Statistician of Tasmania, for many valuable suggestions'.

Lazarus and Dives

Wilson did not pursue the exchange with Isles. His critique of Isles was only a passing broadside. His leading concern was the publication of the contents of his DPhil and PhD: *Capital imports and the terms of trade examined in the light of sixty years of Australian borrowing*, that was published in 1931 by Melbourne University Press, through the good offices of Giblin and Copland, after Angus and Robertson had declined it. His debt to Viner, Wilson imposingly admits: 'Where I have disagreed with him I am probably wrong. If I am right the triumph is not mine but my master's'.

Wilson's thesis addressed this question: 'How is a country's terms of trade affected by the flow of capital in (or out) of it?' Will a country sending sums abroad find its imports cheaper, or more expensive in terms of its exports? This had become topical in the post-war world, with the prospect of large sums flowing from Germany to the victorious powers. But the question was as old as Mill. And the received answer was also as old as Mill. International borrowing ('capital imports' or 'capital inflow') improves the borrowing country's terms of trade: its imports will become cheaper relative to its exports. This is because to borrow from abroad allows payment for part of imports by means of the loans from abroad. The borrowing country is, therefore, relieved of the necessity of exporting a value equal to its imports. Exports are consequently contracted by the home country. And with an unchanged world market for its exports, that reduction will make its exports more valuable. The terms of trade improve.

The logic of Mill's argument can be extended to other questions. What will happen when the loan has to be repaid and serviced? Any net repayment means that the country must now export a value *greater* than its imports, in order to pay not just the imports but also the debt service owed to the foreigners. The terms of trade must fall. This conclusion about debt service had an easy application to the consequence of German reparations to the Allied Powers. As servicing debt is like a reparation, reparations will necessitate a depreciation in the German terms of trade, which will amount to an additional burden to be carried by Germany. This phenomenon – reparations deteriorating the terms of trade and making the burden of reparations even worse – was known as the 'Transfer Problem', and generated a considerable literature.

Wilson announced in *Capital imports and the terms of trade* that he would 'contest the accepted views' on this issue. There was, he said, 'no theoretical grounds' for Mill's assertion. However, said Wilson, there did exist a strong theoretical expectation concerning a distinct, but related, question that classical theorising had never pondered: What was the impact of capital inflows on the prices of goods that could be neither imported or exported? Wilson argued that the price of such 'non-tradeables' relative to other goods would rise with capital inflows. This thesis of his concerning capital inflows and 'the second terms of trade' –

the price of tradeables relative to non-tradeables – was to become a recurrent theme in Australian theorising throughout the twentieth century, and would bear fruit ultimately in the Gregory Thesis.

Wilson's basic insight with respect to capital flows and the terms of trade is that any capital inflow amounts to a transfer of purchasing power from the lending economy to the borrowing economy. This implies that, while the increase in purchasing power induces the borrowing country to buy more of its own export goods and therefore supply less of it to world markets, at the same time the lending country will be buying *less* of the borrowing country's export good, on account of its reduced purchasing power. There is, therefore, a contraction in the *demand* for the export good that accompanies the contraction in its supply. It is perfectly possible that the contraction in demand for the good will equal the contraction in supply. In that case the equilibrium value of the export good is unaltered, rather than increase. A capital inflow need not increase the value of the borrowing country's export goods. Correspondingly, a capital outflow need not reduce the value of the borrowing country's export goods. Hence Mill was wrong in unconditionally predicting transfers and outflows abroad would worsen the terms of trade. One consequence of this conclusion was that the 'Transfer Problem' might be an imaginary terror.

Wilson argues his claims in terms of the beggar Lazarus and Dives the rich man in the parable of the rich man and Lazarus, (Luke 6:19–31) 'clothed in purple and fine linen, and fared sumptuously every day'. It is then expounded in cumbersome numerical examples. But if Wilson's theoretical methods were obsolete, his empirical technique was modern. With the methods he had been taught in Chicago, he used Australia's lavish borrowing as a test case. 'In this as in other directions Australia has almost turned herself into the social and economic laboratory which is often sought but rarely found' (Wilson 1931b, p. 3). With data for borrowing and the terms of trade for 1893–1913, Wilson computed the coefficient of correlation between capital imports and the ratio of export to import prices to be -0.29. Borrowing *deteriorates* the terms of trade (the opposite of what Mill maintained). [16]

Capital imports and the terms of trade was reviewed in the *American Economic Review* ('closely reasoned'), the *Journal of Political Economy* ('an important contribution to the literature of international trade'), and by Harrod in the

---

[16] How so? In Wilsonian logic a negative correlation between capital inflow and the terms of trade would be explained by the British demand for Australian wool being reduced by British loans to Australia: Britons have no money to buy wool because they have lent it to Australia. Modern intertemporal analysis would suggest the negative correlation is explained by causality running from the terms of trade to capital flows: a fall in the value of exports induces Australia to borrow from abroad in order to smooth its consumption in the face of a negative income shock.

September 1932 issue of the *Economic Journal*. Judging the book to be 'extremely interesting and suggestive', and 'a valuable contribution to the literature on international trade', he seized on Wilson's suggestion that the terms of trade impact of capital movements was ambiguous, and re-presented the case with a greater lucidity than Wilson. Hicks wrote to Harrod to say he was 'very interested in your review of Wilson'.[17] More cautiously, D.H. Robertson told Harrod: 'I haven't yet coped properly with your review of Mr. Wilson on capital transfer, and am wondering whether you aren't between you really saying the same thing as Pigou in his highly concentrated and still unpublished paper'.[18] Indeed, in the following (December 1932) issue of *The Economic Journal*, the kind of ideas Wilson was exploring were presented by Pigou definitively, if rather laboriously, in mathematical terms.

But the burgeoning literature on capital flows and the terms of trade ignored the second theme in Wilson's logic: the relations between capital inflows and the 'second terms of trade' – the price of tradeables to non-tradeables – a theme that was to have resonance in the 1970s, with notions of the 'Dutch Disease' and the 'Gregory Thesis'.

Wilson's deliberations on this issue began with the simple distinction between 'exportables' and 'domestic' goods, or, in equivalent modern language, 'tradeables' and 'non-tradeable'. A cigar is exportable. A haircut is not. It is a non-tradeable. Undeniably, British demand for German non-tradeables (say, German haircuts) must be lower than German demand for German non-tradeables (the German haircut). Therefore, any transfer of purchasing power from Germany to Britain must reduce demand for German non-tradeables, and so reduce their price relative to German and British exportables. By a parallel logic, the transfer of purchasing power to Britain would increase the value of British non-tradeables. Such a transfer of purchasing power would comprehend not only 'reparations' but also foreign aid, capital inflow ('capital imports'), or the discovery of some natural resource that earns large economic rents. In all cases, the relative price of non-tradeables in the country receiving the inflow will increase. Gratifyingly, while Mill's thesis about capital flows and the terms of trade was not verified empirically, Wilson could report that 'some verification is found in Australian experience for the proposition that imports of capital tend to be positively correlated with increases in the ratio of "domestic" price level to the price level of "international" commodities'.

It was Australian economists who were to cultivate Wilson's ideas on the 'second terms of trade', especially Trevor Swan (1918–89), who was appointed in 1950 as the foundation professor in economics at the Research School of Economics

---

[17] http://economia.unipv.it/harrod/edition/editionstuff/rfh.11e.htm.
[18] http://economia.unipv.it/harrod/edition/editionstuff/rfh.117.htm#10924.

at the Australian National University (ANU), after Wilson had declined the post. Swan was no protégée of Wilson. In Australia his teachers were R. C. Mills, Ronald Walker, S.J. Butlin, John La Nauze; and overseas Michal Kalecki, James Meade, Nicholas Kaldor, Richard Stone, and Arthur Smithies. Nor had he received Wilson's patronage: Coombs performed that role for Swan. But in early 1950s Canberra, the new professor was in regular contact with the now senior mandarin of the Treasury, Roland Wilson. It was a source of pride to Swan that he, the professor, regularly lunched with the policy-maker Wilson. [19]

The first fruit of Swan's digestion of Wilson's thesis was the 'Swan Diagram' (Swan 1955), which demonstrated how, in a neo-Keynesian context, capital inflows would necessitate an appreciation in the value of services (that is, non-tradeables). Wilfred Salter (1929–63), at Swan's department in the ANU's Research School of Social Sciences from 1956 until 1959, recast the same ideas in neoclassical form in the 'Salter Diagram' (Salter 1959). Perhaps the subsequent development of Wilson's ideas closest to Wilson's original approach was that undertaken by Allan Ross Hall, appointed in the early 1950s to the Research School of Social Sciences, in his paper 'Capital imports and the composition of investment in a borrowing country' (in Hall 1963). In this paper Hall wrote that 'conclusions of Roland Wilson's *Capital imports and the terms of trade* ... have not been fully appreciated by Australian economic historians (including the present writer a dozen years ago)'.

But the most significant revival came with Trevor Swan's return to a public stage in the early 1970s, after some 'difficult years', with his review of 'Overseas investment in Australia. Treasury economic paper no. 1' in the *Economic Record* (Swan 1972). According to Swan:

> This paper might be labelled No.2, for the first on the subject was published by Roland Wilson in 1931. Wilson even then, before he had actually been recruited by Treasury, was an outstanding Treasury officer and economist. In 1931 he disputed and overturned the established views on capital imports and terms of trade held by Taussig, Viner, Keynes.

Swan subsequently notes in his review:

> An important condition for running such a [current account] deficit, transmuting paper assets into real resources, is that our domestic costs and prices should rise relative to the prices of importables and exportables. This truth ... is the one asserted against the previous orthodoxy by Roland Wilson in 1931.

---

[19] Warren Hogan, a PhD student of Swan in the 1950s, recalled years later his shock at being grilled at a social function by Wilson on the content of his thesis. Trevor Swan, observing the harried student from another corner of the room, crossed the floor to be present at the cross-examination.

The key application of the notions that Swan had cultivated was now about to take place, in the 'Gregory Thesis'. R. G. Gregory had joined the Research School of Social Sciences at the ANU in 1971, having trained in international economics. In his 1976 paper, 'Some implications of the growth of the mineral sector', Gregory pressed a simple but socially significant implication of Wilson's thesis: that an increase in the value of non-tradeables would cause a depression in the production and incomes in the import-competing sector. The paper resonated sharply with current events. Booming values in the prices of fuels during the 1970s and 1980s and the associated inflows to develop them had raised the prospect of de-industrialisation.[20]

Miles from anywhere

Wilson did not pursue his own ideas. Viner had expected Wilson to undertake an academic career in North America. With an Oxford DPhil and Chicago PhD he had formidable qualifications. His Tasmanian peer Arthur Smithies was to show what path Wilson could have taken. Smithies (1907–81) had attended the University of Tasmania shortly after Wilson; had won a Rhodes Scholarship shortly after Wilson; had studied PPE at Oxford shortly after Wilson; and then, like Wilson, transferred to an American university, Harvard. There he was supervised by Schumpeter, who had by then left Bonn, and had ended up with an Australian doctoral student after all. (Schumpeter took it upon himself to write to Giblin about his 'Tasmanian' whom he had 'got know so intimately'. 'He has a remarkable aptitude for clever and efficient handling of statistics', and possessed 'quite unusual merit on a theoretical subject'). After completing his doctorate, Smithies joined Wilson at the Bureau of Census and Statistics in Canberra. But there the two careers diverge. After a stint at Michigan, Smithies wound up at Harvard, published prolifically in *Econometrica*, the *Review of Economic Studies*, and the *Quarterly Journal of Economics,* did important work on the 'inflationary gap' (Smithies 1942), and became editor of the *Quarterly Journal of Economics* and the *Journal of Economic Abstracts*.

A career like Smithies was possible for Wilson. Toronto offered him a first job. But a life in learning was not the most important thing to Wilson. He always wore his doctoral robes very lightly, even when such a distinction was a rarity.

---

[20] In the 1990s much attention was given to the notion that capital inflows appreciate the 'real exchange rate' (i.e. the purchasing power of foreign currency in terms of the goods and services of the home country). This is just another application of Wilson's thesis. The thesis implies that a capital inflow into Britain makes British non-tradeables more expensive relative to tradeables. The purchasing power of German currency in Britain has declined. The British real exchange rate has appreciated.

[21] Much later, in a graduation address to the University of Tasmania in 1969, he disowned any vocation for academic life, saying that: '… I myself can lay no claim to scholarship in the deeper sense of the term. I never felt deeply attracted to scholarship for its own sake' (Address to University of Tasmania 2 April 1969).

[22] He would begin as a Lecturer at the University of Tasmania from 1 August 1930. Wilson evidently felt a tug of something other than purely professional calling.

> When he informed Jacob Viner that he was returning to Tasmania, the famous economist expressed great surprise, remarking that 'Tasmania is miles away from everywhere', to which Wilson replied: 'It's not miles away from Tasmania. (Cornish 2002, p. 16).

---

[21] 'I have, of course, attracted a few degrees, mostly of a technical or specialist nature, but most of those in this assembly will know that even earned degrees do not always go hand in hand with scholarship.' Wilson appears to have always styled himself Mr Wilson.

[22] Wilson added, however, that 'my dear friend and teacher, the late James Brigden did try to inculcate in me some of his own love of scholarship'.

4. Economic science and political power

'We are out to put Australia on the economics map.'
L. F. Giblin

'It is my duty as an economist to talk about costs.'
J. B. Brigden

Wilson was to rejoin neither Copland, Giblin nor Brigden on his return to the University of Tasmania in 1931. By then all had left.

Copland had been the first to go. His professorial peers at the University in the early 1920s included several men who would occupy their chairs well into the 1950s. Copland had no such settled temperament. He was reaching for the wider world. In October 1923 he applied to the University for one year's leave, to study either in Britain or the United States. He was refused. Perhaps the Council believed that their young man had already been rewarded well enough. They underestimated Copland's keen sense of entitlement. In July 1924 he applied for the new Chair of Commerce at the University of Melbourne. His application included an impressive list of nine referees, including Giblin. The London-based selection committee had 'unanimously recommend[ed]' his appointment, 'for the first time choosing a candidate who was not born in Britain and had neither studied nor taught in a British university' (Selleck 2003, p. 606). He resigned his Tasmanian chair with effect from 15 December 1924.

Just thirty years old, Copland was now established as the sole Professor of Economics in Melbourne, the business capital of Australia. But the study and research of economics was almost defunct in this commercial centre. Copland was to set about reviving both, creating for the first time a professional voice of Australian economists: The Economic Society of Australia and New Zealand, with its journal, the *Economic Record*.

Melbourne was also the political capital. It was the seat of the national parliament, and would remain so until 1927. Melbourne could also claim a youngish Prime Minister as her own: Stanley Melbourne Bruce, forty-one years old, of commercial background, impressed by 'scientific' American business methods, concerned with efficiency, and constantly pouring memoranda into his dictaphone.

The stage was set for a liaison between political power and the infant Australian economics profession. Over the remainder of the decade, economic inquiries, commissions, and bureaus of economic research were summoned forth by prime-ministerial wish, and manned with economists. From the time of Copland's arrival and until the close of the 1920s, political power was to furnish personally a patronage of the discipline seldom matched elsewhere. And yet, after five further years, political power was rudely to cast aside that patronage.

Town and gown

At the time of Copland's arrival, the University of Melbourne was only just emerging from its late Victorian chrysalis. The wearing of gowns was theoretically compulsory for the undergraduates, and turning out for the weekly parade of the University Rifles practically inescapable. *Farrago* and the Melbourne University Labor Club were yet to be born. It was 'a demi-rural retreat ... a resort, also, for sons and some daughters of gentleman and a few others', in the words of one student from the early 1920s (Fitzpatrick 1961, p. 9). Historians of the University have tended to portray it at this period as provincial, introverted, unambitious in its teaching, and (outside the natural sciences) desultory in its research (Fitzpatrick 1961, Blainey 1957, Selleck 2003).

Indeed, by the time of Copland's arrival, economics had been, in the words of one historian, 'abandoned' (Selleck 2003). It was not strictly extinct: a solitary economic historian taught one course on 'political economy'. But Copland was accurate in informing the readers of the *Economic Journal* that there was 'scarcely' any economics at Melbourne. Copland's appointment was intended to promote a resurgence, and even before arriving he energetically began to organise that. He would create a Bachelor of Commerce. It would – very deliberately – have the underpinnings of a quality degree; students could not obtain a BCom without doing either mathematics, or science or a modern language. He informed the Registrar: 'You may consider it a rather ambitious program but I thought it wise to state at the outset my ideas regarding the work of the school' (UMA DBC 3 October 1924).

He was 'dramatically' successful. Not long after his arrival he wrote: 'We are finding the popularity of economics a little embarrassing. So many students are seeking admission, and just at present our time is occupied with incessant interviewing' (UMA DBC 19 March 1925). He obtained 323 students for the new BCom in 1925. He firmly headed off rival claims for resources (such as a putative sociology department),[1] and pushed for more of his own. He wanted a 'cinema machine' to allow students of Industrial Organisation to observe factory operations without necessitating an excursion, and obtained £50 from the Chamber of Commerce for a duplicating machine.

---

[1] In 1925 Copland vigorously attacked a proposal to found a Chair of Sociology. 'In no University of the standing of Melbourne is such scant attention given in the Faculty of Arts, to the subject of Economics ... Under present conditions it is necessary to develop the study of economics and psychology before proceeding further with sociology' (UMA DBC 31July 1925). See Crozier (2002).

This last gratuity was not accidental. Part of Copland's strategy was to 'establish good relations with the business community from the very beginning of his time in Melbourne' (Scott 1988, p. 3). Despite the fact that Melbourne was the seat of most company headquarters, the university had no links to business. Now faculty meetings were to be held on occasion at the Chamber of Commerce. The new faculty was to include Sir Robert Gibson, the new power in the Commonwealth Bank. Perhaps with an eye to successful alumni Copland was active in the Commerce Students' Society, and succeeded in tempting the Prime Minister to accept an invitation to address it.[2] Copland drew a creditable harvest from his cultivation of business interests.

Copland also moved to provide a professional society for economists. No society or organ had existed in Australia since the *Australian Economist* had expired in 1898 with the ebb of the 1890s slump, and the redirection of controversy towards Federation. The Australian and New Zealand Association for the Advancement of Sciences did maintain an Economics and Statistics 'Section', but it was 'somewhat anaemic'. However, at the 1924 meeting of the section the economists 'attended in force', and with 'an almost evangelical fervour' received Copland's proposal to establish an Economic Society. Nineteen twenty-four, said Giblin, 'might perhaps be called A.E.1 – the first year of economists in Australia' (Giblin 1947, p. 1). With his 'characteristic drive' Copland set about founding a society, with a Central Council of the Economic Society established at the University of Melbourne in August 1925, and Copland duly elected President.

The next step was to establish a voice of the profession – the *Economic Record*, whose first issue appeared in November 1925.[3] 'From the first number', Copland with his co-editor R. C. Mills, 'read every article, every note and most of the reviews that were offered for publication', and did so for 22 years (Giblin 1947, p. 2). The 1000 copies of the first issue were 'soon exhausted'; a reprint of 500 was ordered, and another 150 sold. Given Australia's population was six million, that volume of sales compares very decently with the 3000 copies that, Keynes told Copland, the *Economic Journal* sold. Years later Giblin was to venture accurately: 'it is fair to say that in no other branch of studies, literary or scientific, has Australia produced another journal so highly recognised and esteemed in other countries' (Giblin 1947, p. 4).

The *Economic Record* reflected Copland's vision, as Australian economics engaged in problem-solving rather than science-building. In Copland's conception the *Record* would have no brief to pursue and extend pure theory. Its concern was

---

[2] Bruce: 'I would very much like to accept the invitation because I know that at such a gathering I would have an opportunity of speaking to people who realise the importance of economic research at the present time in Australia' (UMA DBC 22 August 1924).

[3] Brigden originally foresaw it would only be an 'annual volume'.

Figure 4.1. Copland dazzles in Melbourne

Source: uma/I/1967

with a particular question that had become socially significant. New adventures overseas in matters of pure theory were ignored. By way of illustration: in the late 1920s and early 1930s the theoretical issue of monopoly was an international preoccupation of economic theorists. Under the 'applied', problem-solving approach a problem of pure theory could never occupy the attention of Australian economics.

Complementing the problem-solving approach was an outlook that was historicist rather than universalist. No single theory could apply in all circumstances. The universalist theory that the classical economists pretended to follow was in fact a legacy from British conditions in the nineteenth century. The truths in Australia would differ. As Brigden wrote in the inaugural issue of the *Economic Record*:

> The classic theory of international trade has been derived from English circumstances ... [but] there is ... no analogy to be drawn from either British or American experience, and Australians must think out their tariff problem for themselves. (Brigden 1925, p. 32).

Consequently, the elucidation of the Australian circumstances was critical. An accompanying stress on empiricism is pervasive in the *Record*, which may be said to be possessed of a 'somewhat naïve faith not untypical of the time that a knowledge of "the facts" would point the way to the proper course of action' (Richmond 1983, p. 250).

Finally, the Australian economists adhered to a 'summary' repudiation of *laissez-faire* as obsolete.

> It will be sufficient to say rather summarily that the policy of *laissez-faire* in any country allows the natural inequalities of capacity, and the acquired or inherent inequalities of property, to operate to the fullest extent to the diminution of welfare. (Brigden et al. 1929, p. 93).

Refusing liberalism, they did not embrace socialism. The vision of Brigden, Copland and Giblin was of a publicly regulated but privately owned economy.

The *Record*'s first issue of November 1925 carried a paper that was to epitomise these attitudes, and to provide an assault on some classical precepts that was to have repercussions internationally. This was Brigden's 'The Australian tariff and the standard of living' (Brigden 1925). It advanced the heterodoxical thesis that a tariff may enhance the living standard of the average inhabitant. Copland and Giblin had urged Brigden to submit the paper to this inaugural issue of the *Record*. 'You have argued the case with great ingenuity', wrote Copland, without actually accepting the case himself. Brigden took up the proposal: 'It is a sporting challenge ... Although I risk myself, the Society may benefit from the interest aroused' (quoted in Harper 1989). It provoked the first controversy in the *Record*, and Brigden was to spar with free trade advocates, such as F.C. Benham

(1900-1960), in the *Record* through the mid-twenties (see Benham 1926; Brigden 1927a, 1927b; Giblin 1927a).

What was Brigden's argument? 'The Australian tariff and the standard of living' actually contains two separate protectionist arguments: a 'terms-of-trade' argument, and a 'returns-to-labour' argument. Both arguments assume a two-sector economy; in our terminology, 'food' and 'manufactures'.

The terms-of-trade argument holds that a reduction in tariffs on manufactures would increase food output, and by glutting the world market, reduce the value of food in terms of manufactures, so that an actually smaller amount of manufactures could be imported, despite the increase in food exports. In brief, a tariff cut reduces the terms of trade. On a theoretical level, the terms-of-trade argument is a familiar article of textbooks, and unproblematic.

The returns-to-labour argument turns on the marginal productivities of labour. That marginal productivities might be such that a tariff reduction could reduce real wages had been previously anticipated in 1887 in the *Principles of political economy* of Henry Sidgwick (1838–1900). He considered a country producing manufactures under protection, and food such that 'additional food produce could not be obtained except at rapidly increasing expense' (Sidgwick 1887, p. 497). If protection to manufactures is abolished, then labour will be reallocated to food, and marginal productivity in food will diminish so 'rapidly' that the purchasing power of the wage may fall, despite the rise in the amount of manufactures a unit of food may purchase.[4]

Sidgwick's argument was reported, with much pooh-poohing, by Charles Bastable in various editions of *Theory of international trade*. Edgeworth then took up the defence of Sidgwick's claim against Bastable's not-very-telling criticisms, and skirmishes between Bastable and Edgeworth continued in the *Economic Journal* between 1897 and 1900. Any diligent reader of past issues of the *Economic Journal* would already be well aware of Sidgwick's theoretical argument. And as Brigden had been a student of Edgeworth, and one to whom he 'owed much' (Brigden 1926), it is more than plausible that Brigden became acquainted with this controversy directly from the man whom 'no heterodoxy could shock' (Brigden 1926, p. 144).[5]

---

[4] In 1903 J.S. Nicholson (1850–1927) had advanced an argument for the deleterious impact of free trade on labour that is similar to Sigdwick's, but with more arbitrariness and less clarity. As Sidgwick later acknowledged, a similar argument for the benefits of protection had been previously advanced by Torrens in 1821 ([1965] 1821).

[5] In addition, the controversy was amply covered in Bastable's *Theory of international trade*, which Copland used as the Bridgen guide to the theory of protection.

But Brigden provided a novel path by which assumptions about productivity could yield the result that tariffs are improving of worker's welfare. The 'Sidgwick Assumption' – a 'rapid' deterioration in the marginal productivity of labour in food – is refused. Instead in Brigden's argument, labour is assumed to operate with diminishing marginal productivity in food, but with constant marginal returns in manufactures. Given this, increasing tariffs will not reduce the marginal productivity of labour in manufactures (by assumption), and so will not reduce the wage in terms of manufactures. However, with manufactures now more valuable in terms of food, the marginal product of labour in manufactures evaluated in terms of food is higher. This induces a reallocation of labour from food towards manufactures. The marginal product of labour in food is thereby increased. The upshot is that the manufactures wage is unchanged, and the food wage is increased. The utility of the worker (that is, the 'standard of living') must rise, as long as the worker consumes some non-zero quantity of food. Four further implications may be demonstrated (see the appendix to this chapter) and are simply noted here:

1. *Wage maximisation implies autarky*. Brigden's argument implies the maximisation of the worker wage would be secured by the maximisation of the tariff; that is, an increase in the tariff until autarky is reached, and international trade ceases.
2. *Protectionism is wage reducing with a small population*. Brigden's argument does not imply that protectionism would increase real wages for *all* population levels. The population may be so small that the marginal product of labour in food will exceed the marginal product of labour in manufactures even if *all* labour is allocated to food. In this, all labour will be allocated to food, manufacturing will not exist, and the argument cannot proceed.
3. *Autarky does not prevent wages decreasing as population increases*. Protection does not remove the decline in wages caused by the population pressing on scarce land. It only makes the decline smaller than it would have been under free trade. It does so by creating a manufactures industry at a level of population at which manufacturing would be non-existent under free trade, and thereby diverts part of population increases from food (where diminishing returns operate) and into manufacture (where no diminishing returns operate).
4. *The social inefficiency of protection*. Protection is 'pareto inefficient'. There are winners, but the winners cannot compensate the losers. In more specific terms, the decline in rents on land used in food would be larger than the increase in the wage bill.

'The Brigden report'

Brigden's argument was to become the key idea in an enquiry into the tariff commissioned by Bruce, that was to prove an enduring landmark in Australian economic history, and, perhaps, in the development of 'modern' trade theory: *The Australian Tariff: an Economic Enquiry*, often known as 'the Brigden Report'. (See Cain 1973, Manger 1981a, Samuelson 1981, Irwin 1996).

The genesis of the *Enquiry* lay in a sudden increase in protectionist sentiment and action in Australia in the aftermath of the First World War. The average tariff rate rose from about 10 per cent in 1918 to about 20 per cent by 1927 (Dollery and Whitten 1998). Bruce, a moderate protectionist, seemed to have increasing reservations about the wisdom of the protectionist trend. 'The cry of "Let us make everything in Australia" is quite enough to prevent [men] seeing the effect of a policy of that character carried to extremes' (Bruce quoted in McDougall and Bruce 1986, p. 443).

Bruce wanted a 'scientific protection'. The notion of applying scientific methods to problems of national welfare was popular. Shortly before, Bruce had brought to fruition something that resembled a 'national laboratory', a notion earlier championed by Prime Minister Billy Hughes, awed by German technological prowess in the First World War. This was a council of scientists and industrialists in the form of the Council for Scientific and Industrial Research (CSIR). A council of economic scientists might promise to be equally useful. In this spirit, in September 1927 he asked Giblin, C. H. Wickens (the Commonwealth Statistician), and the 'businessman-ideologue' E. C. Dyason to undertake a statistical investigation of the effects and success of tariff policy. In mid-December 1927 this group of three invited Brigden and Copland to join them. This was to result in *The Australian tariff: an economic inquiry*.

The authorship of the *Enquiry* was protracted, difficult and unhappy.

Copland had put himself under awful strain at the University. His letters record him as 'busy', 'very busy', 'frantically busy this week'. It was not just teaching: Copland's professional bibliography runs to around 120 items, a magnitude few economists from the inter-war period (or today) could match. Copland at this time was often an irritated, exasperated man.[6] And it took a toll. Harvard University's C. J. Bullock counselled him: 'your recent troubles were largely due to nervous strain' (UMA 23 November 1926).

There was also significant physical, stylistic and doctrinal distance between the five authors. These divisions (following Marjory Harper and N.G. Cain) might be summarised by way of a contrast between a 'Melbourne Group' (with Copland the leading member) and the 'Hobart Group' (with Brigden the leader). The Hobart group was distinctly protectionist, while Copland's Melbourne Group was more equivocal. Copland was empirical, Brigden more theoretical. Copland

---

[6] Copland's letters of the time are full of his querulous reports of himself being 'puzzled' at 'strange' and 'curious' actions.

wrote as if drafting speeches for a public meeting; Brigden tried to write as if penning letters to a friend. The difference in opinion between Hobart and Melbourne was never successfully resolved. Circumstances were against it. The *Enquiry* was 'written piecemeal, with few meetings of the whole committee' (Harper 1989, p. 8).

An initial three-day meeting in Hobart in January 1928 distributed tasks to the five co-authors. But on 13 March 1928 Bruce demanded the report within a month. To meet Bruce's pre-emptory demand for its conclusion, a draft of the enquiry (a 'Melbourne Report') was prepared by Copland, and submitted to Bruce without 'Hobart's' knowledge. Brigden appears to have suffered this high-handed treatment very meekly.

According to one close student of the *Enquiry*, Bruce 'proposed to publish the document, with addenda from Hobart, seemingly without reading the Hobart material. As Giblin and Brigden objected to publication without considerable revision, they were permitted to redraft the Report to incorporate their work' (Harper 1989). An examination of some of Bruce's correspondence paints a different picture. In a letter of 27 August 1928 Bruce explains that the Melbourne Report 'would not convey much to the ordinary intelligent individual' (Bruce quoted in McDougall and Bruce 1986, pp. 654–60). He dispatched his secretary to Hobart, where all five authors were conferring, with the instruction 'they must do better', and a request of Brigden (not permission') to redraft it (Hytten 1971, p. 52). Bruce declared Brigden's consequent redraft 'an incomparably better job of work than the original one'.

Copland did not share Bruce's judgement. 'So began a low key power struggle' between Brigden and Copland (Harper 1989). 'By the end of 1928 all members of the Committee were rather discouraged'. Giblin told Eilean: 'I'm still rather breathless. The tariff will not get finished. A section I am supposed to be doing rather vital to the whole thing, won't come clear… It has been rather a nightmare at times' (NLA LFG 20 January 1929). The difficulties did not subside. On 11 March 1929, Giblin (then in Melbourne) explained: 'Doubts arose and we wired Brigden to come over for another discussion'. Copland complained to Brigden, 'The new draft on incidence leaves me as puzzled as ever' (UMA 8 April 1929). On 22 May 1929 Giblin wrote: 'Brigden will be over on Saturday, and we must settle things then or never' (NLA LFG 22 May 1929).

Copland's impatience outweighed his doubts. Copland wrote to Brigden: 'The sooner it appears the better. Each time we meet to discuss it doubts and difficulties arise on minor issues and we could, apparently, go on altering the words indefinitely' (UMA 28 June 1929). In the low-key power struggle, 'Hobart' had outworn 'Melbourne'.[7] Years later Hytten summed up: 'Brigden and Giblin wrote that report … no one else had much of a hand in it … Brigden wrote, Giblin criticised … to pacify Copland his essay on free trade was added as an appendix' (Hytten 1951, 1971 p. 53).

Giblin with great care took the corrected proofs to the printing works himself. *The Australian tariff: an economic inquiry* appeared first on 19 July 1929. 'Melbourne was very interested and crowded the bookshops. The first edition of 3,000 has nearly gone and I have written to Bruce about further editions. It is externally quite impressive – looks like a 10/- or 15/- book and sells for 3/6 … The [protectionist] Age leads its article National Policy Vindication and the [free trade] Argus counters with Medicine for Fanatics' (RBA 9 July 1929).

The *Enquiry*'s conclusion is distinctly presented on its first page: in Australia's present circumstances free trade would lower the 'standard of living', that is, the real wage. The *Enquiry*, therefore, distanced itself from the strong tendency of theorists to assert that tariffs would not harm labour as long as it was mobile between import competing and export sectors.[8]

The trenchancy of the *Enquiry*'s theses is not matched by the lucidity of its argument. It was a 'compromise document' in which differences of opinion were concealed. This commitment to compromise discouraged any attempt to secure agreement to some clearly stated argument. This commitment to compromise muffled the *Enquiry*'s presentation of the Australian 'case for protection'.[9]

The theoretical significance of the *Enquiry*

The *Enquiry* has sometimes been judged to be significant for the development of twentieth-century trade theory. Thus Paul Samuelson has judged that the *Enquiry* helped 'set off an analytical controversy that has helped shape the discovery of what has come to be known as modern international trade theory' (Samuelson 1981, p. 147). By 'modern international trade theory', Samuelson means mid-twentieth-century trade theory, which is distinct from both the classical trade theory of Ricardo and the 'post-classical theory' of Mill and Marshall. In classical trade theory, labour was the only factor of production.

---

[7] Copland wrote in a tone of self-exoneration to Cannan: 'I must confess that I endeavoured to explore every possible error that we might have made in coming to our main conclusions. It worried me a good deal for a long time, but eventually I could see no other reasonable conclusion from the facts we have before us' (LSE DBC 21 December 1929).

[8] For example, Gottfried Haberler, one of the fresh breezes in inter-war trade theory, maintained that the suggestion that protection increased wages 'does not merit serious discussion'. 'Free trade seems to be in the interest of the working class'(quoted in Ohlin 1933, p. 202). See also Stolper and Samuelson 1941, p. 61.

[9] The report is 'exasperatingly' 'loose and incomplete' (Cain 1973).

The post-classical theory of Mill and Marshall discarded the labour theory of value, but effectively retained labour as the only *variable* factor. Between 1933 and 1949 Bertil Ohlin and Paul Samuelson recast trade theory by analysing trade in a general equilibrium framework with (at least) two variable factors: capital and labour.

One of the landmarks in the modern theory of international trade was the 1941 proof of Samuelson and Wolfgang Stolper that higher tariffs would unambiguously increase real wages if the country's import-competing sector had a higher labour–capital labour ratio than the export-competing sector. Thus the old protectionist notion that 'protection protects high wages' seemed suddenly to have a solid theoretical foundation. The *Enquiry* of 1929 seemed highly significant here because it had annoyed certain authorities in neoclassical trade theory (such as Jacob Viner) by contending that higher protection *did* increase real wages. On this ground the *Enquiry* has been presented by one commentator as 'a final step between neoclassical trade theory and Ohlin's treatise of 1933' (Cain 1973). Nevertheless, Samuelson himself has written: 'I have to testify it was Wolfgang Stolper's original insight that the Ohlin [1933] analysis provided some vindication for the view that the US tariff might raise real wages here, and not the almost simultaneous ... analysis of the Australian problem, that spawned Stolper-Samuelson' (1981, p. 150). Samuelson describes the episode as 'a plum pudding of Mertonian doubletons of quasi-independent analytic discoveries' (1981, p. 158). 'In my view some of the Australian experts *independently* stumbled on some of what are today known as Hecksher-Ohlin-Samuelson notions that free trade can lower real returns on a factor where it is "relatively scarce"' (private communication to the authors).

What conclusion might an adjudication of this clash of testimony yield about the likely significance of the *Enquiry* for modern trade theory?

An adjudication would begin by noting that the authors of the *Enquiry* strived to bring it to the attention of the intellectual centres. Review copies were sent to overseas journals, with complimentary copies to Keynes, Clapham, Pigou, Ralph Hawtrey, Hugh Dalton, Lionel Robbins, Cannan, Wesley Mitchell, Frank Taussig, and others. But this had little effect. Keynes did write to his friend Giblin to say the *Enquiry* was 'of the highest interest and a very brilliant effort' (quoted in Harper 1989). But it was negatively reviewed in the *Economic Journal*. Viner gave his own cool, forensic and almost relentlessly negative review in the *Economic Record*.[10] Australian academic opinion was not more enthusiastic.

---

[10] Brigden had written hopefully to Copland: 'I am looking forward to Viner's article with great interest, but thought Keynes' comments to Giblin were rather feeble' (UMA JBB 24 October 1929). Copland broke the bad news: Viner's review 'is by no means exciting, and raises many problems that troubled me' (UMA DBC 11 November 1929). Viner contended that there were 'strong

Shann complained that the authors of the *Enquiry* had 'thrown the mantle of their authority' over 'pleas for monopoly' (Shann 1938, p. 412). Leslie Melville (1902-2002) judged the *Enquiry* to have produced an 'ingenious fantasy that is not wholly fantastic'. Although its thesis was 'theoretically attractive', 'the calculations of the Committee have not materially strengthened the argument' (Melville 1929).

When in 1931 Copland sought (with Taussig's encouragement) to ventilate the matter in the *Quarterly Journal of Economics,* his paper was sensibly entitled 'A neglected phase of tariff controversy'.[11] The *Enquiry* seems to have been preserved from oblivion by an attempt of a disciple of Taussig, Karl Anderson, to ensure its oblivion. In 1938 Anderson sought to comprehensively dispose of the 'Australian case for protection' in a paper in the *Quarterly Journal of Economics* (Anderson 1938). Anderson had absorbed the literature: Brigden's 'The Australian tariff and the standard of living'; the *Enquiry* (he quotes from it); Copland (1931b); Viner (1929); and Loveday (1931).

In 1939 Marion Crawford Samuelson (1916–78) advanced a riposte to Anderson's attempted rebuttal of the *Enquiry* (Samuelson 1939). But Samuelson's paper is almost entirely devoted to the terms-of-trade argument, and only refers to the returns-to-labour argument by way of a concluding comment. This suggests that her acquaintance with the *Enquiry* and literature in the *Record* was not close.[12] In referring to the Australian 'case' M. C. Samuelson never mentions names or publications. Paul Samuelson later wrote: 'With great probability, M. C. had never read the 1929 *Report*' (1981, p. 151). There are doubts if she read the Copland paper that Anderson was seeking to obliterate. As we have noted, she stresses the terms-of-trade argument, although Copland completely ignores it. Samuelson merely says, non-commitally, she 'may have' read Copland (Samuelson 1981, p. 153).

In 1941 Samuelson wrote with Stolper, and Marion as amanuensis, 'Protection and real wages' (Stolper and Samuelson 1941). The authors review the literature on this issue, the great bulk of which is hostile to the thesis that protection increases real wages, and refer to Bastable's note of the Sidgwick argument. The

---

presumptions' that the 'very special' assumptions of the case for protection were false. Giblin told Keynes that Viner was not helpful 'on the essence of the argument' (KCLA LFG 5 December 1929).

[11] The *Enquiry* is not mentioned in Ohlin's *Interregional and international trade* of 1933. But this was only an English language translation of a thesis written in 1923, well before the *Enquiry*. Nevertheless, it is interesting that Copland recognized nothing kindred in Ohlin's thought: there was, he said, 'nothing new' in Ohlin.

[12] Samuelson (1981) appears to take it as a rationalisation of the conclusion of the *Enquiry*. However, as a rationalisation for the *Enquiry* it is problematic, since the terms-of-trade argument says that free trade is not Pareto-efficient: there is always some optimal tariff.

authors do not refer to the *Enquiry*, and Samuelson later stated that he had not read it. In the conclusion he suggests the Australian economy may be illustrative of the Stolper-Samuelson theorem, and refers the reader without any further explication to the papers of Copland, M. C. Samuelson and Anderson.

What is to be concluded? It is helpful to make a distinction between the *thesis* of the case and the *argument* of the case.

We contend that the *argument* of the case had no significance for the development of 'modern trade theory'. Firstly, Samuelson had not read the argument in the *Enquiry*, or any of the surrounding literature, with the possible exception of Copland (1931b). Secondly, Samuelson was in any case already aware of the older literature of Sidgwick and Bastable expounding the 'Sidgwick Sufficiency Condition'. Thirdly, and most importantly, the case was irrelevant to the argument of modern trade theory. Modern trade theory turns on the mobility of capital between sectors. But capital and its mobility, is totally ignored by the case.[13]

Nevertheless, it is plausible that the *thesis* of the case was significant for the development of 'modern trade theory'. In the expectant and restless atmosphere of post-war theorising, the *Enquiry* provided the spectacle of 'distinguished economists' (Irwin 1996) boldly pressing the unorthodox notion that protection increased real wages. This notion was effectively defended from one line of criticism by Marion Samuelson. In other words, M. C. Samuelson had shown there could not be an 'impossibility theorem' regarding the notion. A possibility had materialised. In Samuelson's own words: 'I at least had very much in mind at the time of the Stolper-Samuelson investigations the definitive 1939 findings by Marion Samuelson that verified the correctness of the 'Australian case for the tariff''' (Samuelson 1987, p. 241).

The significance for Australian economics

Whatever its importance for theory, the *Enquiry* was a major event in economics in Australia. In instituting the *Enquiry*, the Prime Minister had chosen economists to investigate a topic of controversy, and had included three professors in economics and the President of the new Economic Society. 'Practical men' (that is, men who were only practical) were excluded. It may be described as

---

[13] It should be allowed that:

(i) the Brigden case is a 'degenerate' special case of the Stolper-Samuelson economy (that amounts to two constant returns industries and mobile labour and capital), where the import-competing sector has no capital requirement at all.

(ii) Benham in 1935 wrote a paper on taxes and factor prices that some have seen as anticipating Stolper-Samuelson results (Benham 1935; Manger b1981). One can only speculate what debt this paper owes to his exchanges with Brigden in 'intellectually dead' Australia.

economists' first prominent step on the stage of public life in Australia. And for our authors it was their first prominent step on the stage of public life, in Australia and internationally. Further, the *Enquiry* was not a preliminary essay or an aside. The 232-page *Enquiry* was a work of intensive joint authorship that was intended to serve as an exhibit of good economics. The *Enquiry* certainly served Copland and Giblin's active concern to advance professionalised economics within Australian life.

> They saw the Tariff Report as a showcase for economists' wares, and therefore decided to produce as a far as possible, a non-apologetic consensus document.[14] (Harper 1989, p. 9).

The *Enquiry* remains an anomalous and curious event. It is so because of the heterodoxical character of its thesis: that tariffs promote living standards. The *Enquiry* had been an opportunity for the newly professionalised economists to voice a rejection of protectionism, as their worthy economist forebears had almost always done. Instead, they supplied a 'comprehensive manifesto for moderate protectionism' (Glezer 1982, p. 11). They declined the participation of the Sydney economist R. C. Mills (1886–1952) in the *Enquiry* on account of his inclination to free trade. And in advancing the case, Brigden did battle with a free trade partisan, the young F. C. Benham, then at Sydney University (see Benham 1926). Whereas Benham subjected the Tariff Board to ridicule, Brigden believed the Board could be reformed, and made a worthy institution within the Commonwealth. It is ironically illustrative of the anti-liberalism of this approach to economics that, at the beginning of the Great Depression, the most forward adversaries of protection in the Australian academy were an Englishman (Benham) and a historian (W. K. Hancock).[15]

It is true that to voice a biting rejection of protectionism would not have been popular. The *Enquiry* is more a politic than impolitic document. It is never strident, lecturing or tactless; it is never 'unrealistic' or visionary; grim or alarming. This is not to say it was complaisant; its trouncing of Imperial Preference disproves any eagerness to gratify Bruce.[16] Neither was it daunted,

---

[14] Doubtless, the unfortunate impression created by a conflict in the authors' positions is one reason why the conflict was glided over.

[15] Later Copland was to purchase of copy of Mihaïl Manoïlesco's *The theory of protection, and international trade* of 1931, an ambitious attempt to refute the theory of comparative advantage and multilateral free trade.

[16] The *Enquiry* repudiated Imperial solutions to the trade problems of Australia. Its Appendix S, on 'Preferential trade', rejected basing trade policy upon the Empire (for example, Empire Custom Unions, Imperial Preference). 'The young industries of the Dominions require protection against imports of manufactures of Great Britain' (Brigden et al. 1929). Thus there is 'no common basis for action' between the Dominions and Great Britain.

or dissimulating. But the *Enquiry* was reconciled to what it considered to be political realities. As Copland said:

> It was the political difficulty of raising the subsidies by taxation that inclined the committee to the view that in practice the same result could not have been achieved that way. (Copland 1931b, p. 20)

It can be debated whether this attitude amounts to 'political economy' or 'politic economy'. But the *Enquiry* saw little hope in 'political difficulties' being altered by it adopting an educational role regarding the tariff. Courtesy would be more useful than correction.

This care to evade political difficulties produced a report which managed a compromise. Protection should not be reduced (a victory for the protectionists), and it should not be increased (a victory for the free traders). Copland complained: 'I suppose it will be considered an attempt to be all things to all men' (quoted in Harper 1989, p. 9). And in some measure it was: both the protectionist *Age*, and the free-trade *Argus* welcomed the report.

The Bureau of Economic Research

The *Enquiry* was a trial for a more permanent presence of economists in senior counsels of government.

In 1926 the Victorian Government Statistician, supported by Brigden, successfully moved that the Central Council of the Economic Society form a committee 'to formulate a scheme for the inauguration of a Bureau of Economic Research for submission to the Commonwealth' (Scott 1988, p. 16). In early 1928 Bruce requested Copland to submit proposals for an 'Economic Service'. Copland (with Giblin) proposed that such a service be independent and permanently endowed. Bruce appears to have favoured its being made a branch of the CSIR. But the British Economic Mission of 1928, 'summonsed to quell fear in the City of London about Australian debt', also pressed for independence. The ultimate outcome was the *Economic Research Act*, submitted to Parliament in March 1929. It proposed to establish a Bureau of Economic Research that would:

1. carry out economic research,
2. investigate the 'granting of assistance for the promotion of economic research', co-operation with a academic bodies, and studentships and fellowships in economics, and
3. publish results and an annual report.

Its critics pointed out that the Bill did not give the Bureau power to collect information, or call witnesses, or make public inquiries. Evidently the model for the Bureau was the *Enquiry*, and not the Tariff Board.

The Labor Party was firmly opposed to the Bill and four future Labor Prime Ministers rose from the opposition benches in the House of Representatives to deplore it. The speakers may be divided into two groups: Protectionists and John Curtin.

Protectionists

The most common objection to the Bureau is that it would snub protectionism.

J. H. Scullin:

> Are we to take it that the Economic Research Bureau which it is proposed to set up shall investigate the general effects of the protectionist policy of Australia? There is no need for a bureau to do that. The text books teem with the opinion of so called economic experts of the world on the subject of free trade and protection ... in spite of the glooming forebodings of certain so called leading economists both the people and the Parliament of Australia have determined in favour of protection.

J. B. Chifley:

> Whoever is appointed to the director of the bureau will be a man whose views are known, but I do not think he should be allowed to interfere in any way with tariff matters ... The tariff is not a matter to be decided by economists or even by this Parliament: it is to be decided by the people of Australia, who have pronounced definitely in favour of protection. I stand absolutely for a policy of full-blooded protection.

F. M. Forde:

> We are strenuously opposed to the appointment of a director of economic research under the conditions set out in the bill, for we fear that he may become the tool of the Government for tinkering with the tariff ... It would not be difficult to find a gentleman with free trade tendencies, who would call into question, for instance, the continuation of the embargo on the importation of sugar. He might recommend that sugar grown in cheap black labour countries should be admitted to Australia. He might also advise the Government that it is economically unsound to pursue our White Australia policy and to keep up our barriers against New Zealand butter or Fiji bananas.[17]

---

[17] The future Home Affairs Minister, Arthur Blakely, also rose to protest: 'Up to date I have not yet heard of any economist who is a protectionist ... The Prime Minister had merely 'endeavoured to hide the intention of their govt by repeating that blessed word 'economics' in every second sentence of his speech ... This nebulous science, which is still to be the subject of controversy between those who profess and practise it, is to be loaded onto our people'.

Thus far the case against the Bureau is not, to modern eyes, very formidable. The Bureau might recommend against the White Australia Policy. It may favour the admission of New Zealand butter or Fijian bananas. A speech of a higher level was provided by the newly elected MP for Fremantle, John Curtin. He did not once mention Protection. 'I believe that a case can be made out for a Bureau of Economic Research'. He did not think, however, that 'an adequate reason' had been 'furnished by the Prime Minister'. 'I do not object to the establishment of a bureau of economic and social research, but I cannot support the bill in its present form, limiting, as it does, to scientific and technical inquiries, and excluding the examination of social problems as such'.

The 'economic and social' research Curtin had in mind included: women in industry; housing and efficiency; vocational guidance (there was infinitely greater waste from the neglect of such guidance than from any wrong decision on tariffs); industrial health; and the distribution of wealth.

This is not the concession to economics that it may seem. Curtin made it clear that, in his hypothetical bureau, economists would not be called for, and he had no interest in bestowing any public patronage on them. 'It is not true that Australia is destitute of those that serve the science'. The Economic Society was 'very influential' (a suggestion not then quite as laughable as it would be today), and it published the *Economic Record*.

What did they have to offer, in any case? Curtin advances a critique of economics reminiscent of the historicist critiques that had gained wide currency in the late nineteenth century. 'The doctrines that have been promulgated in the name of economics during the last 100 years have been weird and extraordinary. Such doctrines have been the basis of the writings of Ricardo, Jevons and Malthus'. There is, in truth, 'no such thing as the economic man. The individual living entirely by himself, and for himself, is not to be found on earth'. More generally, there is no such thing as an 'Economic law'. 'The contention that there are laws which dictate the trend of economic development, and these laws must be obeyed is belied by the course of economic history'. To Curtin's mind 'the remarkable disrepute into which economists fell as a result of their predictions before the war' had 'a good deal of justification'. 'Economists by and large' said Curtin, 'are conservative minded, and are fearful of change'. 'The truth is that every new proposition that has been advanced, particularly in the last 50 years, for the amelioration of social conditions, has been opposed by economists'. What these were Curtin leaves unenumerated.

Curtin then advanced the remarkable assertion that 'Every reform that the world has had, and which has been of benefit in the long run, has had to run the gauntlet of established knowledge, whether political, theological, scientific, or other' (Commonwealth Parliamentary Debates 19 March 1929, p. 1462) To Curtin, learning was not an active agent in human progress. It was an obstacle. This was a strange doctrine for a quasi-intellectual such as Curtin. But in a quasi-marxist fashion Curtin seems to have held that *established* learning was not interested in progress. No progress would come from there.

There is no need to search for the source of Curtin's anti-economics; it was a pervasive idea-cliché of the intellectual climate of the late Victorian world from which he had acquired his world view.[18] But he also had had one much more recent encounter with economists that would not have strengthened his confidence. In 1928 he had been appointed by Bruce to be one of five Royal Commissioners assessing the merits of introducing a national scheme of 'child endowment'. They took evidence from two of the economists: Brigden and Copland.[19]

Brigden put to the Commissioners that a scheme of child endowment was 'desirable', but that the 'details need to be very carefully framed'. In a carefully weighed appreciation of a hypothetical scheme he contended that any system that had the endowment cease upon the child reaching the school leaving age (14 years) would be 'disastrous' to education. It would mean that children would be 'thrust upon the labour market to earn their own maintenance'. The moral was that an endowment scheme cannot be usefully done on the cheap. At the same time the scheme should not be so ample so as to make 'production of children as remunerative as the production of income'.

In his evidence, Brigden, who was childless, was alive to the fact that any scheme of child endowment amounted, at bottom, to a transfer of income from those who do not have children to those who did. In contemplating this transfer, Brigden wanted the Commission to give thought to the costs of this to:

- those who have already finished child rearing – without any support – and are now to be taxed to support those who have not finished
- to single men who are using their income 'for some purpose no less admirable than the maintenance of other men's children'
- to the infertile. 'I am not sure that bringing up children is entirely a cost' (Royal Commission on Child Endowment or Family Allowances –Minutes of Evidence, p. 671).

Copland's evidence assailed the prospect of child endowment with strokes that were heavier and less adroit. He sought to insinuate doubts about any scheme in the circumstances of the time. He warned that 'an ambitious social policy involving more expenditure on consumption goods must not be embarked upon without very definite evidence of real social and economic gains from the policy'.

---

[18] John Curtin's library contained the anti-economics polemic of John Ruskin, *The political economy of art: unto this last: the crown of wild olive*. Lyons had given *Unto this last* as a gift to his wife Edith.

[19] Bruce paid 25 guineas for his appearance.

With no obvious connection to child endowment, he then launched into a summary of his researches into the Quantity Theory and purchasing power parity.

A very close exchange followed between Copland and Curtin. Curtin made the most of the difficulties of attempting to establish a relationship between the money supply and the exchange rate by means of 15 years of annual data. Was not the Australian exchange rate most appreciated when her money supply was most expanded? Had not prices in the United States and Australia risen by the same proportionate amount between 1913–21?

> Curtin: I am afraid there has been an unpleasant catch in the matter?
>
> Copland: I am unable to find it.
>
> (Royal Commission on Child Endowment or Family Allowances-Minutes of Evidence, p. 1260)

Curtin then pursued Copland on his affirmation of the Millian doctrine that capital inflows improve the terms of trade, and the cessation of such inflows will worsen them.

> Curtin: On p.5 of your statement you say 'As borrowing ceases import prices will rise and export prices fall giving less favourable, and perhaps unfavourable terms of trade'. What do you mean by that?
>
> Copland: That is a very difficult matter to explain in a few words. It is a categorical statement which has been proved to be true. Both in theory and practice.[20]
>
> Curtin: I am not disputing the correctness of the statement, but I would like to know its bearing on the question of the capacity of Australia to meet the annual expenditure of a system of child endowment'
>
> (Royal Commission on Child Endowment or Family Allowances 1929, p. 1258)[21]

---

[20] Wilson's critique of this Millian doctrine Copland had not absorbed, or had rejected.

[21] Eilean Giblin also gave evidence in her capacity as Vice-President of the Women's Non-party League of Tasmania. She favoured child endowment, but believed part of it should be paid in kind. She also aired some eugenic concerns.

EG: It seems to me it is a very serious problem indeed for future citizens of Australia that the mentally deficient should be propagating themselves. Some hear of various schemes such as sterilisation of the mental deficient, or limiting their freedom.

Commission: Do you approve of segregation?

The majority report of the Royal Commission on Child Endowment or Family Allowances recommended against introducing a national child endowment scheme. Such a scheme was to wait until July 1941 for its introduction, by Menzies, and partly on the advice of Roland Wilson, but in the context of entirely different macroeconomic pressures.

Whoever was the victor in the encounter of Copland and Curtin, the *Economic Research Act* was assented to on 22 March 1929. A search then began for the Director. A salary of £1500 was offered, rather better than any professorial salary. Brigden seems to have won Bruce's confidence; he had in Bruce's opinion 'the best and most practical mind'. But Brigden was not favoured. In 1971 Brigden's close colleague Hytten gave this account of the matter.

> Mr Bruce made a very flattering offer, but told Brigden he wanted it to be kept absolutely confidential. Very naturally he showed it to Giblin and me: we were his closest associates. But Giblin thought he ought to tell Copland as one of the senior economists. I urged him against it, as Bruce had asked him to keep it confidential, and Copland would probably go straight to the PM and ask why he had not been given the offer. He had done something similar previously. But Brigden took Giblin's advice with the inevitable result. As I had forecast Copland went straight to Bruce and demanded that he be considered for the position.[22] Bruce then told Brigden to forget about the offer.[23]

EG: Yes, I think that on the whole segregation would be the most satisfactory, in the form of colonies or such like.

Curtin: Who would draw the line between mental deficiency in a slight degree and mental deficiency to such an extent as to warrant segregation?

EG: There would have to be a board to decide the point.

Curtin: There is a dividing line between those two points. It is a very serious responsibility.

EG: Modern psychologists know a good deal about these things, and have their own tests.

(Royal Commission on Child Endowment or Family Allowances –Minutes of Evidence, p. 703)

[22] There is a letter of Copland to Julian Simpson, a Nationalist politician, in which Copland angles for the appointment. 'May I, therefore, put the matter quite bluntly to you in this way? If the Government decides to establish this service I should be glad to have the opportunity of considering all the attractions relating to it' (UMA DBC 29 June 1928).

[23] In the matter of the offer, Hytten is not repeating hearsay; he states Brigden showed him the offer. It was also Giblin's opinion that Brigden was offered the position (see letter of Roland Wilson to Giblin, RBA 2 November 1950). Wilson believed Giblin was mistaken in this, as Condliffe had told Wilson that he had been offered the position. But clearly, Condliffe receiving an offer of the position at some point in time is entirely consistent with Brigden also receiving an offer.

Yet Bruce had something with which to console Brigden. He recommended Brigden to the Overseas Shipping Representatives Association. Part trade association, part cartel, the Association spoke the language of rationalisation and the elimination of waste (Bach 1976, p. 301). 'So far as competition was wasteful, it [rationalisation] meant the elimination of that competition' said Brigden.

Giblin believed that: 'Brigden is probably the better fitted to the [Director's] job ... The trouble is however that B is inclined to prefer the shipping job – thinks there is a more hopeful result of getting a practical result ... He is being strongly urged by his friends to hold out for five years, or at least three years engagement ... He may in the end take it without the guarantee – he is strongly attracted and would like to gamble on it (NLA LFG 21 April 1929)'. In the end he did take the gamble. Brigden presented his appointment to the press as another symbol of the arrival of the economist. It was simply a 'sign of the times'.[24]

But, in the meantime, who was to fill the empty chair of the Director of the Bureau of Economic Research? Others were considered, including Horace Belshaw (1898-1962), the founder of the New Zealand Institute of Economic Research. But according to Hytten, J. B. Condliffe (1891-1981), another Canterbury College protégé of James Hight, was ultimately offered the position.

In the end nobody was to be Director. On 10 September 1929, just 11 months into his third term, six Nationalist members crossed the floor of the House of Representatives to defeat the Bruce Government's attempt to transfer industrial relations powers to the states. The government was entitled to battle on, but Bruce decided to call general elections. 'I think he is riding for a fall' Giblin told his wife. (RBA LFG 1 September 1929). On 12 October Bruce lost his own seat in a Labor landslide victory. The Scullin Labor Government took office. The Bureau was a dead letter.[25] The new government was to be uncontaminated by economic research.

Wall Street's 'Black Thursday' was 12 days away.

---

[24] 'The war shook our economic foundations so badly that more should be known about them. The chief aim of economics is to understand these foundations. In Australia the subject has grown rapidly, and we have established a status abroad. But in Australia it is still suspected of being associated almost wholly with political theories, a wholly erroneous notion, derived perhaps from the time when the subject was called 'political economy'... My appointment is therefore a sign of the times'. In July 1929 Brigden told Giblin his job was 'shaping well'. 'The various "interests" have been soothed and beguiled', Giblin told Eilean, '– and they have accepted him – in fact made him Vice-Chairman of their Executive' (NLA LFG 4 July 1929).

[25] The Act was not formally repealed until 1950.

Appendix: A rational reconstruction of the Australian case for protection

Brigden's 'Australian Case for Protection' can be formalised as follows.

Assumptions

Let p be the home price of manufactures in terms of food. Let p_w be the exogenous world price of manufactures in terms of food. Then,

$p = [1 + \tau] p_w$

τ = rate of tariff

Let food output, F, be a function of the amount of labour in the food sector, L_F.

$F = F(L_F)$

Let manufactures output, M, be a function of the amount of labour in the food sector, L_M.

$M = M(L_M)$

Labour in food and manufactures sum to the exogenously given supply of labour, L.

$L_F + L_M = L$

Labour is mobile between the two sectors. Therefore, the marginal productivity of labour in food must equal the marginal product of labour in manufactures (evaluated in terms of food), as long as both food and manufactures are produced.

$F'(L_F) = M'(L_M)p$

The impact of a tariff

These five equalities in five unknowns imply the impact of a tariff on living standards. Defining f as the wage in terms of food, $F'(L_F)$, and m as the wage in terms of manufactures, $M'(L_M)$, then,

$$\frac{\partial f}{\partial p} = \frac{F''M'}{F''+M''p} > 0 \qquad \frac{\partial m}{\partial p} = \frac{-M''M'}{F''+M''p} < 0$$

$$0 > M'' > -\infty, \ 0 > F'' > -\infty$$

Thus the impact of protection will be to *increase* the wage in terms of food, and *diminish* the wage in terms of manufactures. Thus the impact of the tariff of the welfare of the worker is ambiguous.

There are, however, two conditions under which the welfare of the worker has unambiguously increased. The first we call 'The Brigden Condition': constant marginal productivity of labour in manufactures.

$M'' = 0$

This is conveyed diagramatically in Figure 4.2.

Figure 4.2. 'The Brigden Condition'

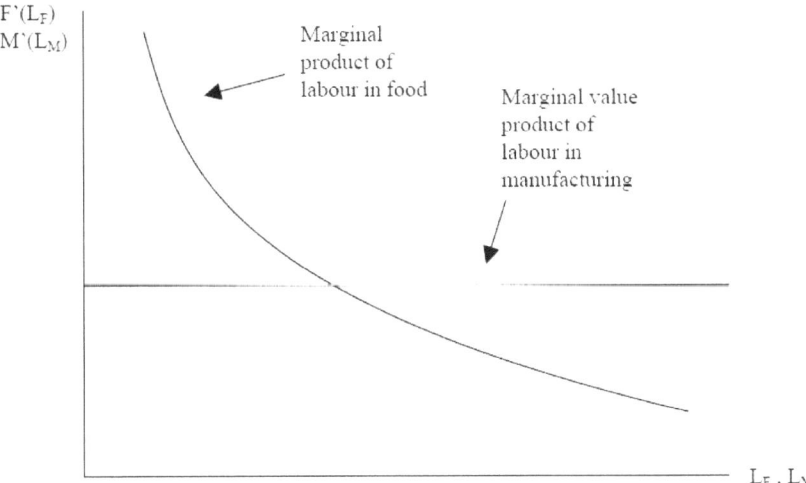

The Brigden Condition implies,

$$\frac{\partial f}{\partial p} = M' \text{ and } \frac{\partial m}{\partial p} = 0$$

These equalities imply that an increase in the price of manufactures will increase the food wage and not reduce the manufactures wage. The marginal product of labour in food is increased and the marginal product in manufactures is the same. In other words, a tariff has necessarily increased the utility of any worker who consumes both food and manufactures.

Figure 4.3. The impact of a tariff under the Brigden assumption

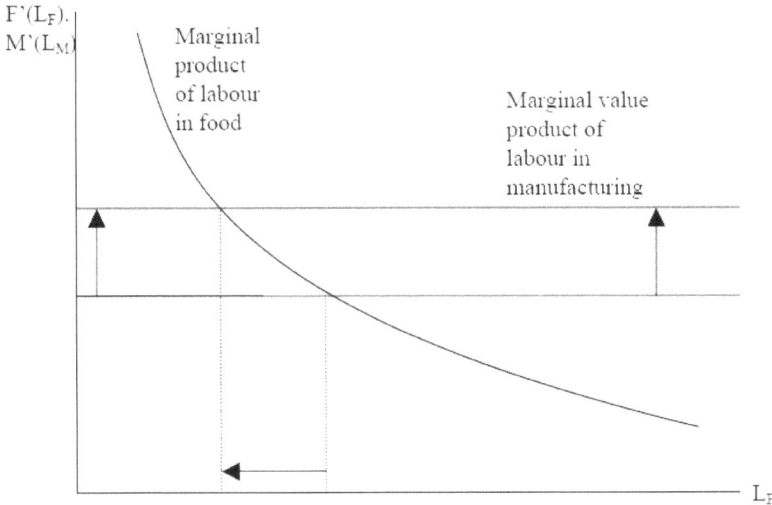

Economic science and political power 81

The second condition for a tariff to increase the welfare of a worker we will call 'The Sidgwick Condition': a discontinuous fall in marginal productivity of labour in Food. This is conveyed diagrammatically in Figure 4.4, and mathematically as,

$$F'' = -\infty$$

Figure 4.4. 'The Sidgwick Assumption'

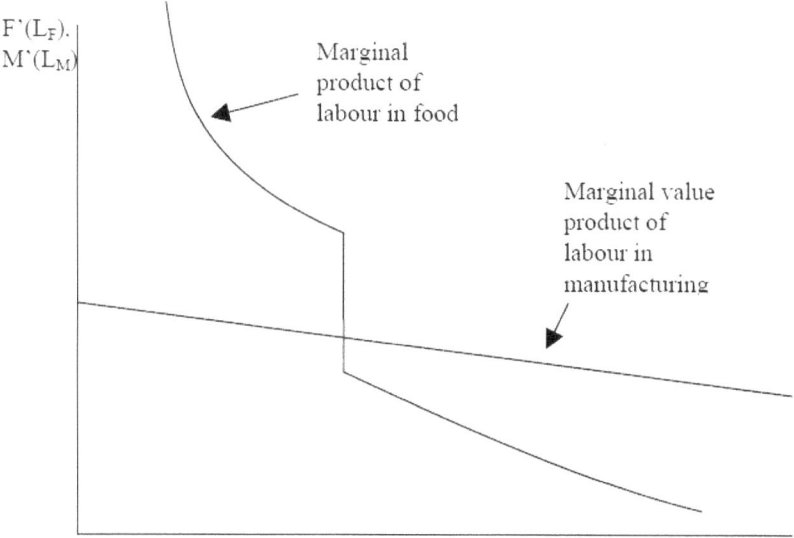

The Sidgwick Condition, like the Brigden Condition, implies,

$$\frac{\partial f}{\partial p} = M' \text{ and } \frac{\partial m}{\partial p} = 0$$

These equalities state that an increase in the price of manufactures will increase the food wage and not reduce the manufactures wage. The logic is that an increase in p increases the food value of the marginal product in manufactures, but labour will *not* reallocate from food towards manufactures, owing to the discontinuity. Consequently, the marginal product of labour in manufactures will be the same. But the food wage (= the wage measured in food) must increase because the food value of the marginal product in manufactures has increased.

Figure 4.5. The impact of a tariff under the Sidgwick Assumption

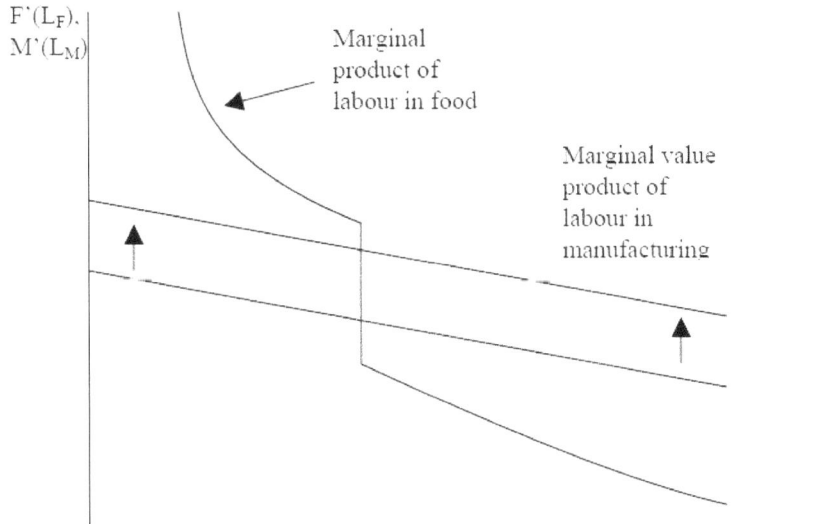

The upshot is that the manufactures wage is unchanged and the food wage is increased. In other words, a tariff has necessarily increased the living standard of the worker.

Under these two conditions, therefore, any increase in a tariff increases worker living standards

The role of population

The contention that the population must be 'appropriately large' if protection is to increase real wages can be easily shown if we make the Brigden Assumption. Figure 4.6 plots L on the horizontal axis and the marginal product of labour in manufactures evaluated in food (using free trade prices), $M'p_w$, on the vertical axis. The plotting of $M'p_w$ is horizontal, since M' and p_w are parametrical to L. The marginal product of labour in food *if* all labour is applied to food, $F'(L)$, is also plotted in Figure 4.6. At $L = L^*$, $F'(L) = M'p_w$, and the marginal product of labour in Food (assuming all labour is applied to food) equals the marginal product of labour in manufactures, evaluated in terms of food at free trade prices.

Figure 4.6. The Minimum Population for a Tariff to be Wage Improving

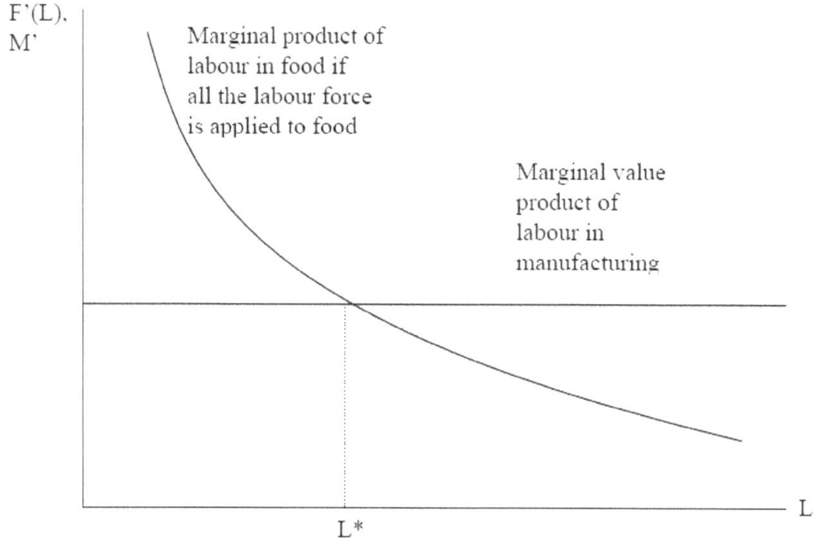

[Figure: Graph with vertical axis labeled F'(L), M' and horizontal axis labeled L. A downward-sloping curve labelled "Marginal product of labour in food if all the labour force is applied to food" intersects a horizontal line labelled "Marginal value product of labour in manufacturing" at point L on the horizontal axis.]*

If $L > L^*$, a tariff will increase real wages, by the argument previously rehearsed.

But if $L < L^*$ a tariff may not increase real wages. If $L < L^*$ then there would be no manufacturing sector under free trade, as *all* labour will be allocated to food.[26] In these circumstances any merely 'small' tariff (that is, one that is insufficient to create a manufacturing industry) would merely raise the price of manufactures, without making local production of manufactures viable. Consequently, the wage in food is unchanged and the tariff has succeeded only in reducing the manufactures wage (that is, the amount of manufactures that can be purchased by the marginal product of labour in food, $= F'(L)/ p_w[1+t]$).

---

[26] There will be no manufacturing since, even though all labour is allocated to food, the marginal product of labour in food is still greater than the marginal product of labour in manufactures (evaluated in terms of food at free trade prices).

5. Giblin and Keynes

> 'I should say that I am writing this in haste before I have thoroughly digested your method of argument, which is, as I have said, quite novel'.
> J. M. Keynes to L. F. Giblin.[1]

By the onset of the Great Depression Giblin had already developed a theory that would afford a valuable insight into this event: the theory of 'the multiplier'. The theory contended that any stimulus to spending will not be cancelled by a compensating reduction in consumption spending, but will lead to an increase in total spending by an amount several times as large – 'a multiple' - of the initial stimulus; a multiple that depended on the proportion of the amount of income not spent.

This tool was also to be developed by Keynes during the first years of the Depression. The striking coincidence of Giblin's and Keynes' near simultaneous conception of the 'multiplier' concept need not greatly perplex. With his Bloomsbury friends, Cambridge education and cultural interests one might be tempted to describe Giblin as an Australian twig of Bloomsbury. And, in sharing their rationalism, 'paganism', footloose radicalism and intuitive modernism, Giblin arrived at a similar sort of sharp revaluation of classical economic wisdom as did Keynes.

Yet, in spite of the similarities, there were important differences between the minds of Giblin and Keynes, and in the circumstances in which their minds operated. Giblin's mind was, in truth, a native growth, which only partly acclimatised in foreign soil. Despite the elements of common heritage and the empathy for one another, this chapter shows that Giblin and Keynes never truly consummated an intellectual relationship.

Giblin and the multiplier

Giblin's priority with respect to multiplier-style concepts has been conceded by authoritative accounts of the multiplier's genesis for many years (Wright 1956; Moggridge 1993; Dimand 1988).[2] Giblin's version of the multiplier was in print, as *Australia, 1930*, in April 1930 - 15 months before the Cambridge multiplier was, and several months before the Cambridge multiplier was even conceived.

How did Giblin come to formulate the multiplier? The germ of Keynes' multiplier theory is easily traced to economic stagnation in 1920s Britain, and to Keynes'

---

[1] KCLA 28 August 1929, JMK/CO/2/184.

[2] Giblin's closest contestant for priority is Jens Warming (Boserup 1969). Attention has also been paid to Hawtrey for his multiplier-like comments on Keynes' *Treatise*. (Davis 1980). For pre-1914 anticipators see Wright (1956), Goodwin (1962) and Hegeland (1954).

arguments in his pamphlet of May 1929, *Can Lloyd George do it?*, in favour of the extensive employment benefits of public works.³ No such line of intellectual descent will serve for Giblin: he had not read *Can Lloyd George do it?*, and suspected it was seeking to defend the discreditable.⁴

A search for the roots of Giblin's ideas tempts us to return to Hobart. In Giblin's youth there lived in Hobart an underconsumptionist, A. J. Ogilvy (1834–1914), who shared the 'left-liberal' outlook of Giblin. He founded the Tasmanian Land Nationalisation Society, and in 1897, the Democratic League, a forerunner of the Tasmanian Labor Party. The author of numerous pamphlets on political economy, in 1892 Ogilvy published *Is capital the result of abstinence?* – answering in the negative – and in 1896 *Saving and spending*.

> Suppose a number of people suddenly determine to save to the extent of a quarter of their income; and let bread, boots and tobacco ... be the articles they have been habitually consuming, and in which they now propose to save ... What now will be the effect on other people? Those who have been supplying the abstainers with bread, boots and tobacco will suddenly find a quarter of their goods left on their hands ... After a while ... the sellers ... will have to reduce their production for the future in view of demand, thereby throwing so many people out of employment. (Ogilvy 1896, p. 209).

But Giblin did not need to notice or read Ogilvy to come into contact with underconsumptionism – almost every unorthodox economic thinker was an underconsumptionist (see Coleman 2002). In any case, Giblin, as we shall see, was not an underconsumptionist.

A stronger lead to the source of Giblin's thought is found in the doctrines of Alfred De Lissa (1838–1913), a London-born Sydney barrister, who, during the 1890s, published a series of papers that not only explored a variety of effective demand notions, but advanced multiplier–style formula and geometric progressions that related the magnitude of an initial spending stimulus to the final total stimulus.⁵ In 1890 he proclaimed the 'Law of Incomes', a 'great

---

³ Keynes wrote in 1938: '*History of the multiplier doctrine*. One must distinguish here between some sort of formal statement ... and the general notion of there being such a thing as secondary employment ... [that] is clearly explained in *Can Lloyd George do it?* ...' (CWJMK, XII, p. 806).

⁴ Giblin to Eilean: 'I was hoping someone would have sent the Keynes Henderson pamphlet on the L. L. G. [=Lloyd George] unemployment scheme, but no one did ... The scheme sounded so like Australian borrowing schemes that I wanted to see a serious defence of it ...The immediate interest is over, but the whole thing seems so full of dangers that it would be instructive to have it for the record' (RBA LFG 4 July 1929).

⁵ De Lissa's first publication was 'The law of income' in the *Australian Economist* 1890 in which he contends the income of 'primary' (= production) industry supports a certain amount of secondary

economic law which appears to underlie the industry of every country', that turned on a 'physiocratic' multiplier concept in which workers in production support workers in services. In 1890 he explained his ideas in an Advancement of Science conference in Hobart in terms of geometric progressions.[6] By 1898 he had generalised his ideas into a formula, whereby total incomes equal value of production divided by the proportion of income spent on services.[7]

When De Lissa spoke in Hobart, Giblin was already in London, studying under Pearson. Thus reason forbids the fancy from imagining the young Giblin absorbing from the stalls De Lissa's multiplier idea. Yet, as one commentator has obliquely put it: 'It is an interesting coincidence that after De Lissa's, one of the first expositions of the multiplier came from L. F. Giblin' (Goodwin 1962). There is something that adds more piquance to the coincidence: during the 1890s De Lissa also wrote on a topic that was soon to become a preoccupation of Giblin's, the special budgetary treatment of Tasmania in the new Commonwealth. De Lissa 'showed that a fair distribution of national revenues in the new federation required adjusting for differences in the economic product in each colony, effectively to compensate for their varying fiscal capacity' (Hancock and Smith 2001). This sentiment is very close to that principle which Giblin was to adopt and champion. Could Giblin's absorption of the controversies over federal finance have brought him into contact with De Lissa's works in general, and his work on the multiplier? One is lost in speculation.

One moves from speculation to fact with the advent in the late 1920s of the Development and Migration Commission, that had been created to appraise government proposals for the establishment of new industries in the light of their potential to support higher immigration. A railway that the Victorian Government had built to open up some wheatlands came to its attention. In 1952 Copland (writing anonymously) recalled:

> It was clear that the traffic on the railway would not be sufficient to meet debt charges, but it was not clear that the building of the railway would be an uneconomic proposition for the economy as a whole. The

---

industry: 'if all the workers in a country are divided strictly into primary and secondary workers ... the products of these primary workers ... will, in addition to the aggregate incomes received by the producers, give aggregate incomes of an equal amount ... to all other workers in the community'.

[6] The example De Lissa favoured was 30 m of incomes of primary workers would yield further incomes 15 then 7.5 + 3.75 +1.875 + ... etc.

[7] De Lissa writes: $\frac{V(\text{value of production})}{R(\text{ratio of expenditure})} = I(\text{total incomes})$. The 'Ratio of expenditure' is what we would call the 'average propensity to spend on production', or (equivalently) the average propensity to not spend on services. So if production is 100, and the 'average propensity to spend' was 0.25, then total incomes would be 400.

addition of, say, £1m in exports of wheat to the national income would result in other and indirect additions to the national income. The new wheat farmers would spend their incomes in a certain proportion on local and imported goods and on such tertiary services as education, health services and transport so that the total national income would be greater than the original addition of the income from wheat ... Copland was aware of these considerations, but was unable to state the problem precisely in terms of the effect on national income as a whole. *He took this problem to Giblin who produced the first formula of the multiplier.* (Anon. 1952, our italics)

In a similar recollection Torliev Hytten (Hytten, 1960) recorded:

I well remember when he first brought the general idea in a page or so of typescript to Brigden and myself for criticism. Giblin was rarely excited, but there was something akin to excitement in him as we discussed and finally agreed on its validity.[8]

Regrettably, Hytten's 'page or so' appears to have been lost, but the three other memoranda survive. These are: 'New farms and population', L. F. Giblin, 9 August 1929; 'The correlative increases in production and population', L. F. Giblin c. 1929; and 'Population supported by 1,000 pounds by new export production', J. B. Brigden, 5 September 1929.

These papers are concerned with the total impact on national income of the new income deriving from a new industry.

'New farms and population' was written at the request of the Development and Migration Commission, which had asked Giblin to analyse what would be the gain to Australia's population of the establishment of new wheat farms. Giblin approached this problem by arguing that there would be both a direct gain and an indirect gain. To analyse the direct gain, he estimated the value of production of each new farm at £700 (after making deductions for transport, interest, raw materials used, repairs etc.). He then noted that, as 'Australian population works out at 1 per £100 of income', the £700 of income accruing to the operator of each new farm would support an additional seven population members. Thus the *direct* population gain would be of seven people for each new farm.

It was in the *indirect* effect that Giblin introduced multiplier analysis. He argued that about two-thirds of the income accruing to the operator of a new farm would be spent on domestically produced consumption goods, thus generating additional income for the profit-earners and wage-earners engaged in the

---

[8] Hytten dates this encounter to 1925, and is surely wrong. The railway issue only emerged in 1928. Giblin later stated: 'The general thesis [of the multiplier] dates from 1928–29' (quoted in Karmel 1960, p. 165).

production of such goods equal to two-thirds of the income accruing to the operator of the new farm. In turn these people would spend two-thirds of their additional income on domestically produced consumption goods, thus generating a further income increase of (two-thirds)^2 times the income accruing to the operator of a new farm. And so on indefinitely. Thus for each new farm established there would be an indirect income gain equal to the direct gain (£700) multiplied by $\frac{2}{3} + (\frac{2}{3})^2 + (\frac{2}{3})^3 + \ldots$ This infinite series converges on two. The indirect income gain for each new farm established would therefore be £1400, so that the total gain would be £2100.[9] The logic of geometric progression, absent from *Australia, 1930*, is explicit here.[10]

Giblin sent 'New farms' to Brigden: 'I should be glad of criticism, – destructive or constructive'. Brigden responded with a two-page comment entitled 'Population supported by 1,000 pounds by new export production', dated 5 September 1929. This is a bolder, starker analysis than Giblin's. It drew the protectionist implications of Giblin's multiplier analysis without hesitation. It pointed out that the reduction in (what would today be called) 'the propensity to import' would increase national income, and consequently suggested that it was through import substitution that any new industries would create employment.[11] It also used the language 'multiplying' and 'multiplied', terminology that Giblin never used.

It is worth noting that Brigden has also been credited by some of his colleagues with turning Giblin's mind away from the positive impact on national income

---

[9] 'The correlative increases in production and population' paper was seemingly written by Giblin: the typescript includes annotations in his hand. It adopts a similar multiplier analysis to 'New farms', but uses a propensity to spend of 0.7. It concludes that, after 'allowing for some other deductions, e.g. part of savings not available for employment', the multiplier would be 3 (rather than the 10/3 implied by 0.7).

[10] 'So that any given number of people, say 90, directly supported by new farms will entail a secondary population of $\frac{2}{3}$ of this number, or 60. And similarly this 60 will employ $\frac{2}{3}$ of 60, or 40, and so on.

For every person supported directly by the new farms we then have an additional population of: $\frac{2}{3} + (\frac{2}{3}$ of $\frac{2}{3}) + (\frac{2}{3}$ of $\frac{2}{3}$ of $\frac{2}{3}) + \ldots$ to infinity.

And this series, by the well-known algebraic rule, adds up to exactly 2.

We shall therefore have about two persons indirectly supported by the farms for every person directly supported.'

[11] 'Certainly an industry which merely diverts demand (such as the cinema) cannot add to our population: but production which takes the place of imports sets going the multiplication of income locally instead of abroad'. It is worth noting that the *Enquiry* of the same year explicitly rejected the notion that protectionism stimulated total employment.

of an expansion of exports, and towards the *negative* impact of a *contraction* of exports on national income. 'It was Brigden who first realized the significance of the multiplier working in reverse gear when wool prices fell ... When wool prices fell at the opening of wool sales late in August, 1929, he was the first to sound the warning of the impending depression that was to follow ...' (Copland quoted in Wilson 1951). Copland states that Brigden's composition of *Escape to prosperity* (1930a) was the occasion of this realisation. The book's opening chapter, 'Australia in 1930', very briefly presents an informal multiplier analysis of the impact of a contraction in exports (Brigden 1930a, p. 5).[12]

Giblin first publicly aired his multiplier ideas in an inaugural lecture for the Chair to which he been recently appointed – the Ritchie Chair at the University of Melbourne.

Giblin had never sought the Ritchie Chair; it would be truer to say it sought him. The Chair had been founded by Mr R. B. Ritchie as a memorial to his son Captain Robert Blackwood Ritchie MC, who had been killed in 1916 while on war service in France. Ritchie had provided an endowment of £30 000 to the University for the purpose.

To fill the Chair, the University established early in 1927 an advisory committee led by Copland, who expectantly told Keynes that they were seeking 'a first class man who would stimulate study generally in Australia'. Keynes soberingly replied: 'My own expectation would be that you would find stronger candidates in Australia than from this country or America' (quoted in Millmow 2005a). A few days later, and evidently quite undiscouraged, Copland shot high, and cabled Edwin Cannan, recently retired from his Chair at the London School of Economics:

> Would you accept invitation new Chair economic research, Melbourne University, see Economic Journal September, Salary 1350 pounds, two years tenure, travelling expenses, 200 pounds each way, two lectures per week during term. (quoted in Milmow 2005a).

Cannan declined, regretfully, '... on account of age and desire to proceed with literary projects'. He further chilled the air by suggesting that younger men would also be reluctant to go to Australia, since, by the time they had returned, 'influential people' would have forgotten them. Cannan's reluctance would not have been diminished by the thoroughly dissatisfied reports of Australian academic life that he had been receiving from Benham, then exiled in Sydney. 'Australia, as I expected,' wrote Benham, 'is intellectually dead' (LSE).

---

[12] It is uncertain when this was written, but as it was published just a few weeks after Giblin's *Australia, 1930* it is further evidence that Brigden was at the very least *au fait* with Giblin's thinking.

In the face of the failure of Copland's straight-to-the-point cablegram, a more deliberate procedure was settled upon. Two committees of three persons were established, one in England (which included Keynes) and one in the United States (including Taussig and Mitchell). Both committees were charged with finding a suitable person, and authorised to approach them. Several worthy candidates were identified, but none was of sufficient stature to satisfy Copland. They were 'simply not good enough', he declared. And the candidates of a stature sufficient to satisfy Copland – such as Viner, who Copland implausibly had hopes for – were not going to be satisfied by Melbourne.

With Keynes' earliest warning seemingly borne out, the search turned to possible candidates from Australia. Copland had been plainly angling for the job himself. 'I am rather attracted to the position myself ... I have hinted to the authorities I would be interested'. However, 'I have the impression the University would like me to stay where I am' (UMA DBC 29 June 1928).

Copland then took a 'revolutionary step'; he would recommend Giblin. This needs no rationalisation. The strong man still needed Giblin, as several points in correspondence highlight.[13] And he admired Giblin's intellectual leadership. He told Taussig regarding his recommendation, that Giblin has 'demonstrated his ability to find a way of measuring economic phenomena which has baffled the rest of us'.

The Council was unanimously persuaded by Copland's recommendation, and on 17 October 1928 the Chancellor of the University enquired of Giblin whether he '... would consider favourably an offer of the Chair'. Giblin, however, would not consider it favourably. He broke the news to Eilean: 'They have offered me the Ritchie chair and I have not read any of their damn textbooks'.[14] But Copland rallied his ally: 'Picture yourself as the doyen of Australian economists!'(quoted in Millmow 2005a).

> Copland reminded Giblin how Brigden and Mills had fared even though they too did not have a thorough background in economics so 'Why not you?' Copland cajoled Giblin to think of the post as his duty and to think of the time he would have to think about real economic problems. It was 'the best economics job in Australia'. (Millmow 2005a).

---

[13] 'I always felt very safe in Tasmania with you', Copland wrote to Giblin at about this time (UMA 6 June 1927).

[14] Clapham, the English economic historian, assured Eilean: 'Economics is mathematics and common sense. We all know about the first and he [Giblin] has more of the second than anybody I know' (quoted in Millmow 2005a).

Giblin was successfully cajoled, and cabled his acceptance of the Chair to Copland. Or so it seemed. For on the same day, 22 August 1928, he cabled again, at 12.40pm.

> Have decided with great regret against Melbourne

An incomplete draft of a letter from Giblin to the Chancellor spoke of his 'amateurish equipment' for the Chair.

But at 2 pm Giblin issued another cablegram.

> Letter Chancellor throws new light cancel previous communication will wire again.

These communications caused 'a little stir' at Melbourne.[15] But Giblin was coming after all. Copland and he were colleagues once more.

Some of Giblin's hesitation to accept is manifested in his prefatory remarks to his inaugural lecture, *Australia, 1930*.

> You may guess my diffidence as a pure amateur in economic studies in attempting to fill an academic chair. I hoped that with the passing months the Professorial robe might come to hang less loosely about me, but I am afraid I am irrevocably an amateur and my surprise at finding myself in this Chair is undimmed. My feeling remains that the action of you, Sir, and of the Council in making the appointment was a tribute to the great Australian genius for gambling on a very speculative event, not, of course, in any vulgar sense, but rather in that suggested by the classical story of George Fox and tobacco. You may remember how in his early journeying through England, denouncing the wickedness of the times, he came one night to a north country inn. A bold young fellow came up to him, sitting quietly in the parlor, and offered him a filled pipe of tobacco. He was minded to refuse according to his habit, but bethought him that the young fellow would go away and say that he had not unity with the creation. So he took the pipe, he tells us, and smoked awhile that it might not be said that he had not unity with the creation. So in respect to gambling I conceived the Council as proving their unity with the creation in making this appointment.

The lecture was delivered on 28 April 1930 in the public lecture theatre of the University. The press was in attendance. The performance was, as the *Argus* truthfully noted, 'long and interesting'. Its 8800 words would have taken a full hour to deliver. The multiplier concept was presented lucidly.

---

[15] So did Giblin's eventual debut at Melbourne. The Chancellor, Sir John Macfarlane, was, according to Copland, 'astonished' by Giblin's appearance.

Cambridge, Tasmania or Cambridge, England?

While Giblin was delivering his lecture, the Cambridge version of the multiplier was still more than a year from publication (in the June 1931 issue of the *Economic Journal*). Indeed it was not even yet formulated. It was to be conceived by Keynes' star pupil, Richard Kahn, during mid-1930, while on a walking holiday in the Austrian Alps.

Giblin's version of the multiplier is indubitably prior. Although this is recognised, Giblin's multiplier is largely ignored in the historiography of Keynes' *General theory*. Patinkin (1993) never mentions Giblin is his chronology of the *General theory*. Giblin's multiplier is referred to only once in Skidelsky's biography of Keynes — and only by implication, and only in a footnote.[16] And there is a good reason for this silence: neither Keynes, nor Kahn, nor any 'Circus' members ever mention Giblin's multiplier. There is no positive evidence that any of these people read it.[17] In fact, there is some positive evidence that they did not read it. First, not long after Keynes began using multiplier analysis in 1933, Giblin wrote that, in doing so, Keynes was following Kahn, rather than himself.[18] Secondly, Keynes baldly states in the *General theory*:

> The conception of the multiplier was first introduced into economic theory by Mr R. F. Kahn in his article on 'The Relation of Home Investment to Unemployment' (*Economic Journal*, June 1931). (Keynes 1936, p. 113).[19]

Yet, on account of his Cambridge associations, it is intellectually legitimate to consider that Keynes and his circle were aware of the Giblin multiplier. And it is intellectually legitimate to be tantalised by the fact that King's College library

---

[16] Dimand (1988, pp. 105–8) does give a detailed treatment of Giblin's multiplier.

[17] According to Dimand, 'Giblin's multiplier analysis was entirely ignored' outside Australia, and even within Australia 'thoroughly forgotten' by 1938. This is a slight exaggeration. A 1939 Canadian survey of Central Banking in the Dominions does note the Giblin multiplier (Plumptre 1940, p. 351). Plumptre had married an employee in the economics department of the Bank of New South Wales. That Hytten ran this department is presumably not unrelated to Plumptre's acquaintance with the Giblin multiplier.

[18] Giblin (1933a): 'Last year [1933], however, Keynes used substantially the same argument [as *Australia, 1930*] in his 'Means to prosperity' — following work by Kahn in the *Economic Journal* in 1931.'

[19] Kahn had few recollections of any cognate literature published in 1930. In 1938 he told Keynes he thought 'there was something analogous published by the Berlin Institut fur Konjunctforschung some time in the same year' (Keynes in JMKCW vol. 12, p. 806). This is presumably a reference to a paper by Alfred Schwoner (1930), which has been noted by historians of the multiplier concept (Hegeland 1954, p. 27).

does contain a copy of *Australia, 1930*. Giblin sent it to them. It arrived in June 1930.[20] Nevertheless, there is no positive evidence that Keynes or any of his circle read, or were aware, of Giblin's multiplier.[21] The two multipliers were 'doubletons'.

A simultaneous but independent formulation of the multiplier is made more likely by the fact that two other economists, in languages other than English, advanced the concept (apparently independently): Jens Warming in 1929–30, and Michal Kalecki in 1933 (see King 1998). The following table compares the various multipliers.

Table 5.1. Multiplier concepts from c. 1930

	Giblin	Brigden	Warming	Kahn	Keynes	Kalecki
Date	'1928–29'	5 Sept 1929	1929–30	June 1931	March 1933	1933
Explanandum	employment, income	employment	employment	employment	income	income
Assumptions	open economy	open economy	open economy	open economy	open economy	open economy
	marginal propensity to absorb of ⅔ –0.7	marginal propensity to absorb of at least 0.5	marginal propensity to absorb of 0.4	marginal propensity to absorb 0.36-0.48	marginal propensity to absorb 0.49	marginal propensity to absorb of 0.3
	mps = 0?			mps of workers = 0 and mps of business men = ⅔ - ⅔	mps > 0	mps of workers = 0 and mps of capitalists > 0
Technique	geometric series	none	geometric series	geometric series	geometric series	calculus
Terminology		'multiplied' 'multiplying'	'roll on'	'ratios'	'multiplier'	
Symbolism	none	none	none	k = 'marginal propensity to absorb'	none	
Multiplier	3	≥ 2	1 ⅔	1.56–1.94, 1.75	2	1 ⅔
Policy	deflation	protection	public works	public works	public works	

Giblin's multiplier and Keynes' *General theory*

Additional evidence for independent creation of the multiplier is the distance between Giblin's macroeconomic views of 1930 and the theoretical structure of the *General theory*.

It might be ventured that there are eight doctrines that the *General theory* was especially concerned to defend, and advance:

---

[20] The King's College copy of *Australia, 1930* records that it was 'Presented by the Author'. The present authors have been unable to discover any other library in Cambridge that holds it.

[21] The then junior PhD student A. K. Cairncross very likely had. In the early 1930s Cairncross was a friend and fellow student of Ronald Walker at Cambridge, whose 1933 thesis drew on Giblin (Cairncross 1998). It was A. K. Cairncross who drew A. L. Wright's attention to the Giblin multiplier.

- effective demand (that is, Say's Law)
- the pervasiveness of 'uncertainty'. To attempt to calculate odds is impossible; we will do better by trusting to animal spirits
- a monetary theory of interest
- a non-monetary theory of prices in situations of unemployment (that is, the invalidity of the Quantity Theory)
- underconsumptionism; the dysfunctionality of thrift
- the dysfunctionality of capital and interest income
- 'disequilibriumism': the economic system does not automatically tend to full employment
- 'stimulationism': public works and monetary expansion as the remedy for unemployment, not wage reductions (except in exceptional circumstances).

How much did Giblin's *Australia, 1930* share this 'larger doctrinal structure' of 1936? Obviously, the multiplier comprehends the first item, *effective demand*. But what of the remaining seven doctrines?

There is no hint of either of *the pervasiveness of uncertainty* or a *monetary theory of interest* in Giblin.

As for *underconsumptionism,* Giblin was not an underconsumptionist. In fact, he was an anti-underconsumptionst. Just six weeks after *Australia, 1930* he published an article in the Melbourne Herald entitled 'The Need for Saving'. 'Saving' Giblin explained to his readers 'becomes capital and we need a lot of it in Australia' He makes his antipathy to consumption quite plain in *Australia, 1930*.

> Three years ago I had the honour of addressing the A[ustralasian] A[ssociation] A[advancement] of S[cience] at Perth on the subject of 'The Road to Ruin'. I conceived it as paved with the extravagant post-war consumption. The case is even stronger today.
>
> Demand seems no longer bridled by the capacity to pay for the desired commodity. Very striking is the new consumption – in motor-cars, movies and talkies, gramophones, tobacco for women, and the increased expenditure in confectionery, and dress, dancing and travelling.

(It will be recalled that Giblin as a student lived on 'ships' biscuits of which he kept a barrel in his rooms', and in maturity 'wore red ties of his own manufacture').

There is nothing of *dysfunctionality'* of capital income in Giblin.

Giblin is not a *'disequilibriumist'*. He explicitly states in *Australia, 1930* that the system would correct itself through wage adjustments. He made it quite clear that the multiplier would be zero if wages (and other incomes) declined.

Giblin in 1930 was not a *stimulationist, either*. In *Australia, 1930* he was a *deflationist*. In 1930 he drew no expansionary policy lesson from his multiplier.[22] On the contrary, the policy conclusion he drew was the necessity of a reduction in wages. '"Wages Must Fall": Professor Giblin's Warning': this was the headline that the Melbourne *Argus* chose for its report on *Australia, 1930*.

Still, for all the distance of his general frame of thought from Keynes' *General theory*, Giblin still developed the export multiplier. But even so, we can ask whether he was convinced of its real world significance? In *Australia, 1930*, after sketching what the concept would imply would be the consequences of an export slump, he asks himself with some perplexity:

> Is, then, this appalling result likely to happen, or is the whole argument affected by a fundamental error?

> The matter is obscure. (Giblin 1930b).[23]

Giblin and Keynes discuss – and don't discuss – the multiplier

This is not to say that Giblin did not raise multiplier issues with Keynes in the years of writing the *General theory*. He did so, twice.

In April 1932 Giblin was acting as Commonwealth Statistician and informal economic advisor to the Commonwealth Government. In that month Giblin sent Keynes a copy of a confidential letter he had sent to his patron, and fellow Tasmanian, the Prime Minister Joseph Lyons.

> 13 April 1932
>
> CONFIDENTIAL
>
> Dear Mr Lyons
>
> I have signed the Report of the Committee on unemployment with some hesitation …
>
> The conclusions of the Report are that money can be reasonably and safely be raised by Treasury-bills for public works … provided that the money so expanded shall earn interest.
>
> The criterion of earning interest must be interpreted with some latitude … I suggest, therefore, that expenditure of Loan money might be held

---

[22] As Cain notes of Giblin: 'In 1929–31 … his attitude to government spending as a recovery multiplicand contrasted with that of Kahn' (1979, p. 109).

[23] In the same vein, the covering letter for 'New farms and population' emphasised that 'this paper was submitted to the Commission as a tentative statement only, and subject to modification and correction'.

open for consideration if it earned ultimately something less than full interest, say four percent, or perhaps as little as three percent.

Our direct loss of income from the lower price of exports, relative to the cost of imports and interest payments, probably about £30m p.a; from cessation of oversea loans it is not more than £30m, making a total of £60m. But the total loss of income is well over £200m. Much the greater part of the total loss of income and employment is due to the indirect effects of the direct loss of purchasing power spread through the community. *The total loss is three to four times the direct loss.*

Conversely any increase of purchasing power directly by government expenditure or otherwise would result in a total purchasing power of three to four times the original amount. If any number of unemployed were put into employment of any kind at average rates of pay, the added number reabsorbed as a consequence in ordinary industry would be two or three times that number, so long as the original expansion continued.

An extreme case may be stated. If an additional £20m was raised by Treasury Bills without seriously disturbing general confidence, and used during one year to employ men at shifting sand at Federal award rates, the result would be the direct employment of more than 100,000 men and the rapid reabsorption into ordinary industry of the whole of the unemployed ... [24] obviously such a policy could not be continued without a ... currency collapse. But if we were sure of a great increase in export prices a year hence, it would be a reasonable policy.

This articulates a very drastic Keynesianism. Was any government in 1932 receiving recommendations to adopt so strenuous a fiscal expansion from such a high-placed and 'official' source? Was anyone conjuring with a multiplier of three or four?

And mark the massive change since *Australia, 1930* in Giblin's confidence in multiplier analysis. Was the 'appalling' prospect that the multiplier analysis *Australia, 1930* conjured up – and which had so alarmed and perplexed him – now vindicated in 1932 as an extraordinary premonition of the Depression? Did this give him intellectual confidence?[25]

Whatever the case, Giblin was boldly pressing multiplier logic at a very significant time in the development of the *General theory*. During that summer of 1932 Keynes was still thinking in terms of correcting and completing the *Treatise on money*. In fact, he was poised to leave it behind and set out on the

---

[24] Italics added.

[25] Or was Giblin – to put a different twist on it – given such confidence by the forthright advocacy of public works on multiplier grounds by Richard Kahn in the 1931 *Economic Journal*?

road to the *General theory*. In 5 April 1932 Keynes had written: 'I propose … to publish a short book extending and correcting' the *Treatise*. On 8 May 1932 he rebuffed Joan Robinson's more radical proposals with the words: 'I lack at present sufficient evidence to the contrary to induce me to scrap all my present half-forged weapons'. On 1 June, the day before he replied to Giblin, he wrote that he planned his new book to 'fill in the gap' in the *Treatise* (see Kahn 1984, pp. 112–13).

So: in June 1932 Keynes is dissatisfied with the *Treatise*, but not completely dissatisfied. He learns that Giblin has been urging the Australian Prime Minister that paying men to 'shift sand' would lead to 'the rapid reabsorption into ordinary industry of the whole of the unemployed'. How does Keynes respond?

> 2 June [1932]
>
> Dear Giblin
>
> I have been extremely interested in your supplementary confidential letter to Mr Lyons … If I understand you rightly, I am very much in agreement with you. I am all in favour of pushing public works programs to the limits of prudence … In my judgement anything that looked liked earning three percent should surely be eligible.

There is something anticlimatic about this reply. Keynes is keen to give his support for public works that earn three per cent. But surely the key item in Giblin's 'supplementary confidential letter' was Giblin's favourable assessment of useless public works (such as shifting sand), which would have a conventionally measured rate of return of minus 100 per cent. But Keynes ignores Giblin's favourable assessment of these.[26]

Nevertheless, most historians of the *General theory* agree that over the next nine months – the autumn and winter of 1932 – the critical transition to the *General theory* occurred.

In March 1933 at about the close of this transition, Giblin's multiplier arrived, after a three-year lag, to Cambridge. It does in the doctoral thesis of E. Ronald Walker, an Australian student at Cambridge, entitled 'Australia in the world Depression', and published as a book under the same title. In Chapter 6, 'The theory of repercussions', Walker draws attention to Giblin's theory of the multiplier, and repeats its algebra. He adds in the foreword that: 'these pages owe much to Mr D. H. Robertson, who read and discussed the whole of the ms … On several points I have had the benefit of the criticism of A. C. Pigou, Professor T. E. Gregory and Mr C. W. Guillebaud'. Thus we may conclude that

---

[26] But Giblin seemed satisfied with Keynes' response. He wrote to Eilean: 'I had a pleasant letter from Keynes, last mail, agreeing very warmly with my attitude. I have sent it on to Lyons' (6 July 1932).

Robertson, and perhaps some other Cambridge names, had became acquainted with Giblin's theory. These are, however, the 'wrong' Cambridge names – Roberston and Pigou – not Keynes and Kahn. And Walker's college was 'the wrong college' – St John's, not King's.[27]

And by March 1933 it was all over, anyway. Keynes had finalised his conception of the multiplier, and published it as *The means to prosperity* (Keynes 1933). This publication was the occasion of a second, more resolute attempt by Giblin to draw Keynes into discussion of the multiplier. In September 1933 he sent Keynes, with apologetic noises, some criticisms of Keynes' multiplier, in particular, its closed economy character. He adds modestly in brackets:

> (I have at times made similar computations here, e.g. on the total increase in income following from a given increase in export production).[28]

He appends four pages of comment and algebra. The day after he sent it, he posts Keynes another note.

> 27/10/33
>
> I must apologise for having sent off to you yesterday – thinking the mail closed then, – a hasty and ill considered scrap[?] on the 'multiplier'. It was done hurriedly in [?] time and I should not have sent it off without more deliberations.

This is, perhaps, not quite the way to market one's thoughts.

Keynes replied:

> Pages 32 and 3 of your typewritten letter are very interesting, but go rather beyond what I was attempting in this short pamphlet ... When I come to write about the multiplier in my next book, I shall deal very thoroughly with the principles on which one should try to arrive at the best possible estimate.

Keynes was not interested in discussing the multiplier with Giblin.[29]

---

[27] Walker was not completely isolated from Keynes. In 1933 he was invited to present a paper to Keynes' 'Political Economy Club'. He 'demonstrated that wage cuts were no cure for unemployment' (Cairncross 1998, p. 49). His argument was presumably the argument for the same claim in his thesis: one that rested on the multiplier.

[28] Is this not also evidence to the effect that Keynes never read *Australia, 1930*? If Giblin had sent it to Keynes, would he need to make this remark?

[29] Keynes was not very interested in discussing the drafts of the *General theory* with anyone outside Cambridge. Ralph Hawtrey and Roy Harrod were some of the very few persons outside Cambridge with whom the drafts were shared.

Nevertheless, Giblin may have succeeded in leaving one foot print on the *General theory*. Upon his appointment to the Commonwealth Bank Board in 1935, Giblin declined to accept two-thirds of his director's fee of £600, and instead allocated £400 it to the establishment of a two-year research fellowship in economics at the University of Melbourne. On 17 September 1935 he wrote to Keynes asking if E. A. G. Robinson – the most senior Cambridge economist with any likelihood of accepting – might be available.[30] He sought to assure Keynes that this new environment would provide Robinson with a valuable intellectual stimulus. For example, in Australia industrial tribunals fixed – or sought to fix – the real wage by law. It is plausible that this observation prompted Keynes to conclude Chapter 19 of the *General theory*, 'Changes in money wages', with a query: what would ensue 'if, as in Australia, an attempt was made to fix by law the real wage' (Keynes 1936, p. 298)? In the absence of such legislation, Keynes' theory implied that the real wage would equal the marginal productivity of labour at that level of output at which aggregate demand equalled aggregate supply. But what if the law attempts to fix the real wage at some magnitude higher than that marginal productivity of labour?

In Chapter 19 Keynes argues that in the attempt to obtain the legislated real wage, nominal wages would be raised. That would produce, however, an equal-sized rise in prices, nullifying any initial increase in real wages. Nominal wages would rise again in a second attempt to increase the real wage, and a wage-price spiral would ensue. The one terminus to this wage-price spiral would lie in an increase in the interest rate, occasioned by the decline in the real money supply, occasioned in turn by the rise in nominal wages. Such a rise in the interest rate would reduce investment, and so aggregated demand, such that the real wage implied by an equality of aggregate demand with aggregate supply is lifted to equality with the legislated real wage.

Whatever the possible impact Giblin's attempt to recruit Robinson had on the *General theory*, Robinson was unavailable for Melbourne, so Keynes suggested that one of his prized pupils, Brian Reddaway, go instead.[31] Reddaway was the chosen apostle sent forth to preach the new gospel. In the words of Alex Millmow:

> Reddaway carried the galley proofs of the *General Theory* on his trip out to Australia. The voyage presented the ideal opportunity to digest the import of Keynes' forthcoming book. Two months after arrival on April 28, Reddaway presented his interpretation of Keynes' theoretical system before the Shillings club, a discussion group of economists, founded by

---

[30] Joan Robinson was included in the invitation.

[31] Copland wrote to Reddaway assuring him: 'You will not find Australia as interesting as Russia, but I think it has many things to interest anyone who has the blood of the pioneering spirit in them'.

Giblin and similar to Keynes' political economy club. His presentation, oddly entitled 'Is the idea of a fair rate of interest a mere convention?' was rushed into print in the June 1936 issue of the *Economic Record*. (Millmow 2003).

On 10 March 1936 Giblin wrote to Keynes that Reddaway had been a great success. Two days later Reddaway wrote to Keynes: 'Altogether the outlook seems quite bright, especially as Giblin is such an extremely likable man' (KCLA BR 12 March 1936).[32]

At about the same time Giblin organised study leave in Cambridge for 1938. The voyage to Britain occasioned, wrote Giblin to Eilean, 'a leisurely reading in one piece of Keynes' *General theory* – with not much more definite result than the need to read it again'.

> In so many places I cannot get the convincing picture of things happening just so – there are so many alternatives and qualifications to be thought out. So much seems to require a careful statistical analysis and testing before one can feel it is safely based. K. is a bit off hand on that side – rather the amateur trusting to the impressions of a shrewd and sensitive intelligence than the professional seeker after facts – and not demanding and relying on the professional investigator as a necessary partner in the business. (NLA LFG c.1938).

On arriving, Keynes was not in Cambridge; he was still convalescing from the crippling 'heart-attack' he had suffered on 16 May 1937. Keynes' absence enabled him to lend Giblin his fully furnished rooms in King's College for the duration of Giblin's stay. Giblin noted they are:

> very magnificent, but a little overwhelming. Duncan Grant's frescoes of nudes cover [the?] side of the long [?] room ... The special merit of these rooms is having its own bathroom which is certainly a luxury ... (NLA LFG 9 February 1938).

> Our belongings got rather mixed up by the bed-maker, who had a fine commercial spirit, and for some years after I had socks and handkerchiefs marked J. M. K. (Giblin 1946, p. 2).

During the first part of 1938 Keynes was only to be in Cambridge between 10–14 March and three weeks in May, (during which time he stayed in his Cambridge Arts Theatre flat). So Giblin set out to visit Keynes at his Sussex farmhouse,

---

[32] KCLA L/36/48.

'Tilton', which neighboured 'Charleston', where Bunny Garnett had been living in 1918.[33]

> Curiously the only other house within a mile – only 200 yards off – I recognised as the house where I first met Keynes 20 years ago. I ran into Lydia at the door, just returned from marketing, and showed me around while Maynard was in his bath. She really is first rate – very jolly and attractive, very sensible and efficient – I was allowed an hour of Maynard who was full of beans – on all things but particularly the inner life of King's over the last 30 years. After an hour I was ejected, not without difficulty for M. was in full spate … His chauffeur, who is not in much use, spends most of his time experimenting with television, with good facilities provided.

Back in Cambridge, Giblin discovered, as others were to later, that key personalities were often inaccessible.

> Dennis Robertson is here but in hiding. Austin Robinson is a bed and breakfast man, spending his days in London; and so on. (RBA LFG 18 July 1938).

Giblin seems to have been most impressed by other visitors, such as Frank Knight - 'certainly anti-Keynes, but not pro anyone else'- one of his precepts being that 'anyone who tried to teach anyone anything was or should be an outcast of society'. Another occasion for visitors was a conference on Tinbergen's pioneering econometric analysis of the business cycle, of which Keynes was fiercely critical. The visiting Oxford economist Jacob Marschak wanted the League of Nations to publish it, but:

> … R[obertson] and C[hampernowne] were rather dubious of its validity. It reaches practical conclusions – such as that interest rates had very little effect on inventory, but the possible errors swamp any certainty in conclusions. [R and C] thought it rather dangerous to publish it. (NLA LFG 18 July 1938).

Giblin arranged for others to visit King's, including an attempt to arrange a meeting between R. G. Menzies and Keynes on the Australian deputy prime minister's 1938 visit.[34]

---

[33] 'I went to David Garnett's at Hilton – with a good deal of cricket – and opportunity to practise left handed bowling for the match [King's] High Table vs [King's]School next week … Garnett is nearly through the editing of T. E. Lawrence's letters, which looks like being very good reading' (NLA LFG 18 July 1938).

[34] There is no evidence that any meeting of Keynes and Menzies came to pass. In March 1941, on a later visit, Menzies did have a 'long talk' with Keynes. Menzies records in his diary that Keynes 'admires' Copland and Giblin (Menzies 1993, p. 88). Keynes told Copland of his own favourable

Keynes did not neglect Giblin. They saw each other during Keynes' brief visit to Cambridge in May of 1938. Keynes made him a supernumerary Fellow. Giblin's King's College obituarist (almost certainly Patrick Wilkinson) records that at this time Giblin 'took the keenest interest in the business of the College, and had many fruitful talks with Keynes'. 'Occasionally', says this obituarist, 'he was proud to think that he had converted Keynes on some points to his own view' (Anon. 1951). But the impression one gets is that their real tie was King's, rather than some shared realm of economic thought.

After Giblin's return to Australia, he and Keynes continued to correspond in the 1940s. Perhaps half of this correspondence is concerned with war finance. In the remainder they share King's College news, swap views on the wisdom of Bunny Garnett's choice of wife, and discuss Giblin's project to establish a National Theatre in Australia.

On Keynes' death, Giblin recorded: 'Keynes had, of all the men I have known, a personality and mind the most fully armed for all adventures' (Giblin 1946). Paradoxically it was Giblin, the hero of the Klondike, who seemed unwilling to join Keynes in his mental adventures. Giblin wished to be the 'professional investigator' – devoted to 'a careful statistical analysis and testing'.[35] The contrast between the *Enquiry* and the *General theory* illustrates the gulf: one a mass of measurement, the other almost free of fact. Keynes cast out into the open sea to pursue his intellectual argosies. Giblin, wishing to keep palpable truth firmly in view, hugged close to the coastline of fact, carefully mapping its shoals and harbours.

---

impression of Menzies. 'I had quite a good talk with him and quickly realised how much he depends on you and other economists' (KCLA April 1941, L/A/3).

[35] In sympathy with this aspiration, Giblin was a member of the Econometric Society, the only Australian academic at that time to be so.

Appendix: A formalisation of Giblin's *Australia, 1930* multiplier analysis

This Appendix advances a model that captures the key features of Giblin's analysis in *Australia, 1930*. In particular it captures the hybrid character of the analysis: containing both a 'Keynesian' emphasis on the benefits of demand, and a 'Classical' emphasis on the benefits of wage cuts.

The modelling assumes the existence two factors of production- labour and land – and three goods: food, manufactures and services. Food uses only land in its production and services uses only labour. All manufactures are imported, all food is exported, and services are neither imported nor exported. The money price of manufactures is normalised at 1. The money price of food in Australian currency is P, and determined by the exogenous exchange rate and world price of food in sterling. The money wage is a given, V. The production of food, F, is given by the fixed supply of land.

National income is the sum of the value of services and food.

$Y = Z + FP$

As there is zero saving, national income in Australian pounds, Y, is entirely spent. As all spending is on services, Z, or manufactures M, we may write,

$Y = Z + M$

The two equalities imply

$M = FP$

But outlays on manufactures (equal imports) are proportional to income,

$M = mY$

Thus,

$$Y = \frac{FP}{m}$$

This last equality captures the leading 'Keynesian' thesis of *Australia 1930*: national income is a multiple of the value of production of the exportable, FP.[36] A decline in FP will produce a decline in national income several times as large. A decline could arise from (i) a fall in the volume of food production, F, (ii) a fall in P due to fall in the pound sterling price of food, and (iii) a fall in P due to the appreciation of the Australian pound. Thus this equality captures the vulnerability of Australian income to world terms of trade, as well as to the nominal exchange rate.

---

[36] So FP is the analog of I in the elementary Keynesian model of national income. And m is the analog of s.

But certain 'Classical' features of the analysis are also apparent. As all employment is located in the services sector, which uses no other factor than labour we may write:

$$LV = Z$$

And since $Z = (1-m)Y$ we may infer,

$$L = \frac{1-m}{m} \frac{F}{V/P}$$

This amounts to a negative relation between employment, L, and the real wage in terms of food, V/P, as hypothesised by 'Classical' economics. Thus the impact of a fall in P may be read in terms of it increasing the real food wage, V/P and thereby reducing employment. The restoration of employment will require a reduction in real wages, that will be secured by a reduction in the nominal wage, V

It may be objected that V/P is not a measure of 'the real wage' when, by our present assumptions, no food is consumed. But the consumption of food can be allowed for without attenuating the negative relation between employment and the real wage. Suppose that c of national income is spent on food. Then

$$Y = Z + M + cY$$

Given $Y = Z + FP$ we may infer,

$$Y = \frac{FP}{c+m}$$

and so,

$$L = \frac{1-m}{c+m} \frac{F}{V/P}$$

The negative relation between employment and the real wage remains.

Two further points about this last expression:

(i) The size of the multiplier contracts as c rises.[37] Thus c operates like the propensity to save in the ordinary Keynesian model, even if the mechanism is

---

[37] In 'Repercussions of changes in income' Giblin states that the fraction of new spending that will become new income in the home country depends on:

1. the proportion spent on imports
2. the proportion spent on exportable goods, when this amount does not increase incomes in the country
3. the extent to which new income cancels old income
4. the extent to which new spending is spent on stocks.

Giblin estimated that imports would amount to £53 in every £240, and consumption of exportables £22.

different. c does not represent an increase in 'leakages' as income rises; it represents a decrease in 'injections' as income rises. For c is the amount by which exports are reduced by an extra unit of income. This implies that if $c + m = 1$ then all of an increase in income goes to either reduce exports or increase imports, and there is no multiplier at all, as Giblin appears to have completely appreciated.[38] The upshot is that the existence of a multiplier requires that at least part of an extra pound of income be spent on the one thing that is neither importable nor exportable: services.

(ii) If $m = 0$ – the closed economy - then the model reduces to the de Lissa model: national income equals 'production' divided by the propensity to spend on production.

---

[38] In 'Correlative increases in production', he wrote: 'When exportable goods are consumed, in general, exports are decreased by the same amount, and there is no additional money for Australian incomes'.

6. The Great Depression and the battle for inflation

'I am sure the Premiers' Plan last year saved the economic structure of Australia.'
J. M. Keynes[1]

'From the economists' side I don't think we have anything of the way of a plan to offer.'
L. F. Giblin

If the welcome reception in mid 1929 of the *Enquiry* heralded the arrival of the economist in Australian public life, they were soon to face a stinging test of their usefulness. In the final months of 1929 the world began its skid into the Great Depression. Australia's national income was soon to decline by 30 per cent; her real national product by 18 per cent; and unemployment of trade unionists to reach 30 per cent in the second quarter of 1932.[2]

As the nation sought a resolution of economic turmoil, economists were awarded with an unprecedented eminence in national affairs. 'With judges, politicians and bankers all in the new classroom', as Jack Lang put it, the Australian economist became 'the nation's pundit' (Lang 1980). And, in a moderate measure, they became the world's. Keynes publicly hailed the deeds of Giblin and Copland. In 1933 Copland was invited by Cambridge University to deliver the inaugural Marshall Lectures on the subject of the advice of Australian economists in the Depression. In 1936, on the occasion of her tercentenary, Harvard followed with a similar invitation to Copland. Australia seemed to constitute an example to other nations.[3] It was her economists who had plucked a 'Plan' from pandemonium.

Their glory was, however, decidedly short-lived. The economic emergency passed. But the myth of the Plan endured. This was the myth of callous budget cuts and wage reductions decreed by the economists. This coloured Australian attitudes towards economists for at least a decade.

And, within a span of a few years, new economic doctrines arrived from Cambridge that left the prescriptions of the economists' plans looking, not merely

---

[1] CWJMK vol. 21, p. 94.

[2] See Haig 2001, p. 30; *Official year book of the Commonwealth of Australia 1935–6*, p. 395

[3] And Canada: Raymond Priestly noted in his diary in 1936 while touring Alberta: 'There were several humble admirers of Douglas Copland among my dinner companions. They are... great admirers of the way Australia extricated herself from her private mess, and Copland's name is mighty in the land …' (Priestley 2002, p. 173).

'stern', [4] but positively injurious. In the light of these new theories, some elements of the economists' advice caused perplexity. How is it that they recommend spending cuts and tax rises in the depths of a Great Depression? This perplexity is only multiplied by our knowledge that Giblin, Brigden and Copland subscribed to certain 'Keynesian' notions about aggregate demand. Thus almost as soon as the Depression began to abate, questions began to nag witnesses and historians. Was their advice helpful or harmful? Were they Keynesians *avant la lettre*? Or classical economists despite themselves?

We will contend that the thinking of Copland and Giblin was informed by a model that was neither purely Keynesian nor classical, but had elements of both. Yet their use of this model teaches what slippery tools analytic insights can be. Their multiplier analysis allowed them to predict the Depression, but its light was less successful in illuminating the remedy to them.

Perhaps the most arresting aspect of their advice was not how Keynesian or Classical it was — or how right or wrong it was — but how intermittently it was heeded. The urgent recommendations of Copland and Giblin, from late 1930, of a monetary loosening were rebuffed by political forces. Giblin's insistence of fiscal expansion towards the Depression's close was similarly doomed. [5] With the exception of the 'rushed' and improvised Premiers' Plan, their experience, rather than bespeaking power or influence, was in large measure one of frustration.

This chapter, then, tells the story of economists foreseeing, but not always understanding; of their best economic advice being ignored; and of their most heeded advice ignoring their best economics. It is a story knit together by the weave of personalities: of Copland's nervous drive and confidence; Giblin's pessimism and hesitancy; and Brigden's mental crotchets; of Giblin's patient leadership by conciliation; of Brigden's weakness for idealistic and lonely positions; and Copland's presumption of heading the charge.

Our method is for the greater part narrative: we patiently map the twisting track of their advice between the first signs of collapse in September 1929 until the defeat of the Lang Government in June 1932. The chapter traces how, in the first nine months, Brigden, Copland and Giblin spoke almost in one voice to persuade Australia to adopt policies that would minimise the impact of the slump in export prices. 'Adjustment' and 'absorption' were the key concepts here, and policy was 'defensive'. We then show how their unity broke, as Giblin and

---

[4] This was Copland's own description of the policy recommendations of himself and his colleagues.

[5] The knotted mat of those years has been unpicked many times. The Great Depression is surely the most intensely researched episode in Australian economic history. Landmarks in the post-war literature include Gregory and Butlin (1988), Schedvin (1970), Gilbert (1973) and Cain (1982, 1987). The role of economists in the events of the period is exhaustively re-examined in Millmow (2004b).

Copland were increasingly inclined towards an active policy of monetary stimulation, while Brigden remained essentially deflationist. The narrative concludes with Giblin distancing himself from Copland and striking out in favour of bold fiscal stimulus.

The chapter concludes by surveying Giblin, Copland and Brigden's efforts, after the passing of the crisis, to write into the public consciousness their own history of this difficult episode.

The twisted trail

The Constitutional Club and the coming blow

In trying to understand what the four believed, it can be helpful to forget some of what we remember. We remember the Great Depression – it is the founding myth of modern economic policy. But the Great Depression – that almost bizarre and still ill-understood phenomenon – was not the stuff of memory in 1929. What the economists could recall in that year was that, over the previous decade, Australia had seen several conspicuous but doubtful public investments, a popular clamour for tariff walls, and a spread of minimum wages and union militancy. There was, then, great difference between the 'past' that pressed on their minds, and the future that was suddenly to dismay them.

We have a picture of our four's mindsets on the very eve of the Great Depression. On 16 September 1929, at David Jones in Sydney, Brigden spoke to the conservative Constitutional Association on 'The economic position of Australia'. He foretold the approaching calamity with striking prescience. Using a multiplier of two, he predicted that the recent reduction in export prices and capital inflow spelled a fall in national income in 1930 'at least equal to 10%' (Brigden 1929).[6] This would be first felt by exporters, but would inevitably spread to wage earners. Regrettably, 'the present generation of wage earners in Australia has been brought up on the idea that its standard of living is a creation of Parliament. The natural thing to expect therefore is some barren trade union and political resistance to economic conditions taking the form of strikes and political instability'.[7]

---

[6] Real or nominal? 'Both' was probably Brigden's estimate. Since he took wage rates to be a given, he cannot have expected much adjustment in money prices.

[7] By this time Brigden, the former union official, had become a disenchanted detractor of the labour movement. 'I fear that the trade union superstition is so deep-rooted in Australia that anything that, with any show of reason, can be construed into an attack of unionism is bound to fail. Trade unionism has become a religion, and the fact that the priesthood of a religion abuses its powers has never been sufficient to overthrow it' (UMA JBB 10 July 1929, 'New South Wales Industrial Regulation'). In 1928 Brigden had proposed to Bruce that 'Works Committees' be created to replace registered unions as bargaining units. 'Within limits to be prescribed by the Court, and normally excluding standard

What might be done? No solution would be found in credit expansion: 'a permanent reduction in income ... cannot be remedied by an inflation of credit'. Such an inflation would bring only 'temporary' benefit. Here Brigden hoists an anti-inflationist standard that he would keep flying throughout the most miserably depressed years of the 1930s.

The best remedy, claimed Brigden, was a program of import replacement by means of cost reduction – achieved largely by an increase in effort, productivity and removal of restrictive conditions, that could 'get 10 per cent more' out of labour. 'Microeconomic Reform' in the language of a latter day. In addition, he used multiplier logic to assert that the required shift to home production would be much less than the £30m loss in exports faced by Australia; 'for local production would set going a cumulative demand for other products ...'.

His advice, then, is not drastic and avoids many measures later urged by the Platoon. No reduction in government expenditure, no depreciation of the Australian pound, no reduction in interest rates. And, above all, no reduction in wage rates. That is spurned on the very same Keynesian grounds that was later spurned by the four:

> Reduced wages should be the last resource, because while ultimately prices would be reduced, the immediate effect is to reduce purchasing power.

Overall, it might be said that Brigden saw Australia's situation in September 1929 as serious, but not hopeless. In fact, the impending blow would be beneficial. For Australia had not 'roared' in the twenties. The Australian economy of the 1920s was overregulated and underproductive. The public's sense of enterprise had wilted. 'People of all classes seemed to expect the Government not only to spend for them, but to think for them [for example, 'find markets', 'settle disputes']' (Brigden 1928). [8] Australia had in that decade misspent its capital resources on mirages. Now this misconduct would be called to account.

> The crisis will be as severe as the resistance to it, but when it is over it will have weeded out the wasteful growths of the prosperous years, just

---

wages and hours, an Award or part of an Award or Agreement may be suspended by the Court or its subordinate authority on the application of a recognised Works Committee.' This has a resemblance to 'enterprise bargaining' and 'certified agreements' of the 1990s.

[8] In the same vein, Copland early in the Depression expressed the hope that the rigours of contraction would strengthen the economy. 'The conditions of high tariffs, heavy borrowing overseas, and high standards of living are not conducive to enterprise or efficiency. The depression has swept way the shelter under which these conditions developed, and it will undoubtedly bring an economic benefit to the country as a consequence' (Copland 1930b, p. 28).

as a severe winter kills off the pests. In the long run it will have done good.

Brigden provided an example of prescience without policy. There was to be a Depression, but no special policy was urged. The Depression was to be the policy.

Australia, 1930

Brigden's relatively hopeful outlook soon perished. Over the next six months recorded unemployment amongst trade unionists grew from 12.1 to 18.5 per cent. On 28 April 1930 in a radio broadcast from 2BL Brigden told his listeners that 140 000 'breadwinners' (or 6 per cent of the labour force) had become unemployed over the previous 12 months. And things, he warned, would only get worse (*Sydney Morning Herald,* 29 April 1930).

On the same night that Brigden was addressing his invisible audience in Sydney, in Melbourne Giblin was mounting the rostrum of the public lecture theatre of Melbourne University to deliver *Australia, 1930*. Also using multiplier theory, he raised the prospect of an 'appalling result' of the contraction of export prices and capita inflow: one sixth of the population unemployed.

Giblin proposed a 'prompt surgical treatment' for this malady. It did not involve government spending; that was not mentioned. Giblin did moot a depreciation of the Australian pound, but it was secondary.[9] The primary treatment was a nominal wage cut of 15 per cent, which, he said, would amount to a real wage cut of five per cent. This would secure an improvement in the real exchange rate. Thus by April 1930, wage cuts were on the agenda. The 'Keynesian' style argument against wage cuts was now repudiated: '… a transfer of consuming power from, say, wages to profits does not involve a reduction of total consuming power because what is taken from wages is added to profits'. Purchasing power 'as a whole' 'would not be altered' (UMA LFG 30 October 1930 LFG). In the same vein, Brigden was to press on his readers of the *Economic News* (9 June 1932, p. 75) that 'Wage *rates* do not buy anything'; only wage incomes do (that is, the product of wage rate and employment). Deficits were rejected. 'Nor can the Government borrow in Australia from our reduced income without … merely transferring employment from production of goods which people can buy to the production of public works that do not add to income' (Brigden *Sydney Morning Herald,* 29 April 1930). Rather than becoming 'more Keynesian' in the face of the crisis, they were becoming less Keynesian.

In May 1930 Brigden published *Escape to prosperity*, an appeal to the public, priced at just 5/-, that sought to coax them into yielding to wage reductions. This public campaign extended to the 'gratuitous distribution' of three articles on 'The economic outlook' by Copland, from the 19–21 June issues of the *Argus*.

---

[9] In the December 1930 issue of *Australian Quarterly* Giblin supported a free exchange rate.

Also using the multiplier, Copland paints a foreboding picture. He calls for wage cuts, and favourably considers the impact of depreciation, without quite recommending this 'financial heresy'. At about the same time in the *Melbourne Herald* Giblin published some 'Letters to John Smith' that were designed to reconcile the public to the necessary policies.

The high point of this campaign was the so-called 'First Manifesto', a joint statement in May 1930 of the economists attending in Brisbane a meeting of the Australasian Association for the Advancement of Science. Reflecting the need to obtain a document that all would sign, it was a little muted, as Giblin sought a consensus to increase the impact of economists.

The manifesto's recipe had already been made familiar by Giblin in the preceding eight weeks: real wage flexibility is pressed hard, [10] and a floating exchange rate cautiously recommended ('free movement in overseas exchange will lessen the immediate evils'). It warns the 'remedy for our troubles is not to be found in exploitation of the note issue'. A new chord is struck with the recommendation for balancing the budget, on the not very urgent-sounding grounds of 'disorganisation'. This could be done without actual contractions in government programs: greater efficiency in administration and greater taxes on property should preserve a balanced budget. In summary, Australia should face up to the unpleasant reality of 'serious' loss of national income by cheapening her labour and currency, and making government services more expensive.

But the Labor Government that had arrived in power in September 1929 was hostile. The 'Manifesto' specifically rebuffed Scullin's pet remedy – ever higher trade barriers: 'Assistance to production by tariffs, bounties or otherwise should not be granted without careful inquiry into the effect on the costs of other industries'. Without an economic voice or auditor in government, Giblin, Copland and Brigden could do no more than attempt to influence public opinion through public lectures, public books and manifestoes.

But whatever momentum they might have been building was checked by the sudden advent of Sir Otto Niemeyer.

Fighting Sir Otto

On 14 July 1930 Sir Otto Niemeyer of the Bank of England disembarked on Australian soil, and there began one of the weirder episodes in Australian history;

---

[10] The Manifesto: 'A system of machine-made wages destroys the hope of increasing real wages as prosperity increases, and in times of crisis concentrates the burden through unemployment upon the minority least able to bear it … A revision of this practice of wage fixation is urgently desirable'. But it is not just wage rates that need correction, 'some fall in profits and real salaries is inevitable' (in Copland and Shann 1931, p. 16).

a freak child of the ill-conditioned Anglo-Australian embrace of the inter-war years.

Neimeyer's arrival was a 1930s version of an International Monetary Fund 'mission' to a developing country in financial crisis, but without the capital injection. Niemeyer, representing the Bank of England, along with Professor T.E. Gregory of the London School of Economics, had ostensibly been invited by the Prime Minister to 'observe' the economic situation in Australia. During his lengthy stay Sir Otto did not so much observe as decree. His advice was stark, pre-emptory and commanding: the Premiers were to balance their budgets immediately.

Regrettably, Niemeyer was ill-suited to furnish good economic advice. Without a grain of sympathy for the country or any stake in its success, he might not be expected to give good counsel. And in addition, for all his severity, there was basically a lack of seriousness about him; there was a distinct element of performance about his conduct. Nor did his general intelligence preclude a streak of absurdity. During his four-month junket of port drinking and golfing, he floated a series of astringent judgements about his host country that ranged from the dubious to the near asinine. Productivity per head in Australia had fallen six per cent in 20 years; Australia was 'overpopulated'; Australia was a 'poor' country. Finally, the Commonwealth Bank's own suggestion that Britain would soon leave the gold standard was 'staggering'. Niemeyer's resistance to this last contention is understandable: he was one of the chief architects of the ill-starred British resumption of the gold standard in 1925.

The truth is that Niemeyer cannot be taken seriously as an economic advisor, and should not have been taken seriously. But he was. He successfully intimidated the Australian elite and has done so since. The few points of resistance amongst the elite were the 'Melbourne' economists, Giblin and Copland.

Not long after, Giblin recalled: 'I remember fights with both Niemeyer and Gregory from the day they landed in Melbourne' (quoted in Schedvin 1970, p. 219). For himself Niemeyer recorded:

> I thought Giblin pretty disappointing … Giblin, and to some extent Brigden, were still hankering after an extension of secondary industries, apparently by means of further protection, because they had the strange idea that secondary industry in Australia would absorb more people than primary industry … .(Millmow 2004a, 2004b).

This curious statement includes a number of Neimeyerisms. Was it 'strange' for Giblin to think secondary industry could employ more people than primary industry when it already did so?[11] What *is* strange is that Niemeyer could believe that Giblin advocated protection, when Giblin and Brigden had publicly opposed further protection (for example in the 'First Manifesto'). Their hopes for secondary industry lay in cost reduction, deregulation and depreciation. But depreciation was abhorred by Niemeyer. Any influence of Giblin's opinion on this matter vanished in the face of Niemeyer's disgust. To strengthen the Commonwealth Bank against the siren call of inflation, Leslie Melville, perhaps the most committed deflationist at this time amongst the Australian economists, was appointed to the Bank with Niemeyer's blessing. The apparent triumph of Niemeyerism was capped by Scullin's reappointment on 25 August 1930 of Sir Robert Gibson as chairman of the Commonwealth Bank for a seven-year term, just as Scullin was departing Australia to attend an Imperial Conference in London.

The quest for inflation

The overall impact of the Niemeyer event was to raise tension. Fissures became fractures as Niemeyer gave courage to pre-existing deflationist sentiments in financial and academic circles. Back in England, he urged Melville to wage war on the 'dangerous nonsense' of 'Copland and co' (Millmow 2004a, p. 155). So having spent a year fighting off 'the left' over wages and work practices, Giblin and Copland were now facing a newly rallied front on 'the right'. But at the same time, an opportunity presented itself with Lyons becoming Acting Treasurer in lieu of Scullin during his absence.

This was a critical period. The prices of Australian bonds in London slumped in the first three weeks of September 1930.[12] Early that month Giblin had written Lyons a baffled and despairing letter. He was 'much oppressed' 'with the danger of our not getting through without a bad smash with a chance of revolution and chaos'. 'I think the break up of the Labor Party is almost inevitable'. And then a remarkable confession: 'From the economists' side I don't think we have anything of the way of a plan to offer. For myself, as for others, I don't think I see light on the whole problem' (NLA JAL: LFG 1 September 1930). Rather than economists dogmatising as the guardians of some therapeutic plan, they do not 'have anything to offer'. This modesty is very Giblinesque.

---

[11] Secondary industry in 1928–29 employed substantially more people than primary industry.

[12] This may seem puzzling. Lang was yet to be elected premier of New South Wales. And Australia, in the event, was to observe strictly all her debt-servicing obligations to overseas bond holders. Giblin blamed 'ignorance and tendency to hysteria on the part of the oversea investor' (Giblin 1930a). Perhaps more to the point was the fact Australian debt securities had during the 1920s been the subject of an assiduous and well-planned campaign of denigration by certain City finance houses (see Colebatch 1926).

'We are badly scared … I think you are our last hope …' wrote Giblin, sharing a mood that was highly characteristic of the moment in Australia.

Three days later Giblin had evidently rallied, and wrote again, now with firm resolution. [13]

> September 4 1930
>
> *Confidential*
>
> Dear Lyons
>
> … the question of general monetary policy is of such outstanding importance that I must worry you about it.
>
> We appear to be taking a blind course towards deflation and restoring parity with sterling without an adequate consideration of the alternative. We have discussed it a good deal in Melbourne, businessmen and economists, and there is a strong feeling it will be a fatal mistake. We have inevitably a very bad place to get through with our loss of income from exports and loans together. A policy of monetary deflation may add so much to the inescapable difficulties as to make successful issue impossible. (NLA LFG 4 September 1930).

Giblin dismissed the 'scare of inflation'. 'I admit the danger of encouraging wild inflationists, but the danger is really made less by admitting the small amount of solid truth which is in their theories. A policy of drastic deflation might v. well end in an orgy of inflation, when the string gets to breaking point.' 'To be scared of such a policy is as sensible as to avoid a glass of beer for fear of delirium tremens' (quoted in White 1987).

On 18 September 1930 Giblin, Copland, and Dyason submitted *A plan for economic readjustment* (Giblin, Copland and Dyason 1930). The plan reaffirmed the importance of real cuts in wages:

> Of overwhelming importance is the quest of unemployment. We are unhesitatingly of the opinion that without a drop in real, as distinguished from the nominal, wage level the unemployment menace cannot be met; temporary suspension of all awards.

This emphasis on *real* wages is no accident. For the key novelty in the *Plan for economic readjustment* is its identification of a new enemy: 'deflation'. It was the uniform fall in the money prices of labour and goods – deflation – that was the villain. There was an urgent need of some re-inflation, as soon as real wages were reduced.

---

[13] MS366/5/35

If this condition is fulfilled it will then be possible by a sound monetary policy to restore industry, and employment, and thus to counteract the repercussions of the first loss of income and to provide a means of escape from indirect losses.

The 'sound monetary policy' would consist of a 20 per cent depreciation of the Australian pound, and the Commonwealth Bank's support of all commercial bank advances on sound security. The Bank was to re-establish the 1929 price-level, amounting to, they believed, an increase in prices of four per cent. The operation of monetary policy was to remain solely in the hands of an independent Central bank: 'The exclusive control of the note issue by the Board for a period of years might be usefully reaffirmed in a solemn act of parliament'. It is all quite familiar to the present day reader: give the central bank an inflation target, and let the central bank get on with it. The small stimulus they proposed targeting would have the additional benefit of largely solving the 'problem' budgets: 'The main cause of budget deficits is languishing industry and the cause cannot be removed until industry is restored and the fall in national income checked'.

Copland was, it seems, central in the formulation of this plan. It displays his characteristic push. [14] The Plan pronounced: 'We emphasise the urgency of immediate action'. But Scullin, in thrall to Sir Otto and Sir Robert, told Lyons he could not entertain such notions. [15] Lyons pigeonholed the 'plan' (Giblin 1951, p. 95).

Fighting each other

Giblin and Copland's attempt to re-inflate was also hampered by a split amongst the economists. Melville and Shann had publicised their opposition to reflation. Shann had blasted these proposals for leaving 'undisturbed the whole Symian bag of tricks – tariffs, wages-fixation, bounties and bonuses', and for being 'frightened' by 'the very look of falling prices'. 'The proposals of the Melbourne School for a stabilised price level', said Shann, 'will serve as a stalking horse' for a centralised and politicised banking system that is a requisite for socialism.

In an attempt to diffuse this conflict, Giblin 'wired to the half-dozen people':

---

[14] The idea of price level stability resonates with the precepts of the new book of Copland's favored author, Keynes: the *Treatise on money*. But Copland could not have seen this book at the time of the plan. The *Treatise on money* was only published on 31 October 1930. And when he did see it, he was not impressed. 'In February I read Keynes and ran out my own version of his equations. I was not satisfied with my grasp of his theory and came to the tentative conclusion that he did not understand his own theory' (UMA DBC 13 April 1931). A harsh conclusion, but not unjustified.

[15] On 5 November 1930 Scullin wrote to Lyons: 'All this talk about creating credit and inflation is most damaging' (quoted in Shann and Copland 1931, p. 63).

> There has been some difference of opinion between Melbourne and Adelaide on monetary policy, which unfortunately has become exaggerated in public statement. Melville has offered to come over here for a couple days with a view to [removing] our differences (NLA LFG).[16]

Giblin proposed that Brigden, Shann, Hytten and Ronald Walker would, at their own expense, join Melville and himself in conference on 27 November 1930 at Dyason's house in Melbourne. At the conference Giblin pressed the necessity of vigorous credit expansion. Within the 'general scheme of … reduction in wages and salaries and public economy and high taxation of fixed incomes', 'it will be necessary for the banks, Commonwealth, trading banks and savings banks – to take very vigorous combined action to provide money at lower interest rates for all legitimate purposes'.

> Objection has been made to the monetary policy of this paper on the grounds that it will encourage reckless inflationists in the community. The argument runs that as we support an anti-deflation policy we are comparative inflationists, and so opening the door to wild inflation; and secondly sentences would be torn from this context in support of crude inflation. We cannot accept the principles of conduct implied by this criticism which would make for discussion of any subject impossible. There is no proposed policy of any kind that is not likely to be misrepresented … Nothing is to be gained by the somewhat hysterical rantings against inflation that are popular today. (NLA LFG).[17]

But Giblin did not persuade. There was no agreement. The economists remained separated. Giblin and Copland 'reflationist'; Brigden, Shann and Melville 'deflationist'.

The upshot was a weak compromise document, 'First steps to economic recovery – statement by economists', an insipid document, searching for what they could agree on.

Events were soon to widen the fractures amongst economists over reflation. In late 1930 the premiers had appointed Brigden (now working for the Queensland Bureau of Economics and Statistics), Shann, Hytten and four treasury officials, to prepare under Gibson's chairmanship a program for the restoration of public finances. Just as the committee first assembled, word arrived that the Bank of New South Wales had decided to depreciate the Australian pound against the pound sterling, after long resisting market pressure to do so. Copland, Shann and Melville had met the general manager of the Bank of New South Wales,

---

[16] MS 366/5/366.

[17] MS 366/9/101.

Alfred Davidson, at his house in Leura in the Blue Mountains, and urged depreciation.[18] But Gibson was adamantly opposed to devaluation. 'Gibson nearly tore out his hair and whiskers on hearing the news' (Hytten 1971). He then 'sat down, closed his eyes, and with a cigarette bobbing up and down started a seemingly endless tirade against private banks, and the world in general'. In order to disburden themself of this 'chairing', the committee broke into three subcommittees, and a draft report was pieced together.

Brigden's presence was critical in formulating the draft, since he had struck an 'anti-inflationist' posture since 1929, although under implicit pressure from Giblin he attempted to admit something of Giblin's expansionism. 'It is almost certainly impossible for Australia to recover ... without some alleviation through expanded credit' (Brigden 1930b, p. 2). Regrettably, velocity would increase with recovery; there would be an overshooting; the subsequent correction would require a 'heroic procedure'. It was all too tricky to pull off. Brigden, then, had what might be called the 'competence objection' to credit expansion. It was a remedy, but a dangerous one, one that could kill as well as cure; its successful application required more knowledge than actual monetary policy would heed.[19]

As a consequence, the committee's draft report for the February 1931 Premiers' Conference rejected any schemes for reflation. 'It would be only too easy to gloss over our loss of prosperity by a loss of purchasing power of the currency. This is not the road to recovery but collapse' (Brigden, Hytten and Shann 1931, p. 9).

The Giblin–Copland tendency ignored the committee's report. Giblin described it as 'narrowly deflationary in tone' (Giblin 1951). To another later anonymous commentator, probably Roland Wilson, the report 'preserved much of the deflationary tone of Sir Otto Niemeyer's statement' (*1937 Official Year Book of the Commonwealth of Australia*).[20] More than disregard, the committee's report was quietly disowned by most other economists. There is in Giblin's account the definite suggestion that Brigden had nothing to do with the recommendations

---

[18] Davidson had reasons of its own: the Bank of New South Wales was losing customers to non-cartel dealers offering scarce pounds sterling at higher than official prices. 'The economists were among the first to congratulate him on his courageous action' (Holder 1970, p. 686).

[19] Brigden took a simpler message to the public. 'The government might need all its moral strength to resist the demand for currency inflation in the near future. And with unemployment rife and depression upon us it will not be easy to convince ardent advocates that a small inflation is bad' (Brigden, *Sydney Morning Herald* 9 December 1929). Brigden noted that devaluation 'would assist recovery' but is 'dangerous'.

[20] A reviewer of Brigden's *Escape to prosperity* noted: 'Some at least of his criticisms will now be found in Sir Otto Niemeyer's speech to the Melbourne Conference' (Anon. 1930).

of the report (Giblin 1951, p. 91). Yet it is unmistakably Brigden's work. [21] Giblin's apparent disinclination to acknowledge this suggests Giblin's quest to find allies rather than adversaries – to provide a united front.

The Treasurer E. G. Theodore and Scullin repudiated the report: they would not have it signed by their public servants. Gibson then refused to sign it. The report was never issued.

The first attempt of economists to provide a solution under the auspices of government had been defeated. The government and the central bank were left at loggerheads. In the face of this impasse, Theodore announced the 'Theodore Plan': a legislative attempt to secure a monetary expansion that the Commonwealth Bank was refusing.

With almost one voice the Australian economists were hostile to the Theodore Plan. Brigden was particularly strident. He had circulated a memorandum among the February 1931 Premiers Conference committee, declaring that Theodore's ideas were worse than Lang's. He attempted to sound the alarm for Australia at large in his February 1931 book, *P.P. On purchasing power and the pound Australian*. He announced:'We are in the transition towards rising prices and progressive inflation' (Brigden 1931a, p55). [22]

Copland was also hostile. This is less explicable, since he had already pressed the case for monetary stimulus. Theodore's declaration that: 'The big task was to get money values back to the 1929 level' is obviously resonant of Copland's 8 September 1930 plan. In June Theodore had told Keith Murdoch he was 'intensely interested in Professor Copland's ideas' on stabilising the price level. And Copland was protesting his own attachment to credit expansion. Yet Copland now maintained that: 'By refusing to accept the report of the experts committee … the Scullin Ministry is raising an effective barrier to economic recovery'. (*Argus*, 23 February 1931). [23] The Theodore Plan, said Copland, would depreciate the exchange rate to 50 to 60 per cent down from the old parity (Copland 1931a, p. 23). Giblin, too, criticised the 'foolishness' of printing notes in his 'Letters to John Smith'.

---

[21] The Brigden archives at the National Library contain a copy of the report (Brigden, Hytten and Shann 1931). At its head is written in Brigden's hand: 'Please keep this as strictly confidential in this form'. It ends with the names Brigden, Hyttten and Shann, and then Gibson followed by six treasury officials. In Brigden's hand the names of Gibson and the Treasury officials are struck out.

[22] 'Everyone is waiting until prices reach bottom, and in waiting they are letting it sink lower still' (Brigden 1931a, p. 50). This sits awkwardly with Brigden's other assertion that the economy is experiencing a 'transition to rising prices', and, indeed, 'progressive inflation has already begun' (p. ix).

[23] Theodore replied: 'The bankers are saying that the prevailing high rates of interest are the direct result of shortage of money. Very well, let us increase the supply' (*Argus*, 24 February 1931).

At this moment of crisis, Giblin – the tireless conciliator – was brought to one of the wings of power. On the morning of 2 February 1931, Wickens – in an attempt to budge the February 1931 Premiers' Conference committee from its 'deflationary tone'– had released, as Commonwealth Statistician, and while the committee still sat, data on the most recent fall in prices. That afternoon Wickens was felled by an epileptic fit. He had been the solitary official in the Commonwealth Government who could claim an expertise on economic issues. Having disposed of the Bureau of Economic Research, the government was now wholly bereft of professional advice. The minister responsible for replacing Wickens, Arthur Blakely, had in 1929 denounced the Bureau of Economic Research in particular, and Australian economists in general. 'The economist is academic, conservative and anti-working class and lives in a world of his own'. He now entreated Giblin to fill the position of Commonwealth Statistician. [24] Giblin replied:

> May I state my own feelings in the matter? I am naturally very loth [sic] to interrupt my work here ... My domestic arrangements, particularly in view of my wife's state of health ... will also be seriously discomposed by a temporary residence in Canberra. On the other hand, if I can be of any service to the Australian Government at this critical time ... I should wish to do my bit. (NLA LFG 27 March 1933).

The plan

Giblin arrived in Canberra at a critical time. The Senate rejected the Theodore Plan. Parliament was paralysed. A new bargain was to be attempted. Shann was asked once more to join the craftsmen, but Brigden and Hytten were dropped. Copland was placed in the chair; Giblin and Melville were added.

They produced the Copland Plan, which was to be the basis of the Premiers' Plan. It recommended a reduction in the deficit from £39m to £11m, to be secured by a £13m reduction in outlays, £12m increase in taxes, and £3m from reduced interest. There was to be a 20 per cent cut in expenditure, and a 15 per cent reduction in interest payments.

The Plan was hardly a policy; it was a deal, a deal specifying how the pain would be shared out; it sought to establish agreement by observing measures of equality of sacrifice. Australian bond holders, public servants and pensioners were all to take a cut. (Bond holders experienced the heaviest proportionate contraction in incomes: legislative fiat reduced interest on government debt by 22.5 per cent.) This universal sharing of the pain made it universally unpopular. It was

---

[24] The falsehood of all four of these contentions is well demonstrated by this volume. Copland complained to Brigden of Blakeley's 'rather sticky article in the Labor press giving economists a hard time' (UMA 23 October 1929).

hated by the left and right, and the principal coming personalities of each ideological current rejected it. Thus Curtin argued that Labor should surrender government rather than accept the Plan (Ross 1983)[25], while R. G. Menzies dubbed it 'the Lang plan plus hypocrisy'.

But this plan was accepted by the federal Labor Government which set about destroying itself by implementing it.

Giblin believed its truest implementation required one specific action by himself. His salary was paid for by the University of Melbourne. It was, therefore, exempt from the cuts applied to public servant salaries. This anomaly left him uneasy. He wrote to the Chancellor of the University of Melbourne, Sir John Monash, requesting his salary be reduced by 25 per cent (UMA LFG 11 June 1931).

Failing with Lyons and stung by Keynes

In the wake of the plan's implementation the Labor Party disintegrated. Elections were called for 19 December 1931, and the United Australia Party (UAP) won them in a landslide. Joseph Lyons, having left the ALP for the UAP, became prime minister.

The political crisis was now solved. And budget discipline recovered. But the economic malaise seemed unresolved. And the new government seemed inert. Giblin told Eilean he was 'rather uneasy about the new Government's general policy – they were talking about further retrenchments and cuts, and the Bank pitched in with a long letter, wind up about deficits, and almost suggesting a new Premiers' Plan' (RBA LFG 17 January 1932).

The context – the establishment of political stability and the improvement in the budget, but continued stagnation and policy passivity – prompted Giblin to make one last attempt for some activism in policy, despite being beset by stress-related illness.[26] In March he privately declared: 'There is a need for bold perhaps desperate, policy to keep things together here' (RBA LFG 9 March 1932). The new government was persuaded to form a committee to provide a 'Preliminary Survey of the Economic Problem'. The committee was to be the same as that of the Copland Committee, with the addition of Sir Wallace Bruce (a past Lord Mayor of Adelaide). But this scheme for membership was disrupted by news from New Zealand in March. 'We shall be without Copland, who has

---

[25] Norman Makin, who was the Scullin governments' speaker and was to come into conflict years later with Brigden, also repudiated the Plan.

[26] A lowered immune system – perhaps caused by stress- had seen Giblin's childhood chickenpox reactivate into shingles. 'I have crashed again' (RBA LFG 20 February 1932). 'I am remaining on as a bed and breakfast patient at the hospital. My scars take some time to dry up and clean up, and I have twice a day spraying and bandaging' (RBA LFG 3 March 1932). He would remain in hospital for six weeks.

just wired from Wellington that he will be weeks more in hospital there.' Giblin took this to be another psychological mishap. 'Copland had a bad break down in New Zealand in March. He had been working at top pressure …' (RBA LFG 23 March 1932). But to Copland's mind it was not, thankfully, a nervous condition. 'I am glad to say there is no recurrence of my old complaint' (UMA DBC 30 March 1932). It was an attack of duodenal ulcer, and so quite in conformity with the theory of the period that ulcers were the bane of hard-driven executives. He had been instructed to neither smoke nor drink for six months. Copland finally returned from New Zealand in April, and Giblin reported to his wife:

> He is convalescing pleasantly, lives well and enjoys life but … has a strict diet, no tobacco and only gentle exercise. He is very disgusted with New Zealand and all her works and most of her men – at least politicians, treasury officials, bankers and businessmen. Thinks she is in for a worse time than Australia because she won't take it and do something. (RBA LFG 18 April 1932). [27]

Copland now believed that if budget deficits were reduced by £8m, then half of that reduction might be properly diverted to unemployment. But Copland was not hopeful about the new enquiry. Of Wallace Bruce: 'Unless his education has improved considerably I am afraid he is not likely to be very helpful' (UMA DBC 30 March 1932). And Copland's replacement by Mills had shifted the committee's composition. As Giblin explained to Eilean,

> The four of us are very fairly agreed in principle and it comes to balancing the best of two courses, both dangerous. Melville's instincts are strongly conservatism, more than Mills, and Shann oscillates, so the balance is on that side. So the prospects of the four coming out strongly for a positive policy are poor … so I am not very hopeful. (RBA LFG March 1932).

Giblin's fears were born out. The resulting report was similar in content to previous attempts to achieve a common position. A 10 per cent cut in real wages was again recommended; as was depreciation. There was approval for some monetary stimulus (advances on debentures to large-scale enterprises for which three-quarters of the needed capital had been privately subscribed). Well and good. But to Giblin's disappointment what it did not do was propose a 'Keynesian' style public works. Instead it timidly mooted a program of public works, but only after cost reductions made it possible for such works to earn interest. [28] 'I

---

[27] MS 366/1/584.

[28] In mid 1932 Copland was still publicly expressing a wish to 'wipe out' government deficits. 'We have been constantly revising upwards our ideas of what is a reasonable deficit. I suggest that this

was still opposed to public works', Melville recalled 40 years later. 'I think that came out in the Wallace Bruce report, didn't it?' (Melville 1973, p. 35).

Giblin wrote to Lyons to express his 'disagreement' with the report.

> It is not a matter of principle but of weighing the seriousness of two admitted dangers – the break-down caused by over-strain on the unemployed and one caused by an unbridled loss of confidence on the side of business finance ... I find each danger equally likely to threaten the social structure and would accordingly without deviation from the principles laid down, put a good deal more emphasis not only on the possibility but on the necessity of active means to reduce the strain of unemployment. (NLA JAL:LFS 13 April 1932).

Giblin urged the Prime Minister to approve 'immediate expenditure on a large scale' on timber and forestry.

Giblin's immediate challenge, however, was not to persuade the Prime Minister to take greater steps, but to persuade the government to embrace even the timid suggestions of the report.

> It scared the government stiff at first, but [Assistant Treasurer] Bruce swallowed it with a gulp ... We have nursed most of the Premiers to some measure of tolerance ... It still has a chance. (RBA LFG 14 April 1932).

Giblin sought to use the press to increase his chances through the support of Keith Murdoch, the proprietor of the *Herald*, and former student of the London School of Economics. Murdoch was sympathetic and had at about that time invited Keynes to Australia for a fee of £2500 (about twice the annual salary of a professor).

> I had a talk over 'doing something' with Murdoch a month ago and he suggested a Press conference in Melbourne at the same time as the Premiers Conference. Last evening, Murdoch collared the editors at Clive Ballieu's, and I talked to them – and Melville and Shann supported. We finished after midnight. Effect I think good ... Murdoch saying he is not sure he agrees but we must go bold-headed for 'something' – some plan – and this is the only reasonable plan in the field.
>
> Tomorrow, the economists talk to the premiers about it, in Conference, and that will be ticklish. (RBA LFG 14 April 1932).

---

is bad for our morals, and that it involves an abuse of credit ... it ought to be possible to devise a plan that will reduce deficits substantially for next year and to wipe them out altogether in the following year ...' (*To-Day*, 25 June 1932).

As the days passed he grew 'uneasy'. 'Banks, Chambers of Commerce, Trades Hall and Mr Lang abuse it in terms of equal intensity' (quoted in Millmow 2000, p. 144). Giblin had one other card to play: his acquaintance with Keynes. He sent the 'Wallace Bruce Report' to Keynes (and Clapham). But Keynes' response was to very publicly stymie it. In the *Melbourne Herald* of 5 June 1932 Keynes wrote:

> In truth I am a little disappointed with the [Wallace Bruce] report. The reasoning in it seems too *simpliste*. The statistics seem to show that the position of Australia is in many respects better than that of many other countries. I should repeat my advice that the main objects of statesmanship should be to stagger along somehow until the rest of the world pulls itself together.

It seems that Keynes was affronted by a strategy where one country – in this case, Australia – seeks to improve itself by a reduction in its costs relative to another country – a 'beggar thy neighbour policy'. More specifically, he found general wage cuts were objectionable. And the report's assertion that export prices were currently 20 per cent below costs factually incredible. Giblin glumly conceded to Copland: 'I am afraid the statistical case is hard to make convincing'.

Giblin's last foray had failed. [29] His audience was reduced to the students' Shillings Club of the University. [30] The Club's secretary minuted: 'At the July [1933] meeting, professor Giblin treated us to a further instalment of the expansionary policy which we suspect is dear to his heart'.

The very last scene belongs to Jack Lang, the punchinello Premier of New South Wales. Giblin had never anathemised Lang. 'Lang is bad, but so far as the Premiers' Plan is concerned Q[ueensland] and W.A. are very little better' (RBA LFG 2 February 1932). And Giblin was doubtful about the confrontationist posture the new Lyons Government adopted towards Lang. 'It seems to me to be perfectly mad, to destroy Aust. Credit in this way with nothing to gain by it. They seem to have rushed into it ... Part of the feeling that they must do something different from Scullin and Theodore' (RBA LFG 2 February 1932).

For his part, Lang was happy on stage to conjure up Giblin's spectre, anathematize him - and then absolve him. As Giblin recorded,

> On one occasion, he mentioned my name to one of his enormous audiences and there was a storm of boos. 'Oh no' said Lang, 'you must not boo him. If it had not been for him it would have been much worse' And then there was an equal storm of cheering. (RBA LFG 15 June 1932).

---

[29] Not entirely failed. At the Premiers' Conference of 14–21 April 1932 it was decided to raise a loan of £2 400 000 for expenditure on unemployment relief works.

[30] The 'Shillings Club'? See Rule no. 2: 'There shall be no more than 20 members of full legal tender'.

The roots of this degree of mutual toleration are not clear. But Giblin had never been aghast at the prospect of not servicing, in the present circumstances, foreign debtors exactly as contract stipulated. Had not the Premiers Plan repudiated the contracted debt service for domestic debtors?

Lang was defeated massively in June 1932. Order had been secured. Unemployment slowly subsided. Finances improved. The fire slowly burnt out.

With the wisdom of hindsight

Why wage cuts?

This policy was the one in which the economists were united, and which they repeatedly pressed. This was the single most controversial measure, and differentiated them most sharply from the 'Keynesians', who thought wage cuts were, at best, unnecessary, and at worst counter-productive.

Why did the four recommend them? Characteristically, Giblin advances his advocacy (in *Australia, 1930*) with considerable caution:

> This belief that wagesmust fall comes too easily to many of us. Easy beliefs are dangerous. This is the best I can make of an answer to John Smith, and you see I have made but a poor job of it. All this will not be very convincing to him. It is all too uncertain, too much a matter of good judgment based on experience and knowledge.

This is perhaps a record for public humility, even if followed by a less humble, implicit claim of authority.

What do their own models predict? Not all their models imply a need of a real wage cut.Indeed, the shock which Australia had experienced in 1931 – a decline in the price of food, for a given price of manufactures - will *increase* real wages in the *Enquiry* model. This is because the decline in the price of food induces labour to shift from food to manufacturing. This does not reduce the marginal product of labour in manufacturing, as marginal productivity in that sector is assumed to be constant. Thus the manufacturing wage is unchanged. But as food production has declined, the marginal product in food has increased. The food wage has increased. Thus workers have benefited from the slump in food prices. Landlords, of course, have suffered.Thus in the *Enquiry* model there is no need for any fall in price of food to be 'shared', as Giblin's endlessly urged during the Depression: its burden falls entirely on the owners of land. Worker consumption increases, although by less than landlord consumption decreases.

By contrast, the formalisation of the *Australia, 1930* model (contained in the appendix to chapter five) does imply that living standards of labour must fall in the face of a fall in the money price of food, if full employment is to be preserved. This is because a fall in the money price of food requires the money wage to fall, if full employment is to be preserved. And as the money price of manufactures is unchanged, this fall in the money wage implies a fall in the real wage in terms of manufactures must fall. T. M. Fitzgerald once suggested that, in using the multiplier to rationalise wage cuts, 'Giblin drew the most perverse conclusions from his multiplier'. Not perverse in the present analysis, but wholly consistent.

Why spending cuts?

The cuts in government outlays recommended by the report of the Copland Committee were extraordinary by modern standards, amounting to two to three per cent of GDP. With a multiplier of two, that might have been responsible for a five per cent reduction in GDP. Copland himself allowed for the existence of an impact of government spending on activity: 'Economy in Government expenditure, whether from loans or revenue, will mean some increase in unemployment immediately' (Copland 1930b, p. 24).

There are, however, several exonerations of this radical tightening of fiscal policy in the depths of depression:

First, 'everyone' favoured cutting. The majority of the Labor Party, as well as the Opposition, approved the Plan's cuts. Scullin was against all but 'revenue-producing' public works. And Theodore told the *Argus*: 'I have not argued against substantial reductions in government expenditure'.

Second, by the time the Premiers' Plan was agreed to (the last days of May 1931), the contraction in GDP had already taken place. The worst was already over. Australia had already hit rock bottom, earlier than most other economies; 1930–31, not 1931–32, was the trough year in Australia in terms of real GDP. Thus cuts may have made things worse in a *ceteris paribus* sense, but they cannot be blamed for the 20 per cent fall in GDP between peak and trough; that had already occurred by the time of the plan.

Third, the fiscal integrity of the state may have necessitated the cuts, regardless of their contractionary impact. If a government's debt is not to blow out to an unlimited extent, the present value of government outlays must equal the present value of its revenues.

$$G + \frac{G_1}{1+r} + \frac{G_2}{[1+r][1+r_1]} + \ldots + D[1+r] = T + \frac{T_1}{1+r} + \frac{T_2}{[1+r][1+r_1]} + \ldots$$

The reduction in terms of trade, if nothing else, would have reduced T, tax revenue, and so reduced the magnitude of the right-hand side. If government debt, D, was not be renounced, a reduction in the present value of government spending, G, or an increase in the present value of taxes, was compelled. And if that had a contractionary impact, then that impact was one price of preserving solvency of the state. And to preserve that solvency was necessary to preserve foreign investors' confidence in almost everything in Australia. It was to this 'confidence' that sacrifices were to be made.

Fourth, although the *Australia, 1930* model has an export multiplier at its centre, it does not so easily assimilate a government spending multiplier. The marginal propensity to save is zero, recall. So the private sector does not wish to spend less than its income; there is no 'gap' for government spending to fill. At the same time, owing to the absence of capital flows and the shortage of foreign exchange reserves, an attempt to create income by government spending would produce a foreign exchange crisis.

Finally, a favourite theme of Brigden in the mid-1930s: the cuts weren't true cuts at all. They were cuts in inverted commas: 'cuts'. Presumably by his use of inverted commas, Brigden is saying that while the Plan involved reductions in money wages and incomes, these were only rolling back the increases in real wages and incomes that had taken place since 1929, on account of falls in the cost of living which, until the Plan, had not been matched by falls in money wages and incomes.

None of these considerations makes an overpowering case for the cuts. To err with everyone is still to err. To be not blameable for the fall in national income that had already occurred, does not make for blamelessness: the cuts may have cut short an incipient recovery and prolonged the trough. The preservation of government solvency in the face of a declining tax base does not require an increase in *current* tax rates; a (credible) undertaking to restore taxes in the future would have equally served to preserve solvency.

A full absorption of Keynesian notions would have overpowered these considerations. But their multiplier ideas still left them a long way from the Keynesian conception of the generation of national income. Brigden seems to have fully held the 'Treasury view' on government expenditure. 'The amount of credit used for ordinary government expenditure will decrease the amount of loanable funds in the community and make less available for capital expenditure' (Brigden, Hytten and Shann 1931). In this vein Brigden stated in the midst of the Depression that excess savings were not a problem.[31] At the same time Copland expressed a similar attachment to the 'Treasury view': 'What is required is ... a reduction in public expenditure as would enable the banks to divert some of the credit they are now creating for governments to industry' (Copland 1931a, p. 23).

---

[31] Brigden's position seems to have been that 'supply' is necessary for 'demand'. He blamed the Depression on interferences with supply. 'The world as a whole is suffering to-day from 'depression' caused as much by unprecedented post-war tariffs as anything else', (*Australian Quarterly* June 1930). To Giblin the Depression was 'due primarily to failure to ration the available supplies of gold and the hoarding of the US, Argentina and France'.

Their approach to the Depression was founded on the simple instinct that in adversity one must suffer to make the best of things. The collapse of the value of Australian exports had made Australia poorer, and it would only be made worse by not consuming less. That consuming more might be a solution offended this respectable and simple intuition.

Writing the history

The struggle to capture the history of the Depression began as soon as it had passed its crisis point. The first move was made by Copland with his delivery of the inaugural Alfred Marshall Lectures in the University of Cambridge during October and November 1933. The lectures had been established by the Faculty of Economics and Politics the year before, and have since usually been delivered by an outsider, but very rarely an Australian.[32] His topic was to be the economic policies that Australia had pursued. Copland gave eight lectures – comprehensive, lucid, and factual; confident without being arrogant. Australia, he declared, had undertaken '… a bold and unorthodox policy at a time when most other countries either refused to take stern measures, or sought to conceal from their people the fact of the depression'.[33] He claimed a triumph.

But it was his auditors in Cambridge, the very hosts of his triumph, that produced a new logic that allowed a doubt to creep over the whole 'policy' of the Plan. Very soon Ronald Walker, just returned from Cambridge, was articulating the new understanding of saving and investment in the pages of the *Record*, and Copland seemed quick to absorb them. By 1934 he was writing,

> The Paradox of Saving
>
> It has been assumed, all too frequently, that the mere act of saving would itself lead to investment, but experience of the past four years everywhere in the world has shown this not to be so. If investment stops, the national income must fall. During 1931 in Australia we reached a position when investment almost reached a standstill. (*To-Day*, 16 October 1934)

This sits ill with the Plan.

But the gap between this new thinking and the old was widest over the policy the economists pressed longest and longest – wage cuts. This was manifested with the arrival in Australia of Brian Reddaway, in 1936, with some proofs of the *General theory* in his luggage. He began making appearances before the

---

[32] Trevor Swan is the only other Australian to have been a Marshall Lecturer.

[33] 'Australia refused to take the half-measures of deflation that are usually recommended to countries in similar difficulties. That was deliberate choice. She also refused to pursue the course of inflation taken by so many nations after the war. That also was deliberate choice. She pursued a middle course that had not hitherto been fully explored.' (Copland 1934, p. 10).

Arbitration Commission, arguing the legitimacy of wage rises in the light of Keynesian theories of effective demand and the economic recovery that had, by then, taken place.

In 1936, not long after Reddaway's arrival, Copland supplied an unexpected interpretation of the Plan.

> The orthodox portions were only smoke screens for things that were really done under the Plan. The things included a depreciation of the currency, the heavy and substantial reduction in interest, the conversion loan of August 1931, and the definite inflation which took place in 1930 to middle of 1932. It was a tragedy that wages and salaries had to be reduced. (Reported in *Westralian Worker,* 21 August 1936).

With Brigden, there was no talk of 'smoke screens' or tragic necessities, but of paradox. 'The Australian Plan' he said in 1937 'was a paradoxical programme of cut and spend', but it 'suited the facts and the ebb tide turned' (Brigden 1937 p. 5).

Whatever Brigden was doing in this statement, he was not making any concessions to permeation of the climate of opinion in the late 1930s by Keynesian ideas. He remained resolute in opposition to any notion of 'excess savings'.

> The menace of thrift is a new vice that has sprung up in the last few years. I think Mr Keynes and his school suffer from the same disability as Adam Smith did in his time, in that they have looked too closely within the range of their own national experience. Great Britain is a country exporting capital, and it is just possible that there may be too much saving for the good of the people of Great Britain. But I do not see the time coming very soon when we here shall be saving too much, enough to do without the importation of capital from abroad. (Brigden 1939b, p. 147).

Brigden's lack of assimilation of Keynesian theory is evident in this argument. In an open economy the menace to full employment lies not in the possibility of an excess of saving over investment at full employment – that, certainly, has rarely happened in Australia – but in the excess of saving + imports over investment + exports, at full employment; another proposition altogether.

Brigden's rebuff of Keynesian theories of national income was complemented by his steady resistance in the late 1930s of Keynesian theories of the price level.

> I understand the new orthodoxy [i.e. Keynesianism] to declare that the continued expansion of credit does not lead to inflation until there is full employment. I understand the new credit theory has been acted upon very successfully in Nazi administration ... It seems to require the same conditions which were available to Dr Schacht ...

>(a) a closed economy with neither free migration of men or money
>
>(b) severe labour discipline with wages pegged at or about depression levels
>
>(c) a comprehensively controlled social system such as the German; and
>
>(d) a popular willingness to work under such conditions
>
>I deny the theory is a good working basis for any sort of thinking in a democracy. It is just another mistake, and none the better for being a fashionable reaction from older mistakes. We in Australia can make our own mistakes. We do not need to import them. (Brigden 1939a, p. 237).

Giblin had no concern to fight Keynesianism, but as late as 1942, he was concerned to defend the plan.

> Unemployment began to improve from the date of the Premiers Plan. That it did not improve more quickly is due chiefly to the fact that the Scullin government, which recognised the value of monetary expansion in promoting employment, was defeated and went out of office at the end of 1932. [34]

That Giblin thought it was worthwhile to defend the plan ten years later in drastically altered economic circumstances shows how much reputations had – perhaps unwittingly – been invested in the plan. It shows the tenacity of resentment. The economists had attracted some very specific parliamentary billingsgate. John Cain senior (later to be Labor Premier of Victoria) used the chamber in December 1933 to accuse Copland of a very personal hypocrisy in refusing the reduction in his own salary that he had proposed for others. 'The professor of economics has been advocating reductions for everyone else, but does not want to share the responsibility ... He was one of those who advocated at the first Premiers Conference that there should be a 20 percent reduction in adjustable government expenditure, including the salaries of public servants ... I feel that I should ... give the professor a taste of his own medicine'. [35]

---

[34] NLA LFG 6 November 1942, 'The Premier's Plan Myth, MS 366/2/228.

[35] It was recorded in the next day's debates that the Registrar of the University of Melbourne 'pointed out that Professor Copland had not only accepted a salary cut but was the first member of the University staff to propose it. His salary had been reduced 120 pounds a year'.

7. Open letters and private correspondence

> 'For God's sake, don't feel that [this] demands any answer. It is enough to have got it off my chest.'
> *L. F. Giblin to E. M. Forster*

Giblin, Brigden and Copland were not scholars immured in library stacks. Nor were they government officials, hidden in invisible annexes to the corridors of power. They were public figures. And they were never more public than in the 1930s, when they took to podium, platform and pen. They were the public intellectuals of the decade.

These public appearances were not a matter of striking an attitude, of being merely a lamenting chorus to the drama of the protagonists. They entered the amphitheatre to put to field a force that would win an important battle – the struggle between thought and prejudice. They believed, in the manner of the Enlightenment *philosophe*, that an important social dynamic lay in the conflict between a calm and supple reason on the one hand, and a hot and hard unreason on the other.

The urgency of this struggle had become more urgent with the advent of democracy, and the transfer of power from an educated elite to the uneducated mass. This transfer encouraged in late-Victorians doubts about the worth of democracy – doubts that both progressives (such as Giblin's hero, George Bernard Shaw), and reactionaries shared alike. Giblin sometimes entertained a Shavian displeasure with democracy. What actual value Giblin placed on democracy – in the sense of majoritarianism – is unclear. But as the 1930s progressed, and as anti-democratic forces drew vigour from unreason, the causes of Democracy and Reason coalesced.

Giblin, Brigden and Copland were not entirely pessimistic about democracy successfully drawing on the rationality that anti-democratic forces despised. The three had some confidence in their capacity to soften 'dense' unreason of the public with their emollient wisdom. But diplomacy, tact, discretion would be at a premium. Polemic they completely avoided; the darts of Keynes', *The economic consequences of the peace,* were very deliberately not imitated.[1]

---

[1] The thirty volumes of *The collected writings of John Maynard Keynes* contain at least four volumes of 'popular' communication. A greater resemblance, and perhaps a model, lay in the popular economics of Stuart Chase (1888–1985).

They were assisted by the apparently easy access they had to newspapers and radio.[2] They were also assisted by the fact that their adversaries professed *economic* theories; the Douglasites and the Marxists, all considered themselves distinguished by their special economic insight. The simple dismissal of the economic criterion that was to confront a later generation of economists was not their difficulty.

At the same time their task was also made both harder and more necessary by circumstances. In Australia the teachings of political economy had never been received with a reverent hush. Political economy's precepts on trade had long been violated by colonial tariffs, and Federation merely violated them in a larger context. For several years an appointment of the first professor of economics at Sydney University had been delayed on account of an apprehension that a free trader might be chosen. (One Chancellor of that University described his resistance to economics teaching as his regular 'scotching the snake' (Groenewegen and McFarlane 1990, p. 43)). At about the same time the appointment of a professor of economics at Melbourne was thwarted by the requirement that the appointee must be Australian. And Australia had until the inter-war period never raised a single 'economist' who had become a prestigious public figure. 'Economists are heretics', Brigden noted (*Economic News* 9 June 1932 p. 108). There were few resources deployed in the dissemination of 'economic intelligence'. Textbooks with an Australian reference were non-existent. As Brigden wrote: 'For the student of Economics in Australia there is, as yet, no satisfactory text book dealing with Australian conditions' (Brigden 1922). And the financial press was undeveloped. The *Australian Financial Review* only came into being in 1951. Even the *Statistical Bulletin* of the Commonwealth Bank did not exist before 1937. It was partly in the light of this paucity that the *Economic Record* was originally conceived, not so much as an academic journal, but as a 'record' of otherwise deficient information.[3]

To this backdrop, the Great Depression arrived. In the view of the four, popular economic illusions exacerbated the Depression. The crux of the crisis did not lie in society's economic machine: 'Capitalism is ourselves', said Brigden (1932a, p. 13). The economic machine was not broken, it had been halted. And it had been halted (to pursue the metaphor) by political obstacles laying in its path. '[The financial system] does not mix well with 'politics' – that is, politics which ignore

---

[2] The press was not always available. Brigden had become *persona non grata* in the pages of the Hobart *Mercury*. The Editor of the *Mercury* told Copland that Brigden had a 'narrow and warped' view of the press. 'Brigden' he said, 'took up the extraordinary view that it was probably a good thing that the press was suppressed during the General Strike'.

[3] Brigden anticipated that the *Record* 'would afford members information on the world's economic happenings during the year' (*Mercury* 8 April 1925).

economics, try to evade economics, and fail' (1932a, p. 26). These 'politics' reduce to public opinion. This opinion, inevitably, became more obdurate in times of stress. And in addition to the older, local devotions (such as the 'living wage'), there arrived in the 1930s new mystery religions (for example, Douglas Credit), and frenzies (for example, the notion of the Depression as a conspiracy).

These illusions, said Wilson in 1931, indicted Australia's 'education system' for failing to acquaint her citizens with 'the hard facts of our economic environment'. Consequently, Brigden believed 'his principal duty to be the dissemination of elementary economic knowledge and principles to an Australian public in which, at that time, both labour and business opinion were indifferent or hostile' (Wilson 1951).[4] In the same vein, Giblin believed the Depression to be a 'great opportunity to bring home economic thought to the Australian people' (Giblin 1947, p. 2).

This chapter, then, begins by telling of the homilies the four issued in the early 1930s to shepherd the flock away from cliffs towards which it was blindly cantering. The 'texts' of these sermons were, above all else, the system of award wages and the monetary system, and to a lesser extent, sugar and railways.

The chapter goes on to show that the secular homily was used not only for weaning the public off economic vice. Politics, censorship and art became matters of 'open letters', especially from Giblin.

But it tells more. For Giblin the 'letter' form was not a literary exercise. Giblin was an addicted, almost obsessive, letter-writer. It was his most preferred form of expression, for private relations as well as his public ones. The chapter closes with some of his personal correspondence. We move, therefore, from the glare of publicity to the recesses of privacy.

John Smith

When Giblin was a young 'socialist', the pre-eminent literary success of socialist agitation consisted of a series of 'letters' by Robert Blatchford to one 'John Smith of Oldham, a Hard-Headed Workman, Fond of Facts'. John Smith was also a Liberal voter, and these addresses were intended to explode the Manchester School in John's eyes, and convert him to the socialist cause. First published in a newspaper in 1893, they were later collected in book form (*Merrie England*), priced at one penny, selling 850 000 copies by 1895, and ultimately two million, with translations in Dutch, German, Swedish, Italian, Danish, Hebrew, Norwegian, Spanish, and Welsh.

---

[4] Downing, the former pupil and assistant of Copland (and Giblin): 'He was essentially a publicist and believed fervently in leading his community into wiser ways of economic thinking and policy' (Downing 1971, p. 466).

Giblin had used Baltchford's letters to Smith for his discussion circle in pre-war Hobart. In the Great Depression Giblin decided to write his own addresses to 'John Smith', with the intention, it might be said with pardonable exaggeration, of restoring the Manchester School in the eyes of the 'hard headed workmen'. Between 8 July 1930 and 18 July 1930, ten 'Letters to John Smith' appeared daily in the *Melbourne Herald* above Giblin's signature. They were republished as a collection by the *Herald* with the sub-title: 'telling in simple language the facts of the economic situation that has arisen in Australia, and showing how our problems can be solved'.[5]

Giblin's fundamental purpose was to persuade his readers of the wisdom of wage rate reductions. The word 'wages' appears in eight of the ten titles. 'The basis of wages' (letter 1); 'Wages can be too high' (letter 3); 'Why wages must fall' (letters 4 and 7); 'More about profits and wages' (letter 6); 'How to get higher wages' (letter 8); 'Making terms about wages' (letter 9); and the 'Limit to wages' (letter 10).[6]

Wage rates, says Giblin, are based on productivity. And the basis of profits? To explain profit, Giblin expounds the simple classical theory that interest and profit is the reward for abstinence.

> Naturally we have to pay people to save – to refrain from spending – and we call the payments 'interest' ... The rate of interest is fixed by the need we have for someone's savings; it must be high enough to induce people to save enough to keep industry going. (Letter 5).

His explanation of wages and profits is the preface to his ultimate purpose of eliciting assent to wage cuts. But then suddenly he notes:

> I have said, 'Wages must fall', and I have not given you any precise reason for the necessity.

This was correct. No reason had been given. But Giblin was cautious. He did not say: 'I give you one'. Instead he backed away with:

> ... are we quite sure of the necessity? Everybody says it – but a considerable number of people always have said it, all through recorded history. Probably Adam in his later centuries was very apt to say of his descendants of the nth degree, 'These boys eat too many figs, and they don't work the way poor Abel used to. I shall have to cut down their rations' ... .(Giblin 1930d, p. 17).

---

[5] A few weeks earlier there appeared *The Economic Outlook*, a reprint of three articles by Copland, which appeared in the Melbourne *Argus* on 19–21 June 1930.

[6] And one of the two in which 'wages' is absent from the title (letter No. 2) is, nevertheless, about wages.

Anything approaching a 'precise reason' for believing that unemployment would go down if wages went down is hard to find. Would not John have detected an evasion?

Would not John have felt that he was being patronised? Opinions on this last are various. (see J.M Garland in Copland 1960). An aspiration to 'enlighten' must assume some sort of position of superiority to those being 'enlightened'. But it is fair to judge that Giblin's assumed superiority lay in knowledge, not intelligence, rationality, or responsibility.

A similar diplomacy is found in Brigden's complementary public lectures, *Escape to prosperity,* later published by Macmillan and sold at the 'lowest possible price'. Brigden drew here on a radically new and apparently powerful way of communicating: the radio. The newly found and briefly lived predecessor of the ABC – the Australian Broadcasting Company – had already, by 1930, 'considerably developed' the radio talk. By 1929 there were 300 000 licensed listeners.[7]

But Brigden's 'strategy for escape' included little economics. Brigden avoided it due to a concern not to lose his listeners. 'I decline to say that Compulsory Arbitration should be abolished forthwith partly because I want this book to be read by people who are arguing about it' (Brigden 1930a, p. 184). Instead he warns his listeners against the tendency of Australians to refer to, and depend upon, the state in economic matters; and then exhorts his countrymen to show in the economic emergency that hardy resourcefulness that was to be found in the 'old pioneer spirit' and 'Mont St Quentin'. His exhortation is good-humoured, homely, and nudging. It is also frequently trite in sentiment and tired in phrasemaking: ('It is time …'; 'Let us …'). *Escape to prosperity* may have made passable listening, but it was a lost opportunity to convey some economic logic.[8]

It is not surprising that Brigden's *Escape* was ignored, while Giblin's letters – dense in simple economic principle – provoked John Curtin into writing his own 'letters' in reply. Curtin begins with a thoughtless conflation of the positions of Gibson and Giblin. 'It is the policy of Sir Robert Gibson and of Professor Giblin that has to answer to the community; for it is their programme which has been, and is, in function' (*Westralian Worker* 12 December 1930). He then turns

---

[7] Brigden gave six talks over October–November 1933 for 4QG, including 'Competition: old theories and new facts', and 'The utopia of economic stability'. They were all 'live'.

[8] *Economic News* was a more decided attempt of Brigden to enlighten the public in economic matters. A monthly production of the Queensland Bureau of Economics and Statistics from June 1932, it furnished economic journalism of a standard not previously seen in Australia. 'Many things done for this book have not been done before' (*Economic News* 6 June 1932, p. 3). The first number describes itself as a 'book' and did constitute by itself an introductory text. Brigden feared *News* may suffer from unpopularity. In fact the *News* was protected from this by its lack of position.

upon Giblin's thesis that it was the deterioration of the terms of trade which is responsible for Australia's troubles. It is not relative prices, says Curtin, but a decline in all money prices that is the source of the difficulty. 'It is not the relation of tea to flour ... that has radically altered, but all of them to money that has given us world-wide depression ... Why then does the Professor leave the money question sacrosanct?' Curtin invokes Keynes as an ally, no doubt thinking of the recently published and much discussed *Treatise on money*.

Giblin drafted a reply. He addresses Curtin as 'my friend'. He suggests that Curtin is mistaken in supposing a significant difference separated the two of them. He, like Curtin, favours going off gold. '[Curtin] would even make me responsible for the present economic structure of society and challenges me to defend it. I probably agree with Mr Curtin in most of the criticism he would make'.[9]

But Giblin defends his identification of the reduction in the terms of trade as the source of Australia's ills. Flour may not have changed relative to tea. But tea made up little of Australia's imports. The average prices of exports had fallen by 50 per cent, says Giblin, while the average price of imports by only six per cent: 'much the greater part of our loss from exports is a real loss, which cannot be made up from monetary policy'. And Giblin contradicts Curtin's notion that private interests are blocking a socially improving monetary policy. 'I am not convinced that "private interests" have hitherto had very serious effects. The question of technical competence is more important'.

Giblin's dismissal of the powerful vested interest seems a precondition of the usefulness of any attempt to shape public opinion. If 'public opinion' is just 'public propaganda' – just an attempt of the man in the street to blind others rather than see himself – any attempt to 'enlighten' opinion would seem totally misguided. As the three always had some confidence that they could enlighten, they must dispute the role of interest.[10] But could vested interests be so confidently dismissed?

Roland Wilson noted tartly in a column in the *Statist* (September 29 1932) that that the UAP Government had announced that pensions were to be cut from 17/5 to 15/-, while simultaneously confirming farmers were exempt from sales tax.[11] With relief he records: 'the movement towards a reduction in costs has at last extended towards the sugar industry'. Sugar was the object lesson of vested interest, commented on by Giblin and Brigden as well as Wilson. For, at

---

[9] JCPML 00653/151/9.

[10] 'This book may leave the Bureau with no friends at all who are accurate and influential'.

[11] In 1932 Wilson wrote four articles (at the request of Shann) on Australian economic conditions for the *Statist: a Journal of Practical Finance and Trade*, founded in 1878, presumably as a competitor to the *Economist*.

a time when Australia at large was in deep economic distress, the Queensland sugar industry was in a state of unnatural prosperity, on account of its protection from the Great Depression by subsidies from Australian consumers.

The preservation in the post-war period of abnormally high wartime sugar prices, by means of import prohibitions and bounties, had underpinned the 165 per cent increase in sugar production between 1921 and 1931. Although Australia was an importer before the 1920s, Queensland's production had long outrun the capacity of the Australian market to absorb expensive Queensland sugar. The inevitable resort was to pay the foreigner to buy Australian sugar. In 1931 Brigden estimated that 49.8 per cent of all production would be exported. The very simplest calculation of the cost of the policy was £8.7m.[12] This compares with £600 000 of public funds spent on capital works in schools in 1930–31, and £150 000 of public funds spent on housing (Butlin 1985, pp. 34–5). £8.7m amounted to 1.5 per cent of GDP. It was equivalent to £1100 per farm (when average earnings in Australia came to £220 pounds per year).[13] It was Wilson's belief that this hefty transfer from South to North was in considerable measure responsible for the unusually low rate of unemployment in Queensland compared with the rest of Australia (Wilson 1932).[14]

Brigden's *The story of sugar* (1932b) seeks to reconcile Australian opinion to this expensive policy, and Queensland opinion to its mild reform. Yes, the Australian consumer pays Queensland producers a premium over the world price. Yet during the First World War a prohibition of the export of sugar to a sugar-starved world had kept Australian prices below international ones. 'This is a fact that Southerners should remember – and Queenslanders forget' (p. iii).

Brigden could certainly not go further – this was a publication of the Queensland Bureau of Economics and Statistics. It is surprising that he ventured as far as he did. Yet the fact remains he did not venture further. The fact remains that *The story of sugar* is an apology for the 'virile industry in the North'. An industry that was not so virile, however, as to be unrequiring of the generous support of the effeminate South. Brigden closes by rebuking the 'indignant' propaganda' (p. 9) of the South against the sugar subsidy. It was impossible for Brigden to join the South's rebukes. But it was possible to avoid this slight of a well-founded resentment.

Railway economics (1931c) was another attempt by Brigden to gently persuade. It traces the roots of financial troubles of the Queensland railway system's

---

[12] £8.7m = £2.7m in export bounties *plus* £6m in subsidy for home production. This sum measures the cost to the consumer. But it does not include the loss caused by the misallocation of resources.

[13] This is pointed out to 'John Smith' by Giblin.

[14] Wilson reported that rate of unemployment in February 1932 as 18.2 per cent in Queensland, 31.8 per cent in New South Wales, and 28.3 per cent in Australia as a whole.

over-investment in track. 'For its sparsely populated area Queensland is lavishly equipped with railways.' But all this capital was not effectively exploited owing to regional squabbling. He traces the beginnings of wrangling over the railway system to the unification of the Southern Division of the railways (Brisbane to Charleville) with the Central Division (Rockhampton to Longreach). This enabled wool to be sent direct to Brisbane by rail, and so bypass Rockhampton. Consequently, penalties were imposed to stop wool using the railway route to Brisbane. But these penalties did not restore Rockhampton's financial viability.

Brigden held hopes for *Railway economics* to obtain a wider interest. But, he says, it 'did not contain any political sticks, and it fell flat' (*Economic News,* 9 June 1932, p. 2).

One other attempt of Brigden at public persuasion is *Credit* (1932a), a tract designed to dispose of Douglas Credit theories. C. H. Douglas had gained considerable publicity on his tours in the 1930s, and Social Credit leagues, movements and associations proliferated in Australia prior to the formation of Social Credit Party. Moreover, it had proved popular with sympathisers of Georgists (more through psychological than logical considerations), and with many in the ALP. In Tasmania in May 1931, the Reverend George Carruthers, a penniless Anglican clergyman, won the sixth seat of Denison on the Social Credit platform, purportedly the first Social Credit MP anywhere. Social credit, it seemed, was on the march.

In *Credit,* Brigden launches his own rebuttal of social credit. He makes heavy work of the trivial fallacies of social credit (such as fixed costs affecting pricing in the short run), or its perplexing dicta ('Money used several times in production must necessarily record a cost greater than itself'). Life is added by giving space to two Queensland Douglasites to reply to Brigden.[15] Brigden's intention was much better secured by a public lecture Copland gave to the Commerce Students Society in August 1932, entitled *Facts and fallacies of Douglas Credit with a note on Australian credit policy.* Copland's bony prose spears Douglas' pretensions and evasions.

---

[15] *P.P.* (Brigden 1931a), issued at about the time of the Lang Plan, was another attempt of Brigden to vanquish unsound notions of money. But it does not succeed as advocacy: it lacks an adversary; it is all as if from teacher to pupil. And as a textbook, it is no more successful. It is lacking in theses. Its great vistas of commonplace definition are not compensated by his enthusiastic use of italics, or his easy, conversational sentences.

The practical communist

For all the attempts of Giblin, Brigden and even Copland to practise diplomacy with respect to wages, they received the obloquy of the Left.[16] (See for example, Lloyd Ross.) The irony is that, throughout the 1930s, Giblin displayed an attraction to extreme left ideals.

The Saturday morning readers of the conservative *Argus* on 2 November 1935 would have seen this listed amongst the public notices:

> TWO-DAY CONFERENCE OF FRIENDSHIP WITH THE SOVIET UNION
>
> At Central Hall
>
> Speakers: Miss D. Alexander, Miss M. Heagney, Prof J. N. Greenwood, Mr W. A. Smith, Ex-Senator R. D. Elliot, Mr J. D. Blake
>
> Chairman: Rev S. Evans, Mr Max Meldrum, Prof L. F. Giblin[17]
>
> At Unity Hall
>
> Talk on Art, Chekov, Russian Music

Giblin's participation in this Communist Party front could not have been unpremeditated. In October 1933 Giblin had addressed the Melbourne University Labor Club, another Communist Party front, on 'socialism'. To the student society Boobooks he spoke on the 'The Practical Communist'. In a radio talk (on 3AR) innocuously entitled, 'Shaping the future of Australia', he registers his sympathetic gaze towards 'one country, Russia' that 'was in the process of giving some answers' to questions of planning.

> Russia has adopted conscious direction in the most extreme form for some years. The experience of Russia, carefully interpreted should help greatly. It is too early to draw certain conclusions. We know that

---

[16] The ever-caustic Roland Wilson was an exception to this diplomacy: he did not give quarter to economically illiterate interests. Thus of the Basic Wage Inquiry he wrote:

> Some amusement has been caused to those whom the depression has not robbed of their sense of humour by ... the claim that a wireless receiving set forms one of the essential elements in the cost of living. The pompous seriousness with which such arguments are advanced and rebutted constitutes a major indictment not only of our educational system but of the methods by which we endeavour to reconcile our social inspiration with the hard facts of our economic environment. (*Statist* 15 August 1933).

[17] Max Meldrum was an anti-modernist art teacher who won the Archibald several times, a pacifist during the First World War, and a civil libertarian. J. D. Blake was at that time an ardent Stalinist who attended and defended the Moscow show trials of the 1930s. D. Alexander was married to Ralph Gibson of the Communist Party, and was active in the Kisch case. John Greenwood was Professor of Metallurgy and Applied Science at the University of Melbourne.

production has greatly increased, that unemployment has been abolished, and that the standard of living is now rising. We also know that this has been done at very heavy cost, and that the standard of living is still very low in comparison with western Europe.

At about the same time he penned another letter to John Smith, entitled 'The lesson from Russia'.

Ten years ago Russia appeared to be down and out as a result of the war and the revolution ... Since then progress has been in leaps and bounds. In about three years it looks as if Russian production would have grown to three times pre-war production. It has been possible because Russian leaders recognised the facts. It was Lenin who set the pace. It is useful to remember that Lenin was a statistician. (NLA LFG).

Has the rhetoric of 'facts' ever made such a fool of itself?

How can one explain such a lapse of judgement? In the mid-1930s a trustful indulgence of the Soviet Union was commonplace among surviving members of the Edwardian Liberal-Left. H. G. Wells was one example. So were the Webbs, (also highly enamoured of facts: see Webb 1889). And so was John Maynard Keynes (see Coleman 1992).[18]

For Giblin, the attraction of the Soviet Union may be more particularly traced. The attraction lay in its rigour, its severity. The Soviet Union was delivering to its population in severe terms the necessary austerity that soft-minded Australians were hiding from. While 'Russia the land of dreams getting down to hard facts. Australia, the land of realities, still dreaming about a sacred standard of living' ('The lesson of Russia').

Giblin was never an enthusiast - Russia's standard of living, remained 'miserably low ... the lowest in Europe'. He was an eccentric.

More certain conclusions will probably emerge during the next few years, and will probably penetrate to Australia in spite of censorship. Meanwhile we must keep an open mind, think carefully and experiment boldly.[19]

---

[18] On June 1 1936 Keynes declared on the BBC that the results of the 'new system' in Russia were 'impressive'. 'The largest scale empiricism and experimentalism which has ever been attempted by disinterested administrators is in operation' (quoted in Coleman 1992). This was his position in 1936: Keynes's views on the Soviet Union underwent several fluctuations, as did his views on many things.

[19] Not all Giblin's platform company was left-wing. He was invited by the ABC to debate with R. G. Menzies on the topic, 'Twenty million people for Australia – is it a possibility?' The ABC, however, required that his talk be submitted in advance, examined, and revised in a manner deemed fit by the ABC. Giblin replied: 'I may say that I would be very interested in such a

'In spite of censorship': the modern reader will assume that this is a reference to Soviet censorship. However, it is more likely a reference to Australian censorship which, at this point of time, forbade the dissemination of works deemed to advocate 'the overthrow of civilised government'. These included Lenin. In the 1930s Australian censorship was at its peak of confidence and completeness.

The Lyons Government Minister for Customs, Sir Thomas White,[20] had proved a particularly assiduous censor. In response, a Book Censorship Abolition League was formed in 1934, and Giblin was one of its public speakers. 'Book Anti-Censorship are staging another big show at the Town Hall. Six speakers taking each a banned book and dealing with it – a good representative lot of speakers – Paton from the University taking one of Lenin's books and so on' (RBA LFG April 1935).[21]

The occasion of his memorable protest was the controversy over Aldous Huxley's *Eyeless in Gaza* that appeared in 1936. Harold Holt described it as 'brilliant'; Casey thought it 'dull'. But *Brave new world* had been banned, and White had sternly announced: 'Huxley should not escape the process of the law'. The prospect of banning *Eyeless in Gaza* was floated. This moved Giblin to protest; the protest is worth quoting at some length.

> It would be difficult to imagine a more thoroughly depressing piece of news. The collapse of the wool-market would be a trifling mishap in comparison.
>
> Mr Huxley has for some years been the most interesting of the younger English writers. Enormous promise, expressed often in tentative and experimental form, has left some dissatisfaction with the total performance, despite brilliance in parts. It has for some time been an anxious question whether he was going to get anywhere ... 'Eyeless in Gaza' goes far towards answering this question and dispelling this doubt. The superficial brilliances have in effect disappeared, merged in the high seriousness of the story. I have read no new book for years which comes so near to the Greek tragic idea of purging by pity and terror.
>
> What would make the censorship news supremely farcical, if it was not so revolting, is that Mr Huxley shows himself here as fundamentally a

---

discussion, but I am not willing to broadcast at any time on any subject under the conditions referred to in your letter' (UMA LFG 19 October 1936).

[20] Thomas White (1888–1957), was a son-in-law of Alfred Deakin, winner of the Distinguished Flying Cross, author of *Guests of the unspeakable: the odyssey of an Australian airman, being a record of captivity and escape in Turkey*, and active in the Develop Australia League, the Protect Australia League, and the Royal Empire Society.

[21] Sir George Paton, Vice-Chancellor of the University of Melbourne from 1951 to 1968.

moralist of the old dispensation ... 'Eyeless in Gaza' is a dramatic re-statement in terms of present day experience of the vision opened in the Sermon on the Mount – the most honest and convincing given to this generation. And Mr White is considering whether it should be banned!

It is of course possible to pick out from the six hundred pages a minor incident, a touch of colour, here and there, details necessary for a fair and full presentation of the whole story – and put them violently into apposition as a sample of the whole calculated to disturb the after dinner complacency of the unlettered pater-familias. The same could be done with most great writers.

If one could ascribe this attitude to the blind and dense unreason of a Minister's intelligence, it would not be so bad. Ministers come and go. It is much worse than that. Not only is the Government behind it, but in effect the whole Parliament of Australia. Censorship procedure of the kind we have suffered from would not be possible if there were in Parliament even a solid minority of people acutely conscious of the ridiculous futility of the Censor's antics. It is abundantly clear that there is not, – that with hardly an exception our representatives do not care ... It is this attitude towards the intelligence of the country which spells the breakdown of democracy and opens the road to the worst excesses of either Nazism or Bolshevism.

Eyeless in Gaza was not banned. The retreat on book censorship began the following year. *Brave New World* was unbanned.[22]

Giblin did not only lift his pen to defend art, but also to advance it; not so much as defender, but as patron and benefactor.

The Jindyworobaks were a poetic movement of the late 1930s and 1940s, stirred by Rex Ingamells (1913-1955). The movement has been judged to amount to a resurgence of the literary nationalism of the 1890s, but distinguished by a 'novel attempt to mine aboriginal culture for inspiration' (Bennett 1988).[23] Giblin appears to have been the earliest of several patrons of Ingamells. It seems that he had brought Ingamells to the attention of John Masefield – the popular Poet Laureate, and generous patron of young talent (FUL p. 11) – when Masefield

---

[22] *Love me sailor* left Giblin 'impressed by its qualities'. He told Eilean it is 'ridiculous' to consider it 'bawdy' (NLA LFG 29 March 1949).

[23] The chief organ of 1890s nationalism was *The Bulletin*. Giblin 'had a long standing devotion to the Sydney *Bulletin*' (Copland 1960, p. 12).

visited Melbourne in 1934 for the centenary of European settlement.[24] And he provided Ingamells with a contact for Bunny Garnett.

Giblin also provided the opening 'manifesto' for the Jindyworobaks, in a foreword to Ingamell's first collection of poetry, *Gumtops*. There Giblin makes a bare and brave call for Australian poetry to shun the English literary tradition, which distracts the native poet from the necessary 'direct reaction' to the Australian environment.

> Some individuality of character and habit have developed in Australia in the last 150 years, and the face of nature has always had a unique distinction. But this individuality and distinction are not at all adequately on record in letters or any other art … The contrast with older countries is very marked. In England, of nature and man, the record is so adequate as to raise the familiar doubt as to which came first. The English rustic is shaped in the tradition of Shakespeare and Hardy; rain-clouds on the southern hills have obviously read their Meredith; beeches and wych-elms know all there is to know of Gothic architecture; and the poplars round Cambridge raise their heads in conscious rivalry with King's College Chapel … Our Australian poetry is in striking contrast, and enrichment must be slow and laborious. The problem of even naming the common birds and beasts, trees and flowers, needs the inspiration of a new Adam. Our fathers, in despair at their strange surroundings, and clutching at some pathetic shred of similarity to familiar things, peopled the bush with a dozen different oaks, ashes, myrtles, pears, cherries. A true story is impossible in these terms. (Giblin 1935).

Australian poets, wrote Giblin, 'must forget all they have learned of the poetry of other lands; shut their ears to all the familiar, captivating echoes, and try to give us their first-hand, direct reaction to nature and man as they find them in Australia'.[25]

Gumtops, with Giblin's foreword, was sent to P. R. Stephensen, the doyen of Australian literary nationalism of the 1930s. He declined to publish. The spirit and thought of Giblin's foreword is undeniably similar to Stephensen's nationalist credo, *Foundations of Australian culture*, published in July 1935. The insistence on creation being a matter of first-hand direct reaction, and the implications of this for Australian literature, is common to both. Stephensen is commonly

---

[24] 'Between 1933 and 1935, Prof L. F. Giblin, Mr Edward Garnett, and Mr John Masefield encouraged me to write Australian nature poems'. Giblin told Ingamells: 'You are certainly overgenerous in speaking of my help' (FUL LFG 2 October 1948).

[25] Ingamells says Giblin's foreword articulates the key 'Jindy' concern: 'environmental values'. This expression has an arresting modernity about it. But it does not speak for a wish for man to not shape the environment. Rather, it speaks of a wish for the environment to shape man.

recorded as a 'profound influence' on the twenty-two-year-old Ingamells. The chronology would suggest that Giblin might be more deserving of that judgement.

Giblin recommended Ingamells for a Rhodes Scholarship. But his letter commented:

> It is a queer quality, this power or incipient power, of making poetry. It does not correlate with other abilities. The Committee will find his responses on personal contact disappointing, a little crude. (UMA LFG 27 October 1936).

It appears that Giblin's 'disappointment' became more pungent over the years. He 'drifted into a defensive disinterest' about the 'Jindys'. Twelve years later Giblin wrote to Ingamells to explain 'on why I have kept aloof from your enterprise'.

> 2.10.48
>
> Dear Rex
>
> … the deciding factor was the adoption of the word 'jindyworobak'. It seemed to me to be a very perverse choice – academic in the worst sense. You seem to have exercised a perverse ingenuity in picking out a word with all the [undecipherable] that any word in any language could have … that was my state of mind when I became a victim of the pruning knife. (FUL LFG 2 October 1948).

'I am bound to admit now that I was wrong in thinking you would get nowhere'. But there was little other show of concession in his letter. Giblin judges a recent Jindy collection to contain 'some very poor stuff … General impression was of a poor ability to write English'. A week later he seems to have felt some regret at sending this cool, hard letter, and wrote again. 'I think the criticism of my last letter may suggest hostility to you' (FUL LFG 7 October 1948).

At bottom of his estrangement from the Jindyworobaks is a difference over truth as an artistic value. To Giblin truth was a central artistic value. He wanted 'a true story'. Art was a form of reporting. And when he read one of the Jindys infelicitously compare the cry of a certain bird with a 'chortle', he was 'roused to a fury of scornful protest'.[26]

---

[26] Giblin found no appeal in the notion of Art as a distinct domain, or sanctuary, from Life. Francis Galton – the mentor of Giblin's own teacher Karl Pearson – had taken it for granted that art was to answer to science; thus Galton's scientific investigations of poetry. Giblin, in a similar way, was content to make quantitative investigations of poetry. Late in life he pursued an exhaustive quantitative investigation of poetry, called the Poetry Game, in which reactions to lines of poetry were measured. 'I was not a particularly imaginative child, or bright in the way of fancy'.

'Personal'

Several months after Giblin died, his sister Edith asked: 'Is Copland writing a life? I have almost everything Lynd wrote me while he was away – Klondyke-England –War' (NLA LFG:EMG 21 May 1951). What she could offer a biographer was massive. Giblin was addicted to letter-writing, of all sorts: letters to family, to friends, almost daily letters to his wife; letters to the editor;[27] follow-up letters; letters with codicils; carefully composed, but never sent letters.

To his elder sister, Edith, he wrote more, and more devotedly, than to any other person. His first letter is to her, on the occasion of a visit to the mainland.

> Dear Edith
>
> Did you like Sydney or Melbourne best? Are there many good buildings in Sydney. I thought a couple of days ago that you would not be able to go to Sydney, which would have been awful for you.
>
> The Hutchins School are going to give an entertainment of gymnasium and exercises to parents and friends. Mr and Mrs Justice Giblin & family are invited. We are dreadfully disappointed, Miss E. Giblin, or at least I am, that you will not be there to witness my intended brilliant performance. (RBA LFG 13 June 1885).

In his young adulthood his animated, blithe, copious letters to Edith reveal a wish to share with her his world – and his enjoyment of it. And her own wish for him to share it. He provides minute descriptions on the cityscape of Cambridge. He describes his friendships about which she wishes to learn.

The appearance of Eilean in 1917 created a new correspondent. When they were apart – which was often – he wrote frequently. His letters to her are briefings, extensive and interested. From the front in 1918 he wrote:

> There are queer stories of insubordination among Tommy units going about. One is credibly reported by one of our fellows who was at Harvre at the time. Food very short, complaints, promises to make it better; that evening only a biscuit to eat, and the crowd gathered to protest – 2 Tommy battalions concerned. Second in command addressed men, and has his face cut open with a jam tin, and stuff flew about. A big N.C.O. got up to protect the officer, offered to take on anyone, and he was kicked to death, and cheers followed. There were over 30 killed altogether and finally Australians were turned out to clear up the row, which apparently they did.[28]

---

[27] A sample. To the *Argus,* complaining about its over-crowded columns: 'The orator knows the eloquence of pauses, the musician of silent bars. The architect (except in Melbourne) recognizes the value of a plain space of wall. Even the advertiser in your paper knows that he gets greater effect (and profit) by leaving his paid-for inches blank. But on the 'literary side' the smallest space of virgin white seems to be an unpardonable sin' (UMA LFG 1 August 1933).

[28] Just a rumour? On the night of 9–10 December 1918 elements of British forces in Le Havre rioted.

Figure 7.1. Giblin with young friends

Source: Courtesy of Alf Hagger

His letters to Eilean avoid the bouts of reflection and the minuting of to-and-fro, written to Edith. They also lack the gaiety of those of his earlier life. Perhaps Eilean was not a good foil for blithe spirits. Or had his life lost some joy?

There was a third category of correspondent: youths and young men.

Giblin devoted considerable time to the 'pastoral care' of boys. He was a member of Legacy. He had frequent associations with boys' schools, especially Geelong Grammar[29] and Canberra Grammar School. On his 70th birthday he received a gift from one boy, 'Michael', stricken by rheumatic fever, and bed-ridden for over a year – a pipe.

This sort of association generated a correspondence on several occasions. The correspondents were often the sons of Giblin's academic peers and colleagues. One example is Paul Unwin, a son of Ernest Unwin who arrived in 1923 to be Headmaster of the Friends School at Hobart.

The first letter on file reveals Paul already full of trust and attachment to Giblin.

> I have grown some this term, and am now 5 foot 5 inches high and I weigh 9 stone 9 to 10lbs; is this too much?

Some time later:

> I am so glad that you have decided to visit us these holidays … I will be thirteen when I see you next, so get some work for me to do at the Beach on the farm, or I shall become a newsense [sic].

At about this time Giblin sent Unwin a copy of the freshly published *Enquiry*.

> 31/7/29
>
> Dear Mr Giblin
>
> Thanks for the Tariff book you sent me. It will come in very well to put in my library, even if I never read it right through until I am old man with white locks.

Long before his adulthood, questions of later dilemmas loomed in Paul's mind.

> 10.30am 29/9/29
>
> Dear Mr Giblin
>
> I am sorry to trouble you but as you teach in Melbourne University could you let me know what [are] the conditions of compulsory military service there? Being a quaker I am entirely against, as all our denomination, Compulsory Military Training and for that I am practically debarred from Sydney University.

---

[29] Giblin notes after one visit to Canberra Grammar: 'Boys being encouraged to think for themselves, are doing so, and the results sometimes embarrassing' (RBA LFG 4 April 1935).

Perhaps a career in forestry might evade military training? Giblin gave him some preparation.

> Paul did very well. Ran about lightly with a 25lb swag and was always ready for more. We had three good wettings – one with a very wearisome spell of 3 hours soaked through over long button grass.

Giblin wrote to the Tasmanian Forestry Commission to recommend Unwin as a trainee. 'I feel sure that you will find him a very satisfactory investment'. Giblin knew what he was talking about. Unwin was made a trainee, and in 1971 was appointed Chief Commissioner of Forests.

Having begun with open letters to the throng, we can conclude with one letter which was only ever seen by the author's eyes. On his return from Cambridge in 1938 Giblin wrote, but never sent, the following letter.

Dear Morgan Forster

This impertinence springs from your Henry Thornton article, which like all you write nestles in my mind as very little contemporary stuff does. It's a queer family in which you are for me a member – the saga, Hamlet and the sonnets, some of Miss Austen and a good deal of Meredith, the later Beethoven and the 4th Symphony of Sibelius.

You may just have heard my name. I spent most of last spring and summer at King's: they very amiably made me a supernumerary fellow. In visiting England and Cambridge, I had rather counted on meeting you, and Wedd was confident you would be sometime in Cambridge. In default, I even thought of invading your Surrey fastness, but a sense of decency was reinforced by lack of time at the last. Still, I would like to tell you baldly – and leave it at that – how pre-eminently you have been my refreshment these last 30 years …

That's all and more than enough. It is in fact my first offence of this kind in 66 years. Call it dotage. It will harmonise with second childhood if I adopt the small boy's friendly ending – Love.

L. F. Giblin

8. The seven-pointed star

> 'Federation is a 'compromise between nationality and democracy'.
> *L. F. Giblin*

It was the Great Depression that brought the four to Canberra. It was a budget crisis that they grappled with. But they were soon engaged with a more enduring and more expressly political problem that had been made manifest by the slump: a general incapability of the federal Australian polity that had been created in 1901.

The new state had two weaknesses.

The first was that Australia was both a democracy and an agglomeration. Like any democratic agglomeration, it experienced a tension between the aspiration to unity, and the fact of inequality. Federation was intended to cope with this tension. But under the stress of the Depression, it became an open question as to whether the principle of Federation would contain the tension or succumb to it. In the pit of depression Federation was in crisis, as Australia experienced attempts to proclaim new states and more lawful attempts by existing states to secede from the Commonwealth. The sole doctrinal counterforce to these pressures for disintegration was 'unification', the terminology of the day for the abolition of the states – which would only have made succession inevitable.

A second weakness lay in the machinery of state. In 1901 the machinery of central government did not exist. It had to be created or improvised. This challenge became more critical in the 1920s as the federal state acquired an ever-expanding range of functions, and resolved to exercise them in a make-believe capital on the Molonglo. A critical element of this machinery – an effective public administration – was painfully lacking.

The four were significant – sometimes decisive – in treating these infirmities of the body politic. Giblin, assisted by Brigden, was crucial in heading off the crisis in Australian Federation. All four were closely involved in the attempt to improve the quality of public administration.

But their involvement in public administration also afforded them a painful lesson: that while good public service is necessary for good government, it is also quite insufficient for good government. The ship of state requires efficient machinery, but to steer a course a pilot is also required. In the late 1930s Brigden and Wilson threw themselves into launching inaugural national legislation on banking and social security, only to see both sink ignominiously. Their projects for economic and social reform were wrecked by the absence of strong political leadership.

Making Federation work [1]

Giblin's Tasmanian background might have predisposed him to some degree of zeal for the new federal polity. Giblin's father had, as Premier of Tasmania in 1884, taken a leading role in the Sydney convention that established the Federal Council of Australasia. [2] His father's friend and ally Inglis Clarke had a very substantial influence on the constitution of the new Commonwealth of Australia. In both referendums (1898 and 1899) Tasmania had been the most enthusiastic 'Yes' colony. In 1899, 95 per cent of Tasmania had voted in favour of Federation.

Yet Giblin did not share the enthusiasm of his fellow Tasmanians. A few weeks after Federation he told his sister that Federation 'is only a piece of machinery: efficient (if it is efficient) equally for good and evil' (RBA LFG 10 February 1901). This cool, equipoised attitude towards Federation stayed with him.

But for the first 10 years there was no call for anyone's opinions on the Federation to be staked and defended. The financial relations of the states and Commonwealth seem to have been satisfactorily arranged by the Constitution. These arrangements were highly specific in the short run, and perfectly vague in the longer run. For 10 years the custom duties that were to be collected by the new Commonwealth would be distributed to the states, by way of compensation for what was formerly their revenue. And after 10 years? Section 96 provided in a completely general way for the possibility of Commonwealth financial assistance to the states from 1911. These constitutional directives were an expedient that reflected an impatience for federation, combined with a confidence that things would somehow sort themselves out in the end. This confidence was underpinned by a faith that the states would eventually 'converge' economically.

By 1910, a smooth passage to permanent arrangements seemed to have been secured. Each state was to receive the same grant, in *per capita* terms, a policy that seemed sensible in the light of optimism about convergence. Western Australia was, in addition, given a so-called 'special grant' of a continuing nature in 1910, and Tasmania followed two years later.

It was only amidst the travails of the 1920s that, in the minds of smaller states, Federation was transforming from a panacea to a Pandora's box. In 1925 the Tasmanian Rights League appeared, supported by the Hobart Chamber of Commerce and the *Mercury,* to press Tasmania's new sense of grievance. A League of Small States materialised to link the disaffections of Tasmania, South Australia,

---

[1] Some background for this section is given by the Commonwealth Grants Commission's own history of the body (1995). A scholarly account of the origins of the Grants Commission is provided by May (1971). A more recent history of the evolution federal finance is in Hancock and Smith (2001).

[2] This had its first meeting in Hobart, in 1886

and Western Australia. In 1930 the Women's Non-Party League of Tasmania was established to voice Tasmanian grievances (May 1971, p. 27), and Eilean Giblin was its deputy.

During the 1920s 'the Commonwealth was subjected to a continuous barrage of demands from Tasmania' (May 1971, p. 9). These demands would be met with a request by the Commonwealth to submit a case, which was then referred to an *ad hoc* committee for consideration. Inevitably, this committee's subsequent recommendation was not entirely deferential towards the claimant state. This procedure of specific claim and specific adjudication was one that encouraged ambit claims, and the suspicion of ambit claims.

In August 1926 Giblin proposed an alternative in his Presidential Address to Section G of the Australasian Association for the Advancement of Science [3] (Giblin 1926). The grant-giving procedure might be lifted from political controversy if the decision about a special grant at any point of time 'could be made by Parliament only on the advice of an Economic Committee, with powers and duties corresponding roughly to those of the Tariff Board' (Giblin 1926, p. 158). Two years later Giblin developed this idea before the Royal Commission on the Constitution of the Commonwealth to press the same proposal.

> A special grant ... depends to some extent on how loudly a State squeals ... Would not it be better to have a board, somewhat in the nature of the tariff board, with a strong economic flavour to it, consisting as much as possible of professional people, who could look at the thing professionally, and arrive at an unbiased [sic] opinion with reference to the *per capita* payments. (Royal Commission on the Constitution of the Commonwealth, p. 903).

This 'grants board' would be expert, independent, and permanent; it would not be one of those '... temporary Commissions which investigate the affairs of one State once, and then go out of existence'. It would have a 'strong economic flavour'. And, like the Tariff Board, it would be 'extra-constitutional': Giblin's proposed reform did not involve constitutional change. This was no small point to Brigden, Giblin's constant ally on this issue. It was imperative, Brigden believed, to avoid the mistaken 'legalism' of the Federation movement of the preceding generation. As Brigden put it: 'The remedy is not to embroider words into the Constitution, even if the people would consent to it, but to use economic sense which (it may be hoped) will eventually become a common sense' (1931b). This comment represents a marked change in a man who had pinned such hopes on constitutional amendments in 1910, and reflected the priority Brigden now

---

[3] Giblin wrote to Copland of this occasion: 'Of course, your absence made a big difference. There is nobody else [who] enjoys discussion as you do. Mills and Brigden in different ways discuss it to themselves but don't flow ... (UMA LFG 17 September 1926).

afforded the economic over the legal, and his aspiration to educate the population about the futility of believing that the economic could be altered by legal fiat.

Giblin's proposals were ignored until, under the strain of the Depression, the Federation structure began to creak.

The political chaos and economic distress of the early 1930s reinvigorated the movement to establish a new state in northern New South Wales: New England. In 1932, 'separatists would now come as close as ever to achieving a new state' (Farrell 1997, p. 147). The proposed means were, admittedly, unlawful. An assembly of persons would gather, and presume to pass an 'act' establishing the new state. The precedent of West Virginia in 1861 was cited. A constitution was prepared in readiness. The leader of the Country Party, Earl Page, gave it his blessing.

A more serious threat to the integrity of Federation arose from the campaign of Western Australia to secede. The Nationalist Premier of that state had converted to the cause of 'Westralia' in the face of an aggressive campaign for secession. A referendum was announced. On 8 April 1933 'Westralians' were to be asked: 'Are you in favour of the State of Western Australia withdrawing from the Federal Commonwealth?'. The federal government was not content to gaze. Every elector in Western Australia, South Australia and Tasmania received *The case for union*. Speakers in favour of Federation were dispatched to Perth. But to no avail: 138 653 votes were cast in favour of leaving the Commonwealth, with 70 706 votes against.

The time for action had evidently arrived. A few weeks after the Western Australian referendum in May 1933 a Bill establishing a Commonwealth Grants Commission was passed by the Commonwealth Parliament. Its design was very plainly inspired by Giblin.

This Commission would not be department of the executive, staffed by public servants. Neither was it to have a federal structure, such as the Loan Council. It amounted to the delegation of a power (of recommendation) by the Commonwealth government to an independent body, a 'commission'. The Commission was to consist of three members – a Chairman and two others – who were to be appointed for a maximum of three years. While legislation permitted evidence to be given under oath, its process was to be expert not judicial.

The first appointments to the Commission were made in July 1933. The Chairman was F. W. Eggleston, a lawyer and liberal *philosophe*. Giblin was one of the two other members.

But if this new tribunal was to replace anarchy by order, then some guiding philosophical principles were requisite. Brigden had already stressed that there must be principles upon which to base judgements and recommendations of the Commission. In other words, an intellectual problem underlay the political problem. There were in Brigden's mind three possible guiding principles: *Relief for Deficits*, *Compensation for Disabilities under Federation*, and what is now known as *Fiscal Equalisation*.

Relief for Deficits

This speaks for itself, and had been the prevailing touchstone before the Commission had been created. 'If there has been any principle at all, it is a requirement that the recipient state shall be in a chronic condition of revenue deficit' (Brigden 1931b, p. 296).

Compensation for Disabilities under Federation

This principle stated that Commonwealth should provide financial assistance to compensate a state for any costs suffered as a consequence of Federation. This was a widespread notion and rooted in a popular precept of justice.

The influence of this idea prompted the Tasmanian Government in 1925 to appoint a committee to report on *Tasmanian disabilities under Federation*. Giblin and Brigden were two of the committee's six members, and Roland Wilson was its secretary. The committee's report, written by Giblin and Brigden,[4] contained a detailed discussion of some specific handicaps which federation had imposed on the Tasmanian economy. However, the overall consideration of the advantages and disadvantages did not result in a powerful case for federal assistance for Tasmania. Indeed, there seemed to be no case at all. 'Tasmania received, on the most conservative reckoning, at least some substantial benefit from the relations with the Commonwealth' (UMA JBB 13 May 1929). As Brigden was to try explain to readers of the *Mercury* in 1929: 'the Commonwealth spends less per head in Tasmania than in other States, but it collects still less per head because we have a lower level of income and expenditure'.

Perhaps not surprisingly, therefore, Giblin and Brigden advanced the contention that the criterion, 'Disabilities Under Federation', was too narrow a means for determining the size of the special grant which a state should receive from the Commonwealth. Giblin makes his case by asserting that:

> Federation implies responsibility as well as privileges; and if a state is in financial difficulties not of its own making, consideration and help by the Commonwealth as a whole is just as necessary and proper if the cause of them was, e.g., the unexpected working out of her mineral

---

[4] Brigden: 'I had to draft the thing *in toto*. It has been an awful rush and more especially as I had to explain and fight at intervals, calling in Giblin a couple of times. The pace was so hot that I could not get my drafts before Giblin for criticism. Of course the tables are his, and also a couple of special passages of his have been worked in especially, '"war expenditure and taxable capacity"'. Brigden adds: 'The claim [for Tasmania] is for a shocking amount' (UMA JBB undated).

resources, as if they came from entering a form of Federation which was better suited to her neighbours' conditions than her own. (Giblin and Brigden et al. 1925, p. 9).

The case for assistance was now broadened from costs to a state resulting from Federation to any costs to the state 'not of its own making'.

Giblin was to return to this idea and develop it further, some five years later in *The case for Tasmania, 1930*. This document was a response to the newly elected Scullin Government's decision to investigate Tasmania's financial disabilities through a parliamentary joint committee. The committee of 10 authors was constituted by Tasmanian worthies, with Giblin and Hytten appended – who, of course, wrote it. In Appendix J, specifically written by Giblin, 'State Disabilities – with special reference to Tasmania', Giblin pressed a stage further his belief that 'Disabilities Under Federation' was not a satisfactory principle for determining assistance to the states. Giblin gave a second reason for opposing this concept as a guiding principle. Even if compensation for disabilities was desirable, it could not be implemented: '… it is not practically possible to estimate directly the economic cost of tariff policy to Tasmania, and still less possible to translate the cost into the terms of a loss to the State Treasury'. He went on to claim that '… the same is true of other disabilities due to Federation – a direct measure is not possible' (Giblin 1930c, p. 64).

Fiscal Equalisation

Fiscal Equalisation is the principle that was to win the day, and may be understood as an adaptation to federalism of Louis Blanc's exhortation: 'from each according to his abilities, to each according to his needs'.

In the context of a conglomeration of communities of differing incomes, Blanc's ideal would disallow any principle requiring equal *per capita* contributions to the costs of government. And, as Giblin observed, equal *per capita* contributions was never in fact required of a conglomerations of communities.

> No such basis would ever be assumed for contributions to international organizations, such as the League of Nations. When Ireland received Home Rule, not even the bitterest opponent of Irish-Self Government proposed that she be asked to carry any but a very small fraction of her per capita liability for the public debt of the United Kingdom. No agricultural portion of England or any other highly civilized country could possibly pay its share of the expenses of government on a population basis. (Giblin 1926).

In a completely unified fiscal system, Blanc's ideal could be simply achieved by a uniform tax *rate* of incomes across member communities, combined with a flat *level* of government outlays across member communities. But in a system with both state taxation as well as central taxation, a uniform *federal* tax rate across member communities, combined with a flat level of federal outlays across member communities may not secure this. It would not, for example, if some states had higher tax rates than others. This was, Giblin argued, the case in Australia. He had argued this as early as 1924, when Lyons, the then Tasmanian Premier, had asked Giblin, as Government Statistician, '… to make an impartial examination into the severity of taxation in different States of Australia' (Lyons in Giblin 1924). Giblin responded with a careful and highly detailed estimate, which concluded that Tasmania was the second most severely taxed of the Australian states.

Giblin began by working out state taxation per head for each state, for the fiscal year 1922/23.

Table 8.1. Giblin's taxation comparisons

	State taxation per head, shillings	Taxable capacity	Taxation severity
New South Wales	71.10	1.006	71.5
Victoria	51.2	1.158	44.2
Queensland	84.0	0.789	106.6
South Australia	71.0	1.075	66.1
Western Australia	57.6	0.867	66.4
Tasmania	49.8	0.588	84.5

The first column is not favourable to the suggestion that Tasmania is severely taxed. New South Wales had the largest per capita state taxation, and Tasmania the lowest. But might it not be that the higher-than-average figure for New South Wales reflected a greater-than-average *capacity* to tax? Should not taxation be measured relative to the capacity to tax? The obvious measure of capacity to tax would be income. The 'severity' of state taxation would then be measured by state taxes as a proportion of state income. But Giblin maintained that the capacity to tax varied with the *square* of income, on the grounds that taxation did typically vary with the square of income. Thus a measure of taxable capacity equals the square of *per capita* state income, relative to *per capita* Australian income, factored up by 1000. This produces the middle column. The severity of taxation is then defined as taxation relative to 'capacity to tax' (so defined). This is shown in the third column where Tasmania now has the second most severe taxation.

As an attempt to establish a particular point of fact – that Tasmania had more severe state taxation – Giblin's case is questionable. The critical ingredient in the exercise is the assumption of 'taxable capacity' varying with the square of income.[5] If taxable capacity was supposed to vary simply with income, then New South Wales would remain more 'severely' taxed than Tasmania.

But Giblin's principle that, in a federal system, differences in the severity of state taxation would justify differences in federal assistance to states stands or falls independently of any points of fact about Tasmania.

The idea that differences in severity of state taxation would justify differences in the federal system received a louder articulation in Giblin's appendix to *The case for Tasmania, 1930*. There he provided an (admittedly somewhat shadowy) test for determining whether a State was deserving of assistance.

(1) It should be taxing its people with considerably greater severity than the Australian average.

(2) It should not be attempting social provision on a more generous scale than the average.

(3) Its costs of administration should be below the average.

(4) It should for some years at least have shown moderation and caution in loan expenditure.

If these conditions are satisfied, I submit that the responsibility is on the Commonwealth to make up what is required to enable revenue to balance expenditure. It is not a question of making a contribution towards it. If the above conditions are fairly satisfied, the obligation is on the Commonwealth to make up the deficiency in full as a vital condition for the effective working of Federation.

The thread running through Giblin's precepts is the notion that it is fitting to have the same *level* of *basic* government services across communities, and the same *rate* of total taxation across communities to fund them. Giblin's proposal merely mandated a uniform level of *basic* government services across the states. It did not mandate a uniform level of total government services across the states: states could provide more than basic services if they chose. Even less did his principle mandate a uniform level of *all* goods and services (both public and private) across the states. As Giblin said in *The case for Tasmania*: 'There is, of course, no question of bringing Tasmania up to an Australian level of prosperity by direct help from the Commonwealth' (quoted in May 1971, p. 21). Indeed, Giblin's advocacy of 'fiscal equalisation' was in part underpinned by his

---

[5] A different attempt to justify the assumption of the 'capacity' to pay varying with square of income would draw on declining marginal utility. The utility cost of a tax burden will vary with the square of income under a certain utility function. If $U = \alpha - 1/Y$ then $U(Y) - U(Y-T)$ (= the burden of taxation) $= \frac{T}{Y^2 - TY} \approx \frac{T}{Y^2}$ with a tolerable accuracy for low tax burdens.

pessimism about Tasmania's economic performance. [6] Sunny hopes of convergence were illusory. Tasmania could never afford the level of *basic* services which, as a member of Federation, it was entitled to.

The new Commonwealth Grants Commission did not immediately embrace the principle of 'fiscal equalisation': Giblin pressed it against Eggleston's own instincts. Giblin records this conflict in letters to Eilean.

> Eggleston's fertile pen is turning out reams of draft report – which is good but won't do – and the only effective way to criticize it is to rewrite it in one third of the space. (RBA LFG 23 May 1935).

> A lot of fight and delay over principles. But Eggleston has been very tolerant and prepared to give way even when he is deeply committed. We have an unfortunate difference in mental make up which makes it impossible to harmonise or compromise differences. (RBA LFG 10 July 1935).

> Eggleston has been distraught. Pressure of time has rather forced him to accept stuff I have written which he does not agree with, or rather which does not adequately express his views. It is very unfair to him, and most unfortunate. He has been very forbearing, and [at] a meeting today we arrived at a fair working compromise, but I shall have to go hard to live up to it. (RBA LFG 31 July 1935).

Only in the third annual report of the Commission was fiscal equalisation unambiguously recommended. [7] That report contained an illuminating passage in which the slow adoption of the principle was described.

> In our first report ... [fiscal equalisation was] adopted tentatively, and with some reluctance, for immediate practical purposes. The general discussion on the principles of grants was not summed up into final conclusions, but left with loose and somewhat contradictory ends.

> In our second report we developed the tentative principles of the first, and concluded that the relative financial position of the States, when analyzed with sufficient care and understanding, was the only basis on which special grants should be made.

---

[6] Giblin was inevitably considered by his fellow Tasmanians a disloyal and callous son.

[7] These quotations lead to a different conclusion from that advanced by Hytten. He wrote: 'How much of this work [of the third report] is due to Giblin, and how much must be credited to the equally keen mind of the Commission's Chairman, Sir Frederic Eggleston, is difficult to say, but the honours may be evenly divided. Giblin was always a good team worker, and a master at compromise where opinions were divided' (Hytten 1951). The existence of a conflict has been noted by May (1971, p. 65).

Further consideration and another year's experience have led us to the following conclusions: Special grants are justified when a State through financial stress from any cause is unable efficiently to discharge its functions as a member of the federation and should be determined by the amount of help found necessary to make it possible for that State by reasonable effort to function at a standard not appreciably below that of other States.

The recommendations of the third report were accepted by the Lyons Government. The Opposition Leader, John Curtin, reported himself to be 'astonished' that a 'responsible government should, at the behest of an external commission, abandon its own policy'. But the task was accomplished. The third report set the principle. Any of the Commissions following the first Commission [8] could have replaced fiscal equalisation had they wished, but none have. The Commission and its use of the fiscal equalisation principle remains a monument to Giblin to the present day. [9]

The present day impact of this principle is illustrated by a comparison of the grants recommended by the Grants Commission with what a *per capita* distribution would yield.

Table 8.2. Comparison of grants recommended by the Commonwealth Grants Commission with grants implied by a *per capita* schema, $m, 2005-06

	Commonwealth Grants Commission	Per capita	Difference	Per Capita Redistribution, $
New South Wales	13090	15069	-1979	-290
Victoria	9783	11170	-1388	-274
Queensland	9240	8849	390	97
Western Australia	4603	4490	113	55
South Australia	4107	3412	694	449
Tasmania	1672	1076	595	1222
ACT	822	712	103	316
NT	1921	450	1470	7217
Australia	45238	45238	0	

Western Australia is now barely a beneficiary of the principle; but the Northern Territory overwhelmingly is. Something near two billion dollars is currently transferred from New South Wales to the Northern Territory and Tasmania, and

---

[8] Giblin did not seek re-appointment after his term expired in 1936.

[9] In 1999 the principle received the following articulation by the Commission:

State Governments should receive funding from the Commonwealth such that, if each made the *same effort* to raise revenue from its own sources and operated at the *same level of efficiency* each would have the capacity to provide services *at the same standard*. (Commonwealth Grants Commission 1999, p. 4)

Italics added.

something considerably more than billion is transferred from Victoria and bestowed on South Australia and the remaining states. The 'loss' of Victoria and News South Wales through fiscal equalisation has remained, and has provoked personal attacks on the Commissioners, a mythologisation of its history, and a complete misidentification of fiscal equalisation with the principle of disabilities under federation. [10]

The success of the Commonwealth Grants Commission and its principle of fiscal equalisation calls for some explanation. On the face of it, Giblin's suggestion that an 'independent' Commission of 'experts' would resolve the financial wrestling of the states and Commonwealth seems almost naïve. But some factors behind its success may be hypothesised.

First, the Commission served diplomacy. The states were no longer petitioners seeking charity, or wards seeking the clemency of their guardian. They were equal members of a community.

Second, the Commission reduced wasteful tactics. When property rights are indistinct and contract difficult, the process of negotiation diverts energies from trading possessions towards defending possessions — or coercing them from others. [11] A rule-based system — which amounts to a system of property rights — saves on these activities.

Third, the principle of fiscal equalisation served to reconcile the aspiration to unity and the fact of inequality. It seemed equitable that a state in which state taxation was light received a smaller grant — other things being equal — than one in which state taxation was severe. A Fiscal Commonwealth, like the Lord, 'helped those who helped themselves'. [12] At the same time, it permitted the

---

[10] A recent Premier of New South Wales has described the Commissioners as 'a select priesthood of obscure and mediocre economists' who could not get jobs anywhere else (*Sydney Morning Herald*, 4 March 2004). At the same time a Treasurer of Victoria claimed of the Commission:

> under this outmoded, clapped out system which we've inherited really since the 1920s, Victorians subsidise other states to the tune of more than 1.3 billion dollars each year … It has got its basis going back 100 years, to when … back to tariff protection, to when the states that — the agricultural states, you know, Queensland and South Australia and so on — when they thought that they were penalised by the level of tariff protection, particularly in Victoria and New South Wales. (ABC 3 March 2004)

[11] In 1929 the Commonwealth offered assistance to Western Australia on the condition it transferred its north-west portion to the Commonwealth (Hancock and Smith 2001, p. 31). This sort of shakedown could not take place under the Commission.

[12] The effective subsidy to poorer states could be justified in homely terms — as Brigden did — in terms of 'adjusting for handicaps, just as in a race'.

expression of different preferences. It allowed *non*-basic services to be provided and funded by state taxation if the state so chose. [13]

In 1934, the first year of the Commonwealth Grants Commission, the survival of federalism was doubtful. In that year Brigden sensed that federation as it was conceived in 1901 was 'incompatible with the permanent and characteristic policy of the Australian people'. As federalism restricts the power of state, it belonged to 'a different age', and he foresaw 'unwilling progress towards unification' (Brigden 1934). This was not an entirely inaccurate prediction. It is a moot point whether its degree of inaccuracy – or its accuracy – might in significant measure be traced to Giblin and Brigden. [14]

The machinery of state

A second menace to the Commonwealth lay in the debilitated condition of the central government. In the 1930s the federal public administration was, in Paul Hasluck's words, 'incredibly weak'. This has its roots in three decades of mismanagement.

In 1901 most of the difficulties of the creation of a public administration had been conveniently evaded. The functions of the new federal government were few – post offices, custom houses and a small army – and they were inherited from the colonial governments. They could be just 'rebadged'. But there was a cost to this expedience – the best public servants stayed with the states, and only the 'third tier' of the civil service was willing to risk their careers in a new and puny form of government.

Further, the modicum of planning that legislators did afford the new public service was blameworthy: they deemed only a very modest educational accomplishment was required for general public administration. By law, recruitment into general administration was purely on the basis of an examination that was, as Giblin later put it, 'suitable for the brighter boys of the age fourteen'. Further educational attainment was not only redundant, it was almost impossible since a maximum age for recruits of 16 was initially decreed.

The educational level did not improve with the rapid extension of Commonwealth responsibilities in the post-war world: it deteriorated. After 1918, the Parliament judged that the war veteran was the type most worthy of recruitment into public administration. The veteran was exempted from the standard examination and required to pass only a less difficult one. The age maximum was far more generous for veterans, 51 rather than 23. The health requirements were also less

---

[13] Brigden proposed a federal regime of taxation, with the states permitted surcharges on income tax. This system was implemented in 1976.

[14] Copland was not as involved as Giblin and Brigden. But he reported the development of Fiscal Equalisation in papers in the *Quarterly Journal of Economics*, and elsewhere (Copland 1937b).

demanding. These concessions had an impact. Between 1918 and 1932, only 49 youths were recruited by the standard examination, rather fewer than four per year. Over the same time span, 1031 veterans were recruited. But these veteran recruits did not, as a rule, flourish: by 1939 no veteran had risen to a 'senior appointment'. In the word of the historian of the Commonwealth Public Service, the recruitment policies in the inter-war period were 'disastrous' (Scarrow 1957).

Giblin would have been aware of similar problems in the service of the Tasmanian Government: 'Youths were needed but were largely precluded from employment' (Robson 1983, vol. 2, p. 463).[15] As Tasmanian Statistician in the early 1920s, Giblin had shepherded four junior officers in the public service through Bachelor of Commerce degrees at the University of Tasmania, and had arranged for their fees to be paid on the condition they stayed in the service for five years. Presumably Giblin obtained a more vivid view of the problems of the Commonwealth Public Service when appointed Acting Commonwealth Statistician in 1931. He quickly resolved to break down the barrier to young graduates and admit the first person with a university qualification to general administration in the Commonwealth Public Service. He would use his star pupil: Roland Wilson, BA, DPhil, PhD. He persuaded Sir Harry Sheehan, the Secretary to the Treasury, to appoint Wilson for six months from February 1932 as an 'economics adviser'. How this was done is a mystery: it seems plainly to contravene the legislation, as Wilson was twenty-eight years old. The massive destruction of Treasury files from the period will ensure that this remains a mystery. But, somehow, it was done.

Still, the appointment itself did not clinch victory. 'The thought of bringing a graduate into the Treasury was a very novel and unpopular idea at that time' (Wilson 1984), and it was considered prudent to place Wilson into the Bureau of Census and Statistics 'out of sight of Treasury officers'. Regrettably, the officers in the Bureau seemed to have no more liberal an outlook. On the first day of his appearance in the Bureau, its workforce initiated a sit-down strike in protest.

A more systematic solution for reform was required. For several years there had been a pressure to relax the *de facto* prohibition on graduates. The British Economic Mission of 1928 had favoured doing so, as did the universities, and the University Association of Canberra. In addition, the Commonwealth Bank, with a very similar recruiting regimen to the Commonwealth Public Service, had actually gone so far as to employ a single graduate in 1931 – Leslie Melville.

---

[15] The State public services had never become quite the sanctuary for war veterans that the Commonwealth's had become. Nevertheless, in June 1930, 38 per cent of the permanent staff of the Tasmanian Public Service were returned soldiers.

Giblin entered the fray with his paper, 'The recruiting of the public service' (Giblin 1929). In Britain, Giblin pointed out, the senior rank of the public service is 'enlisted from men with the highest University qualifications ... the first class final honours at Oxford or Cambridge'. In Australia, by contrast, 'practically all vacancies in the Clerical Division of the Commonwealth service have been filled by returned soldiers, from whom no higher test has been required than reading, writing and very easy arithmetic'. As result of this 'criminal short sightedness', 'the service has become the dumping ground of returned soldiers who have failed to make a living in any other way'.

Giblin proposed that 10 graduates per year be recruited. Within 30 years, nearly all of the 300 senior ranks would be graduates. To stimulate this, some suitable 'cadets' would be financed to attend university, while still performing some duties in the service. Within four years of completing their degree, they would be paid £500.

The *Commonwealth Public Service Act 1933* was the fruit of these proposals, and invoked the first modest relaxation of the bar to graduates. The relaxation amounted to permitting a graduate to be recruited up to the age of 25. But that was all. No other concession was made. There was no 'graduate loading' which Giblin plainly wanted: they would be paid exactly as the others. The graduates were to begin at the bottom of the hierarchy. They must also have their degree from an Australian university, a worthless restriction. Finally, a limit was placed on graduate appointments: no more than 10 per cent of the intake.

Despite the modesty of the legislation, it was opposed by both Lang and non-Lang Labor factions in the House of Representatives. 'The Labor left still regarded university training in the main a privilege of the wealthy'(Sawer 1963). Giblin had tried to assuage such sentiments: he pointed out that eight of 13 Cambridge graduates recruited into the British civil service that year had received their secondary education in government schools. In the Senate one Labor MP voted in favour, mentioning his student nephew. The more salient passion was not hostility but fear: 'Labor as a whole reflected the fear of the public service unions that such recruitment would block promotion of those who rose from the ranks' (Sawer 1972, p. 55)

But a signal had been given. Recruitment began in 1934 and between 1934 and 1941 about 10 per year were accepted, or around the number Giblin had envisioned.[16] Regrettably, this slow pace was overtaken by the war, and at its outbreak, 16 of 24 Permanent Heads had no tertiary qualifications (Scarrow 1957).

---

[16] All graduate recruits were men. Women could only be appointed as 'short-hand typists'.

Perhaps more immediately useful than legislation was the intersection of the four with the dapper figure of Richard Casey - Baron Casey of Berwick and of the City of Westminster, engineer, aviator, Bruce protégé, Antarctica enthusiast, man about town, and from 1935, Treasurer.[17]

Casey found 'economic experts' congenial. The first of the species he became acquainted with was T.E. Gregory, during the professor's 1931 tour of inspection: 'a temperamental Jew' he told Bruce, 'with almost every superficial demerit possible, but with great fundamental intelligence and knowledge' (NAA RGC 17 March 1938). With Gregory's departure, Casey turned to the local varieties.

> He was quick to court a little band that encompassed much of the locally available expertise: E. O. G. Shann, D. B. Copland, L. F. Giblin, Roland Wilson, Leslie Melville. He thought highly of them, read their papers, talked to them, corresponded with them. He came to regard Shann as a personal friend, and he held in especially high regard the younger Melville and Wilson. (Hudson 1986, p. 99).

His 'especially high regard' for Wilson arose from Wilson's performance as the newly appointed Commonwealth Statistician. Casey was originally inclined to appoint a Briton to fill this post, but was persuaded by Giblin that Wilson was 'the obvious man'. 'In Wilson, Casey found a mind he could respect, and an undisguised expertise of which he was occasionally wilfully sceptical but more often in awe' (Forster and Hazlehurst 1988, p. 73).

Casey's interest in 'the experts' was sharpened by the poverty of the public service who worked under him. 'There are very few men in the service I would like to have'. When a British official was seconded to his department, he declared: 'It has been a revelation to me to have a first-rate civil servant to work for one – and it convinces me that Ministers in England must live a sheltered and pampered life – as compared with our lives here'.

Consequently, when in 1935 the prospect arose of Wilson resigning in order to fill the vacant chair at the University of Tasmania, 'Casey was aghast ("I could not contemplate losing Wilson") and he persuaded Cabinet to make Wilson as well [as Commonwealth Statistician] an adviser to the Treasury so that his salary would total what was needed to keep him in Canberra' (Hudson 1986, p. 99).

Under Casey, Wilson was to expand the earlier efforts to improve the quality of public service. 'If you wanted a book', Wilson later recalled, you had to tell the librarian 'what size it was, how thick, what colour the binding was, then he'd bring you three or four to pick from!'. Wilson arranged to appoint the first

---

[17] Richard Casey (1890–1976) was elected as a UAP member of the House of Representatives in December 1931. From 1933 to 1940 he held various ministerial portfolios, and in January 1940 he was appointed the first Australian Minister to the United States.

female librarian into the Commonwealth Public Service. He also ultimately succeeded in creating the category of Research Officer to hasten the absorption of graduates.

Banks and social security

Casey was to rely on Wilson in a noisy and futile battle to impose on banks the kind of regulation that, in the mid-century, was imagined to be necessary to rational economic management. The background was the Royal Commission on Banking and Monetary Policy (January 1936–July 1937) which had manifested a general unease at the banking policy during the Great Depression. Something had to be done. Requiring the trading banks to lodge a minimum level of deposits at the central bank seemed in order. Expert opinion to the Commission was mixed. While Copland had favoured them in print(1937a), Giblin was unimpressed by the idea. Brigden declined to subscribe to any theories of control, and favoured gradual accretion of specific measures and powers of persuasion. Conceding no more than that compulsory minimum deposits might one day be desirable, Brigden suggested to the Royal Commission that such powers should be held in reserve until such time as the Commonwealth Bank of Australia considered it advisable to apply to Parliament for their temporary deployment. To Wilson, compulsory deposits 'would be of little use as an instrument of credit'.

But compulsory deposits became a symbol to Casey, and to the banks, of the Commonwealth's right to manage the banking system. Wilson was assigned to formulate a Trading Banks Bill.

Casey told Bruce: 'The Trading Banks will give vent to piercing screams when the contents of the Banking Bill are made known to them' (NAA RGC 17 March 1938). Presumably because of those screams, Cabinet hesitated to back the draft. Banking legislation 'has really given me a headache'. At the close of 1938 the Trading Banks Bill was postponed. In May 1939, the Bill was watered down to remove licensing of banks, and enabling banks to fall below their 'required' reserves for a period of 13 weeks without penalty, and for any length of time beyond that with penalty (Sutherlin 1980, p. 268). Even this version was allowed to lapse. No Trading Banks Bill was ever passed.

Years later Wilson was to comment that Casey was a more efficient engineer than politician. The insufficiency of an expert public service in securing reform had been made plain by Casey's conduct.

The same lesson was to be taught in even more painful terms to J. B. Brigden, in the fiasco over national insurance, perhaps the greatest legislative busted flush of the Australian Commonwealth.

Australia's old age pension system had never been a contributive scheme. It had been funded directly from general revenue since its introduction in 1908 by

Alfred Deakin. Anxiety about the potential burden of its unfunded liabilities had been heightened by the fiscal crisis of the Depression. In October 1932 the Auditor-General produced a contributory plan for pensions. L. F. Giblin with H. C. Green had found fault with this proposal. But the Depression also produced a slump in the birth rate, which raised the spectacle of a shrunken working-age population being burdened with financing an unreduced pensions bill. Casey observed that the proportion of the population over 65 had tripled since 1888, and if these trends continued, then by 1978 there would be 54 old age pensioners for every 100 workers. A continuing budgetary discomfit also harmonised with a current of thought which saw social insurance 'as an instrument which secured intra-class harmony by means of genuine reforms and State supervision whilst leaving the individualist ethos in place in the principle of individual contributions' (Watts 1983).

The time for a contributory scheme of social entitlements had come. In 1937 the Lyons Government declared itself for a scheme that imposed small compulsory weekly contributions on all low-to-middle income employees – amounting to about 1.65 percent of average weekly earnings - to fund sickness, medical and retirement benefits. This scheme of 'national insurance' would require a 'scale and complexity of legislation and administration rare in the Australian context' (Watts 1983, p. 129). It would be, in Brigden's words 'the most ambitious financial project put forward under any national insurance scheme I have been able to discover' (Brigden 1939b p. 147).

National insurance would need a commission to run it, and the commission would need a head. But whom? Casey complained to Bruce: 'As you will realize, the range of choice amongst our existing public servants is limited'. Only one of the heads of the public service was deemed desirable: the Secretary of the Treasury, Harry Sheehan. And that welcome opportunity had vanished, Casey told Bruce, when a Commonwealth Bank officer 'appeared on my doorstep in Canberra last week, breathless with excitement … After shutting all the doors and windows, he broke me the news to me that the Board were unanimous in recommending that Sheehan be appointed Governor [of the Commonwealth Bank]'(NAA RGC 17 December 1937).

> The very paucity of the above led me to try to think of people outside the existing public service. This led me to think of the names of Brigden (Economist and in charge of the Bureau of Industry in Brisbane; now getting 2,000 pounds a year from Forgan Smith), Copland (in charge of the School of Economics in Melbourne and getting from all sources probably about 1,750 pounds per year), and Giblin. (NAA RGC 17 Dec 1937).

Figure 8.1. Giblin at his desk

Figure 8.2. Brigden at his desk

Figure 8.3. Copland at his desk

Source: ANU: UA2000/15, Envelope 44, L13351

Figure 8.4. Wilson at his desk

Giblin told Casey his own appointment was 'out of the question' but suggested Copland 'would be an admirable choice'. Casey took Copland's name to Cabinet, which was a 'little stunned', but offered no opposition. 'He is rather keen about the prospect' (NAA RGC 17 December 1937). But Copland was not appointed. Either a 'stunned' cabinet collected itself, or Copland became less keen, due to the emergence of the real possibility of his being appointed Vice-Chancellor of the University of Melbourne.

Giblin told Casey that Brigden was 'the obvious economist', and Brigden was appointed 'Director' of National Insurance on 14 Febuary 1938. On 6 July 1938, the day the Bill received vice-regal assent, Brigden was deemed 'Commissioner of National Insurance'.[18] Brigden and his colleagues then 'began an exhausting round of conferences and interviews only five days after the NIC was established'. A promotional campaign was launched on 11–12 July 1938 in the Albert Hall in Canberra. 'Throughout July and August Brigden had a whirlwind itinerary which took him to each capital city in a little over a month' (Watts 1983, p. 187). Every major trade union and friendly society was visited;[19] 1.7 million pamphlets were issued.

On 5 September Brigden declared: 'National insurance was no longer a dream ... it is here' (*The Age*, 6 September 1938). National Insurance was, in fact, not there. It would not be there until 1 January 1939, and a diverse array of adversaries was striving to stop it.

These adversaries included ideological opponents. National Insurance embodied what might be called the principle of 'compulsory thrift'; the poor will be compelled to help themselves.[20] By contrast, the Labor Party, and the left in general, favoured what might called 'compulsory charity'; the rich will be compelled to help the poor. This genuine ideological stance could be nicely pegged on a commonplace vexation at compulsory contributions, and a buzzing profusion of small groups attacked the Commission. Thirty-one thousand protest letters were dispatched by representatives of the State Electricity Commission of Victoria. Social Credit claimed to have sent 20 000 letters. G. P. O'Day, the 'red doctor', and author of *Why you should join the Communist Party of Australia*, became 'a tireless speaker against the legislation at countless suburban meetings organized – often by CPA members' (Watts 1983).

---

[18] Brigden was replaced at the Bureau by Colin Clark, who had been brought to Australia by Copland in 1937 to lecture at the University of Melbourne (Healy and McFarlane 1989).

[19] 'Our ageing population ... is a serious problem, one which cannot be treated lightly. Whereas to-day for every person of pension age ... there are four people of working age, in forty years time the latter figure shall be halved' (Brigden 1939b, p. 147).

[20] The contributions would be matched by contributions by employers. This would surely be passed on in time in the form of lower wages.

In addition to these 'ideological' opponents were certain, not necessarily less noble, interested adversaries. General practitioners were dissatisfied. There was to be no 'fee for service' but only a not very large flat annual sum for every patient. Their representatives spent from May 1938 to mid-1939 white-anting the bill. Business groups were also hostile to National Insurance, as they would be required to match the contributions of employees (Hudson 1986, p. 105). At the same time farmers were unsympathetic because they were exempted from its benefits.

Brigden fought the propaganda battle. Thirteen Bulletins were issued by the National Insurance Commission in August 1938, along with 'frequent radio broadcasts', and by December 1938, over one million copies of the pamphlet, *What national insurance means to the wage-earner, his wife and children*, were distributed. Brigden directed his own staff to compose letters to the editor. Two-minute film ads by worthies of the day, including Ernest Bevin, were organised.[21]

It was not all lure and beguilement. Brigden also publicly attacked the means test.

> I feel very strongly on that means test. I think in Australia the means test is a serious problem. It should not be taboo. Is it a fact that the Australian habit of concentrating public assistance ... tends to increase the number of persons in necessitous circumstances? I will not say that it increases the cadgers and scroungers of the country: I would rather let other people use those words. Like the problem of soil erosion, it involves the problem of the erosion of national character. (Brigden 1939b, p. 150).

The battle was wearing. 'National insurance has been a tremendous grind' wrote Casey. Brigden told a public audience that national insurance was proving 'extremely difficult', thanks to the late start, and the elevation of perfection above improvement. 'It may be too ambitious' (Brigden 1939b p. 147). He was frustrated by the lack of public interest. 'The intellectuals in Australia have taken the faintest possible interest in national insurance ... intellectuals do not care whether the cow calves or breaks its Australian neck' (Brigden 1939b, p. 149).[22]

Brigden and Casey were struggling to avoid retreat. Brigden devised a scheme to include farmers, but this was rejected by Treasury. Brigden had 'a key role

---

[21] No trace of them has survived. Two film clips of Casey are extant.

[22] One historian of the welfare state wrote: 'Brigden was at least one of the few people that kept up with contemporary thinking on the subject...There was elsewhere singularly little interest shown 'in the general principles of social insurance' (Kewley 1965, p. 165).

Figure 8.5. One of 1.7 million pamphlets issued to win public favour for the ill-starred National Insurance scheme

Here are the Answers to a few Questions about NATIONAL INSURANCE

What happens if I get out of work?

National Insurance is not unemployment insurance; that must come later. All contributions cease when a man is out of work; they are paid only while he is receiving wages. While he is unemployed he does not incur any liability. A free insurance period during unemployment covers him up to 21 months or more for all benefits for which he has qualified. Even if insured for only a week before getting out of work, he will at least receive free doctor and medicine during the free insurance period.

What about my lodge membership?

National Insurance provides free doctor and medicine for the wage-earner, but not for his wife and family. It is probable that lodge subscriptions will be adjusted to enable the worker to keep his family covered. Continuing his lodge membership does not affect his National Insurance benefits. He will be entitled to receive benefits of both.

Does change of work-place or residence affect my benefits?

National Insurance benefits are the right of every insured person and are available throughout Australia. The worker carries his right to insurance benefits with him from job to job and from State to State, wherever he may go in the course of his work.

What happens when my salary passes £365 a year?

Manual workers remain in insurance no matter what their earnings. Clerks and other non-manual workers are compulsorily insured only while receiving not more than £365 a year. If, after being in insurance for two years or more, their earnings exceed £365, they may continue as voluntary contributors. By paying the joint contribution themselves they may remain covered for all benefits except free doctor and medicine. If a man does not become a voluntary contributor, he will be entitled to a free insurance period during which he will receive all benefits for which he has qualified.

What is the position of a girl who marries?

The average young woman will have drawn on medical benefits and sick pay while working. On marrying, after being insured for four years or more, any woman may become a voluntary contributor for pension only. For a contribution of 1/- a week thereafter she would qualify for a pension in her own right of 15/- a week from 60 years onwards (on the average yielding £690), or for 1/6 a week, a pension of £1 a week (yielding £920). If, later, she should receive the insurance widow's pension, that benefit would be paid in addition to her own pension. If she does not become a voluntary contributor, she will be entitled to a free insurance period.

What steps should I take to enrol?

YOU SHOULD ENROL WITH AN APPROVED SOCIETY WITHIN THE NEXT FEW WEEKS. Lists of Societies are available at all Post Offices. You may choose whatever Society you wish. There is no entrance fee. But you must enrol to ensure payment of your benefits.

If there is any point upon which you desire information call or write to the offices of the National Insurance Commission.

DEPUTY COMMISSIONER OF NATIONAL INSURANCE
Phillip House, Phillip St., Sydney

District Inspectors at LISMORE, ARMIDALE, DUBBO, NEWCASTLE.

What National Insurance Means . . .

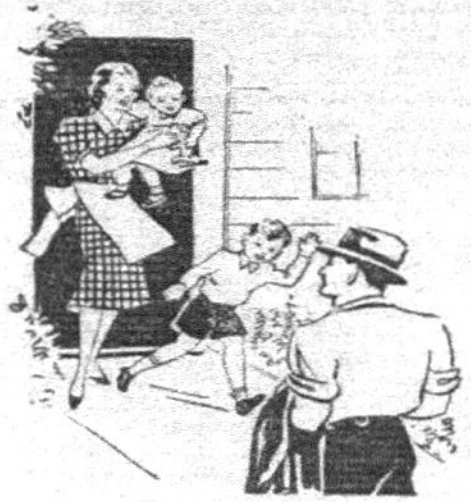

To the Wage-Earner, his Wife and Children

in negotiations with doctors' seeking to reconcile them (Watts 1987, p. 17). In November Brigden persuaded Casey that implementation should be delayed from January until April 1939. 'Casey may well have been working ... with Brigden on a fall back position' (Watts 1983). But restless political forces were closing in on the wounded prey. In February 1939, Earl Page, very lightly discarding the principle of Cabinet unity, publicly urged scrapping the legislation. In a drastic rescue measure, on 15 February 1939, old age pensions were dropped from the scheme, and unemployment benefits introduced.

It was to little effect; Lyons was not backing National Insurance. In truth he had made it known in 1938 that he did not want the legislation passed, and only agreed to its passage in the face of Casey's threat to resign (McLachlan 1948, p. 253). Lyon's sudden death on 7 April 1939, therefore, may have appeared as an opportunity. Had not Menzies actually resigned in March, in protest over Lyons' lethargy over National Insurance? But any such hopeful expectation was soon disappointed. As Wilson remarked later concerning these events, Menzies was never really interested in economics 'unless it was going for him' (quoted in Sutherlin 1980, p. 270).

Casey, Menzies' only rival, was removed from Treasury. The national insurance legislation was suspended in June 1939. And Brigden 'came close to a complete physical break down' (Watts 1983, p. 134). He remained the commissioner of a non-existent commission. To relieve 'the embarrassment of Brigden's position', he was appointed secretary to the newly created Department of Social Services. This was accomplished on 29 August 1939. The passage of a few days was to make the issues of socialservices less urgent.

9. In war and peace

> On the economic side in wartime I think the most influential advisers were ... Giblin, Copland, Melville and Brigden — and perhaps Roland Wilson.
> *Paul Hasluck*[1]

Introduction

It had been the Great War that had first brought Giblin's four together. In 1939 a still greater war was to unite them a second time. For the next six years they were absorbed in shaping Australia's war effort.

They were at the front of the helter skelter dash to build war industries and to marshall a workforce to man them. They educated two Treasurers about the need to consider resourcing the war effort in macroeconomic terms. With the approach of victory, they articulated similar Keynesian notions to preserve full employment in peace. With the global spread of the war, they strived to assure what they believed were Australia's interests in the approaching post-war international order. This was a struggle that culminated at San Francisco in 1945 in a bitter dispute over the place of the 'full-employment pledge' in the United Nations Charter (Crisp 1965). [2]

Yet it might be said that none of the four had 'a good war'. Their successes were mingled with frustration and bitter disappointment.

'Goodwill toward men'

'Fellow Australians. It is my melancholy duty to inform you officially that in consequence of the persistence by Germany in her invasion of Poland, Great Britain has declared war upon her and that, as a result, Australia is also at war.' With a formula of words resembling a telegram announcing a death to the next of kin, Prime Minister Menzies announced the advent of war to Australia. Many listeners shared Menzies' spiritlessness. Most elements of Australian political life had supported appeasement. Lyons hailed the Munich agreement, and had even sought to claim some personal credit for it. John Curtin, as Opposition Leader, congratulated Lyons on his stance. Highly contrary hues in the Australian ideological kaleidoscope concurred on the merit of appeasement, including Eggleston, *The Bulletin*, and the Catholic hierarchy. [3]

---

[1] Hasluck 1997, p. 55.

[2] The economic dimension of the Australian war effort has been extensively investigated by Walker (1947), Hasluck (1952), Butlin (1955), Butlin and Schedvin (1977), Watts (1983) and Ross (1995).

[3] H. C. Coombs has recorded in his memoirs that he was a 'pacifist' even after the outbreak of war in 1939. Giblin and Copland cannot be described as pacifists. Copland caused indignation by urging

In sympathy with this outlook, Giblin shared the widespread disquiet about any policy that increased, rather than reduced, the probability of war. Giblin believed, with Copland and many others, that the Treaty of Versailles had been unjust and inexpedient, and any war for the treaty would be unjust and inexpedient. [4]

On 16 April 1937, Giblin, Copland and four other members of the University of Melbourne, issued a manifesto: *Australia's policy – peace or war*. It was effectively addressed to Lyons:

> 20 years ago we crushed German imperialism, though it was touch and ago, and now Germany seems as strong as ever again. The job cost Australia 60,000 men killed, thousands impaired in health, and down to the present 470m pounds in money while we still owe 280m in war debts. Today aggressive imperialism has three heads – German, Italian, Japan[ese]. To scotch them for another generation is not likely to cost less than it did the last time, even if we succeed. Must we all go through it again in a few years time? Although the League seems at present discredited, war is even more discredited. The British Empire could cut the ground from beneath the feet of the dictators by offering to take steps to remove grievances.

Prominent 'steps' the Empire should take included reducing trade preference and a stricter internationalisation of League of Nations mandates. 'Both of these offers would be contingent upon fascist countries coming back into the League, and supporting collective security'. [5] This was the standard Chamberlain outlook, and in hindsight seems hopelessly thin.

With the advent of the Munich agreement of 1938, Giblin's position diverged from that of both appeasers and anti-appeasers. His key judgement was that Germany was strong and Britain was weak. And because of this strength, a war of any kind with Hitler would be 'madness'. [6] And because of this strength, German domination of the European continent was unstoppable – war or no. Giblin suggested that the most rational course of conduct for Britain was to 'cease

---

military training to be compulsory for Melbourne University undergraduates. Predictably, Giblin's interest focused on military training for schoolboys.

[4] Like many war veterans, Giblin had a less negative opinion of Germans than civilians. At the close of the First World War he had affirmed in a soldiers' debate that Germans should be allowed to migrate to Australia. And while in 1933 he declared that 'Germany has cut herself from civilisation' (Giblin 1933), in 1937 he told James William Barrett (the Chancellor of Melbourne University), that, although Nazi methods were 'distasteful', 'one cannot quarrel with their aims' (4 May 1937, quoted in Roe 1984, p. 83).

[5] Specific reference is made to the Australian 'Mandate' of former German New Guinea.

[6] Why? Because success was uncertain and 'years of attrition' inevitable.

to be a European power', and 'play for an American alliance to keep freedom of the seas'. Such a withdrawal to the Channel would constitute an equilibrium: 'an armed peace for a generation or so, which would give time for reason to be born again in Central Europe, with help perhaps by cautious and indirect evangelisation from the outside' (UMA LFG 24 October 1938). Giblin, therefore, was putting his hopes in a cold war: an Anglo-American alliance that would withstand a continental menace, but with fascism rather than communism as the adversary, and with the Channel rather than the Elbe as the frontier. Europe's ultimate salvation would rest on a slow ideological conversion ('evangelisation').

Unlike the Munich signatories, no part of Giblin's analysis assumed the orderly conduct of Hitler. Giblin did not believe that Hitler had been cajoled, however reluctantly, into concert with other European 'great powers'. Hitler's letter of 28 September 1938, Giblin remarked, 'takes the mask off too completely'. It was 'seething with scarcely concealed contempt'. Did Chamberlain 'really think that in a year – or 18 months – England will be in a position to call the tune?' Thus both Giblin and the anti-appeasers agreed that Hitler would use his power just as he pleased. But their analyses drew different inferences. The necessity of war was inferred by Churchill's analysis, and the necessity of avoiding war by Giblin's. Churchill's policy was the nobler. In the upshot, it was also more expedient. Yet that expedience turned upon the totally unexpected collapse of the Western Front in 1940, and the consequent avoidance of the 'years of attrition' upon which Giblin premised his argument. Giblin had been tripped up by being *insufficiently* pessimistic about British inferiority. The calculus of events had proved inscrutable, even to that subtle reader of wind-scattered leaves.

The reveille

When war came all four were rapidly summoned.

Brigden was quickly made the Economic Adviser to the new Department of Supply and Development that had just replaced the old Munitions Supply Board. On 1 January 1940 he became its Secretary.[7] Copland also became an adviser to government at the outset of the war. Appointed Commonwealth Prices Commissioner in 1939, he was appointed Economic Consultant to the Prime Minister in 1941, and held both positions until the end of the war.

Menzies had intended to appoint Wilson as his economic adviser for the duration of the war. But Wilson had been successfully arguing for the establishment of

---

[7] Brigden was from 1 December 1939, Acting Secretary of the Department of Supply and Development; from 1 January 1940, Secretary, Department of Supply and Development; from 8 August 1940, Secretary, Department of Munitions; and from 1 July 1941 Secretary of the Department of Aircraft Production.

a Department of Labour and National Service, and on a train journey from Sydney to Canberra, Harold Holt, the designated minister for the new department, offered Wilson the position of Secretary. In October 1940 Wilson was appointed (Cornish 2002, p. 23).

At Wilson's urging, Giblin was brought to Canberra at the age of sixty-six to be Chairman of the Financial and Economic Committee (F&E), a committee formally constituted as part of Treasury in September 1939.[8] It was composed of Wilson, Melville and Giblin, with Copland, Brigden and Coombs recruited later.[9] In Wilson's vision this committee would 'constitute a small central thinking committee', with 'its services ... available to Cabinet or to any other department'. The research was done by Wilson, Brigden, Melville, and Coombs; Copland was the conduit to the Prime Minister; and Giblin, 'the one full-time member [who] appears to have served as a one man synthesiser' (Maddock and Penny 1983, p. 31).

The bivouac

Wilson and Brigden left Canberra for Melbourne, where Manpower and Industry would be directed. And, in the opposite direction, Giblin and Copland left Melbourne for Canberra. The two shared digs in the capital, and Giblin reported to Eilean this arrangement was 'going well', despite his vexation at 'German music' being banned from the ABC. In June 1940 after reading some 'very depressing' cables from Bruce about the war in France, and presumably feeling his opportunities for leave from Canberra had suddenly diminished, Giblin beckoned Eilean to leave Melbourne for the capital. The hunt for quarters suitable for a couple began; Giblin discussed the possibility of using the Brigden's house, which was being rented to the United States 'legation'.

The Giblins settled down to the eccentric austerity of wartime Canberra: of meat and butter 'usually unobtainable'; bacon 'unprocurable'; the milk almost bluish in winter; wood hard to get (when seven tonnes might be needed each winter), and mysteriously sudden evaporations of particular commodities – bootlaces one month, envelopes another. But Giblin, of course, enjoyed the physical demands of this life. His letters record with satisfaction his 10 pullets providing eggs; the 130 lb of pumpkin he harvested; and the strawberry patch that yielded

---

[8] It was Wilson who had recommended initially that such a committee be established for the purpose of advising the government on the implications of possible blockades of shipping to and from Australia in the event of a war with Japan.

[9] At about this time Giblin described Coombs as 'a good fellow, solid, no frills, no disturbing ego, very reasonable, though there is ground where I – Wilson also – cannot follow him'. He told Keynes: 'do not take him too seriously' (KCLA LFG 14 May 1943, L/A/75).

strawberries so ample that their consumption would 'require the help of neighbours'.

Each day Giblin, in 'a thick tweed suit, ... a badgeless digger hat; the same red tie, the clog like boots, large pipe ... and the huge bushman's pack' (Reynolds c. 1951) would make his way to the small room on the top floor of External Affairs and Treasury. In this 'sunny corner of the top floor of West Block, Canberra, ... he crouched over his pipe among a litter of papers, [and provided] not only a cell of economic thought but a place where many departmental and inter-departmental tangles were unwound by honest and straightforward commonsense (Hasluck 1952, p. 452). Hasluck later recalled it was a 'privilege' to work 'close to this great Australian, sagacious, humorous, kindly to persons, devastating to humbug (Hasluck 1980, p. 64). Giblin, said Hasluck, 'had a sanifying influence. He showed us the things we had to think about and helped keep the thinking straight. His personality had the effect of sand paper, rough but polishing others' (Hasluck 1954, p. 138).

Churning butter into guns

In Melbourne, Brigden was facing the most urgent problem of the war effort: the arming of Australia's military forces. This could not be done by relying on the arms industries of a larger nation. A heavy armaments industry would have to be created from scratch. In this task Brigden was, from the beginning of 1940, the senior public servant, being appointed the Secretary of the Department of Munitions, and later Secretary of the Department of Aircraft Production.

This was an arduous undertaking, with as many deep frustrations as rewards. The fundamental difficulty was Australia's state of industrial underdevelopment. Manufacturing output had doubled in real terms over the preceding 20 years (Butlin 1985), but manufactures were still dominated by food, clothing and furniture, and unprocessed or semi-processed products (such as steel). As of 1939, Australia had barely produced an aeroplane. She produced no aluminium, extracted no petroleum, and possessed no tankers to ship it. Cotton wool was imported. Newsprint was not produced, and even cardboard could not be made in the absence of certain imported ingredients. 'Nearly all' machine tools and factory plant were imported (Ross 1995).

Figure 9.1. Brigden (left), as Secretary of Munitions sharing a platform with R. G. Menzies

There were also more human difficulties. Australia was distant from technological expertise. Brigden later recalled: 'Frequently there were no blue-prints. Critical parts were explained by crude picturegram'. [10] The factors of production did not always cooperate: one small arms factory was halted for three weeks while three unions fought a demarcation dispute over a single person. Brigden also lamented how the employment of women as factory hands was delayed by men:

> Traditional trade union objections delayed the employment of women elsewhere in Munitions, except as laboratory workers etc, and in a somewhat furtive small way in factories. Yet it had been proved that a gauge lasted at least twice as long in the hands of a women worker as in the hands of a new male worker. (Brigden 1942).

Away from the factory floor, the gathering of sufficient and appropriate personnel for the Department of Munitions was a struggle. The Department grew from 14 persons at the opening of the war to 6259 at its peak in August 1943. Brigden could draw on the formidable capabilities of his deputy, J. K. Jensen. But in general the quality of the existing public service was weak. This necessitated recruiting over 90 per cent of staff from outside the ranks of experienced public servants, which itself produced some difficulties. Essington Lewis of BHP had been made 'Director-General for Munitions' by Menzies in June 1941, and endowed with great powers. But as Brigden commented: 'The man from business finds that public opinion will not allow him to behave in a businesslike way'.

Personnel difficulties extended to the executive. Menzies did not make a zestful commander. He styled himself Minister for Munitions, but seemed not to relish playing the warlord. He had told Bruce at the outbreak of war: 'Those who think about it, all feel sick about it – and those who don't want to feel sick, don't think about it' (DFATHP RGM 11 September 1939).

Months passed into years, but the art of fashioning swords from ploughshares remained stubbornly elusive. By November 1940 Australia was in possession of only 42 'modern' planes; all of them, in fact, obsolete. The project to manufacture Beauforts – that ultimately yielded in the last years of the war 365 Beaufighters – was, said Brigden, 'ill fated from the start'. By April 1941 Australia still possessed no naval mines. By May 1941 only 10 (light) tanks were available (Day 2003).

In a world at war, Australia's effort to arm herself seemed insufficient. As Menzies' Government did not command a majority in parliament, it was vulnerable to opposition assault on this matter. One avenue for the attack was

---

[10] Picturegram = fax. Since 1934 Siemens-Karolus equipment installed in Melbourne had supplied faxes from London. But this service was discontinued in 1942 because of the difficulty of obtaining (German) spare parts.

the role Menzies had given prominent businessmen in the direction of the armament program. On 5 June 1941 Norman Makin, the Labor member for Hindmarsh in South Australia, attacked the role of industrialists, such as Essington Lewis. In August 1941 H. V. Evatt and J. A. Beasley made 'scathing attacks'. 'Both suggested that Lewis was sacrificing his country's needs for his company's profits' (Blainey 1971).

But there was another avenue for attack: Brigden was the onetime advocate of the reviled National Insurance scheme, and still malodorous to some Labor members on account of his support for the Premiers' Plan. On 5 June 1941 Curtin attacked Brigden's appointment as Secretary to the Department of Munitions. On the following day, Curtin's deputy Frank Forde proposed that Brigden be transferred to the position of Director of Economic Co-ordination, 'a fantastic assignment' created early in the war, and abolished as soon as Labor acceded to office in October 1941 (NAA Advisory War Council Minute, 6 June 1941).

When Labor did obtain the government benches, Brigden's position as Secretary of the Department of Munitions was highly vulnerable. Copland was emphatic in pressing on the new government the progress that had been made in armaments:

> In October 1941 the Economic Adviser to the new Curtin Government, Professor D. B. Copland, reported that the speed with which war industries had reached mass production stage had amazed even the experts introduced from overseas to supervise operations. At the outbreak of war, he said, Australia possessed only 1 manufacturer of lathes, two power presses, and one government machine factory. By late 1941 Australia was practically self-sufficient and over 30 firms were manufacturing machine tools. Munitions production had leapt 18 times in value. For every man at a bench or lathe in 1939, there were at least 20 by October 1941. (Page 1963, p. 294). [11]

Copland's ebullience should not be dismissed as self-justification, or simply as aid for a friend in need. Since 1990 a 'revisionist history' of the war effort has emerged that paints a far more positive picture of Australian re-armament than earlier analysts had accepted (Ross 1995). But, however justified Copland's case may have been, his evidence was tainted. Several branches of the ALP passed motions demanding Copland's removal from government service. The future Labor leader Arthur Calwell rose in the House of Representatives to ask if the Copland who was advising Prime Minister Curtin was the one and the same Copland who had in 1931 recommended a 10 per cent cut in wages? [12]

---

[11] Brigden noted with pride the export of machine tools to the United States. Optics, too, were an achievement.

[12] Copland had known the family of Elsie Curtin since his leadership of the WEA in Tasmania.

How to pay for the war

Lying beneath the 'micro' problems of armaments were the more macroeconomic problems of maximising total available resources. In this, the four were significant in introducing a 'national accounting' mentality, and a Keynesian approach to government budgets.

Deficits or doles?

The four's influence relied in large measure on the open-mindedness of the minister responsible for national economic management, Percy Spender, the new breeze in the listless United Australia Party. He had entered parliament in 1937 by defeating the UAP minister for defence. He was quickly recruited into the government, made Assistant Treasurer in April 1939, Acting Treasurer in November 1939, and Treasurer in March 1940. In 1943 he was to stand for leadership of the UAP, and lose by a single vote.

Spender was all energy and new ideas, and was a good foil for Giblin's proselytising of novel Keynesian precepts. There was sometimes tension between the two. On one occasion Giblin told Eilean:

> The trouble is that Spender has no idea of the work involved and will not make or get decisions on essential points of policy. So there is continual recasting of the Financial Statement, and everyone is slaving to make it a decent document – which it can't be at the moment – or at least reduce the indecencies and crudeness of it. (NLA LFG 30 April 1940). [13]

But Spender was a ready pupil of Giblin. [14]

The first lesson involved the appropriate stance of government spending and taxation in the face of unemployment.

Unemployment had remained significant throughout the 1930s. In the September quarter 1939, unemployment of unionists was measured at 10.3 per cent. [15] Shortly after the outbreak of war Giblin drew Spender's attention to current levels of unemployment, asserting that unemployment 'threatens to become quickly an acute embarrassment to the government' (17 October 1939). The outbreak of war, he said, had sent a psychological shockwave through the business community, and consumers had stopped spending. [16]

---

[13] Giblin adds, 'Mac [Secretary to the Treasury S.G. MacFarlane] is in the depths of despair.'

[14] Spender acknowledges Giblin's role in his memoirs.

[15] In 1940 unemployment of unionists averaged at 8.6 per cent. By the last stages of the war this was to drop to 1.0 per cent.

[16] LFG to PS, 17 October 1939, NAA571/1/39/3799.

The government, said Giblin, had compounded the unemployment problem by excessive timidity in defence spending. 'The difficulty', Giblin argued, 'can only be met by more rapid spending – not planning, or commitments or raising loans, but spending; and spending for employment as much as and more than for defence'.

In his notes for the supplementary Budget speech of November 1939, Giblin asserted that: 'This is not the time to provide against the possibility of a deficit either by reduction of expenditure or by new taxation. For the next few months, the unemployment situation will be critical. Reduction of expenditure or increases of taxation would further depress unemployment. This is a proper occasion for deficit financing ... The same reason holds against any present increase in taxation to meet war expenditure' [17]

Treasury, however, was implacably opposed to any further increase in Commonwealth spending. But Spender refused to endorse the view of his own department. In this spirit of dissent, Spender put to Cabinet (13 November 1939) that 'no measures should be imposed now which would obviously have the effect of increasing unemployment'; any further 'increases in direct taxation at this juncture would cause uneasiness and tend to reduce employment'. 'An integral part of this policy is to avoid any increase in taxation likely to depress private enterprise.' [18]

Giblin's concern about aggregate demand was underpinned by a vision that efficient conduct of the war effort required looking at the economy as a whole. The key insight here was that, in an economy seeking to maximise war material, *unemployment was as wasteful as consumption*. Spender took this point readily. Thus, in response to Giblin, Spender wrote to Menzies on 25 October saying that the 'the view of our economic advisers' is that 'maintenance of employment ... is of paramount importance in lessening the burden imposed by war. In short, the burden is the diversion of human labour to war purposes, which can only be lessened, apart from reducing expenditure, by increasing the national income, which in turn can ... be accomplished by bringing into productive employment people not presently engaged therein.' And Spender went on: 'One of the objectives of our present policy is to restore and increase the national income. This will enable us to divert resources to defence without encroaching unnecessarily on existing standards of consumption.' [19] He was convinced that 'Giblin's suggestion means a sound national approach to our national problem,

---

[17] NAA 571/1/39/4105, 'Prof Giblin's Notes', October–November 1939.

[18] NAA PS 13 November 1939, 'Revision of Budget, 1939–40', 184/8/Bundle 1.

[19] NAA PS to RGM 25October 1939, 571/1/39/3799.

which I need hardly say would be of tremendous political value to ourselves'.[20]

A third lesson was the outlook on the government budget. The F&E put to him that the budget should be regarded not only as a device to manage the government's own incomes and outlays, but also as a part of an algorithm that assisted the government to manage aggregate demand in the economy as whole.

In his memoirs Spender found fault with the first Menzies war budget for not recognising this:

> The Budget of September 1939 was, in effect, just another traditional budget that did not vary from the peacetime pattern. There was nothing … to indicate a financial policy geared to war, or any statement of principle or planning as to how the economy of the nation was to be organised for war. (Spender 1972, p. 43).

In contrast, Spender's supplementary Budget brought down in 30 November 1939 was built around Giblin's approach to war finance. Spender argued that:

> In view of the … uncertainty resulting from the outbreak of war and the recent decline in employment, the Government is of the opinion that to increase taxation at the present time would merely delay the recovery of our economy, retard the full utilization of employable labour, reduce the potential of our national income, and consequently interfere with the full prosecution of our war programme. It has been decided, therefore, not to increase further the burden of taxation for defence purposes in this financial year.[21] (Butlin 1955, p. 200).

If there ever was a 'Keynesian Revolution' in Australian economic policy, it may be argued that it arrived at this time and in this way: in 1939, and from Giblin, through the F&E, to Spender.

Reflation or inflation?

A second difference between orthodox finance and the F&E came over the prudence or imprudence of funding some war requirements from central bank

---

[20] To strengthen the Treasury's economic expertise, Spender endorsed the suggestion, put to him by Wilson, that Coombs should be seconded from the Commonwealth Bank in Sydney, where he was Assistant Economist, to become Economist at the Treasury.

[21] Spender's supplementary budget of November 1939 reflected in large measure the approach that had been adopted by the F&E. Unemployment remained at unacceptable levels and therefore it was possible, the Acting Treasurer declared in the budget speech, to fund some of the increased war expenditure from loans borrowed from the banking system, including borrowing from the central bank. Defence borrowing was raised from £19m to £46m, and the reliance on tax revenue was reduced from £6m to £2m.

borrowing (that is, 'printing money'). The Commonwealth Treasury had resolved in its own mind that war expenditure should be financed from taxation and loans from the public. Borrowing from the banking system, especially from the central bank, was to be avoided like hellfire. That expedient had been over-used in Australia – and elsewhere – during the First World War, and had led to inflation or even hyper-inflation, exchange rate depreciation, and economic turbulence.

But whereas the Treasury dismissed such borrowing as unsound, the economists were more ambivalent. Giblin, as chairman of the F&E, helped to forge a common view among economists: as long as resources – particularly labour – were not being used at full capacity, it was legitimate to 'borrow' from the Commonwealth Bank. As Giblin told the Secretary to the Treasury, S. G. MacFarlane: 'central bank credit should be injected in times of depression and withdrawn in times of prosperity and the net result should be zero'. [22]

Not long before the outbreak of war, at the invitation of the then Treasurer R. G. Casey, both Wilson and Brigden had prepared notes on the efficacy of borrowing from the central bank.

Wilson had argued that 'if the economic system is not working to full capacity', 'there is in general a good case for finding money for reproductive works. There may even be a good case for finding money for works which are not reproductive in the financial sense of returning full interest to the Treasuries, but which are reproductive in the wider economic sense.' He declared, moreover, that it 'may well be that this money should come from an expansion of central bank credit …'. It was true that foreign reserves might be depleted in the process; that private enterprise might be adversely affected if interest rates were to rise; and that appropriate labour skills might not be available from among the unemployed. But when 'incomes have fallen and unemployment is increasing', he concluded that 'an increase in public spending, assisted by central bank credit, is probably desirable to stimulate activity'. [23]

Brigden, vigilant as ever in the face of the siren call of inflation, was more wary than either Wilson or Giblin. He did acknowledge that 'present opinion tends … to support the use of central bank credit as a substitute for taxation or as a

---

[22] Giblin's views may be contrasted with those of the Treasury, which early in 1939 had drafted speech notes for Casey on the subject of war finance. The notes referred to recent suggestions that 'defence should be financed by some form or other of national credit'. The effect of that, the Treasury asserted, would be 'to destroy confidence in the existing currency. The currency would depreciate, costs of living would rise and all titles to money – including *Savings Bank Deposits* [italics in the original] would become less valuable. In fact, their value might even go the way of other countries and become almost negative.'

[23] NAA RW to RGC November 1938, 'Finance and monetary policy', 1968/391/140.

means of increasing employment or the national income or both'. But this opinion, he said, had been influenced by the writings of Keynes, and had been based on the assumption that wages would not increase when there was unemployment. Yet in Australia, according to Brigden, 'each degree of increase toward full employment is accompanied by increases in wage rates and ... labour costs'. If central bank lending was resorted to, controls over foreign exchange, investment and labour would be required: 'control must follow as the Government under public pressure, seeks to avoid the adverse consequences of its action'. [24]

As for Giblin, since unemployment existed, he believed it was quite legitimate for central bank credit to be used 'to set working all the unused resources of labour in the country'. 'In general an excessive issue is necessary as a first step followed by a corrective withdrawal of the excess'. [25]

But Giblin foresaw an inflationary pressure. In his notes for the November 1939 supplementary Budget, he wrote that: 'The policy proposed is to use the stimulus of central bank credit to finance the initial period. So far the procedure may be called reflation. If this method were to be continued we should have inflation beginning gently but accelerating to a dangerous rapidity'. As a consequence, 'After the initial period then, say from next May, the war should be financed jointly by taxation and current savings, invested in loans on the market. Only by adhering to this principle of finance can inflation be controlled'. [26]

The end of Giblin's 'initial period' might be said to be signalled by Coombs' F&E paper of 7 December 1940 headed: 'The banking system and war finance'. The banks were now in a highly liquid position and were seeking investment opportunities to maintain their profits. Coombs was fearful that these circumstances might spark a 'dangerous inflationary process'. He proposed that the banks' advance policy and their liquid assets should be subjected to tighter control. Two alternatives were proposed: a system of minimum variable liquidity ratios, or a uniform minimum ratio that would be sufficient to control the most liquid of the banks, bringing the other banks up to that level by exchanging liquid assets for government securities. Wilson suggested, however, that the time might be right for the introduction of what he called the '100% money plan', by which he meant that all increases in bank assets from a particular date should be lodged with the Commonwealth Bank. Later, Wilson's plan was

---

[24] NAA JBB to MacFarlane, 1 June 1939 'Central bank credit and employment', 1968/391/138.

[25] NAA LFG 26 October 1939, 'War finance', 1968/391/139.

[26] NAA LFG n/d but October–November 1939, CP 13/1/C File X111 'War finance: Preface'. Also, NAA LFG to PS 17 October 1939, 571/1/39/3799.

adopted by the Curtin Government as a central device to restrain the impact of excessive monetary expansion. [27]

These ideas were aired with increasing alarm by the F&E at its meeting in December 1940, but already by April 1940 it began to advise the government that reliance on bank credit would soon have to end, and, in consequence, taxation would have to be raised. It was aware that taxation on low incomes would be politically difficult. [28] In response, Spender acknowledged that, with respect to bank credit, 'This possibility is now largely closed. We must in the future rely almost entirely on taxation and public loans'. [29]

By March 1941 the matter had become more urgent. It was in this context that Giblin raised the political difficulties of dispensing with credit expansion. 'With resources fully used', he said, 'there can be no case for further credit expansion in 1941–42 but rather for contraction. Nevertheless it may be politically impossible to finance a growing war expenditure by market loans and taxation, so that immediate recourse to credit expansion may be forced on the government.' [30] Drawing upon the ideas of Coombs, Melville and Wilson, Giblin then put three alternatives to the F&E:

> first to borrow from the Commonwealth Bank, but to limit the secondary expansion of credit by controlling the advance policies of the banks through minimum liquidity ratios;
>
> second, to borrow from the banks, but limit their profits;
>
> and third, to induce the banks to transfer their deposits to the Treasury, or to the Commonwealth Bank acting on behalf of the Treasury [31].

Copland, however, was inclined to seek voluntary cooperation from the banks. But the problem here seemed to be that the banks would define 'cooperation' in different ways, and would be unlikely to accept the Commonwealth Bank's definition. [32]

Since the F&E was unable to agree, it decided to seek political direction, especially on how bank profits might be controlled.

---

[27] NAA HCC 7 December 1940, CP 5/1/Bundle XVII, File CCLXIII, 'The banking system and war finance'.

[28] NAA PS Submission to the Cabinet, 27 March 1940, 184/8/1/Bundle 1

[29] NAA PS 27 March 1940, 'Submission to Cabinet', 184/8/1/Bundle 1. NAA PS to Macfarlane, April 1940 CP 184/1/1/ Bundle 1. NAA 4 July 1940 PS to LFG, CP 5/1/ Bundle XV11, File CCLX111.

[30] NAA LFG c. March 1941, 'Inflationary loans', CP 5/1/Bundle XV11, File CCLX11.

[31] NAA CP 5/1/Bundle XVII, File CCLXII.

[32] NAA, 'Inflationary loans', CP 5/1/Bundle XV11, File CCLX111.

Taxes or 'contributions'?

The new Keynesian approach did not mean unconditional deficits and low taxes. With the end of unemployment and the inexorable rise in war expenditure, the convenient policy of low taxation became more doubtful. Not because it meant deficits, but because it meant an excess of demand over supply.

The F&E became increasingly preoccupied with calculating the gap between expected war expenditure in the months ahead and the resources required to meet the increased demands from taxation and loans. The use of the so-called 'gap' methodology was initiated by Giblin, drawing on the terminology and method of Keynes in *How to pay for the war* (Keynes 1939, 1940). He corresponded frequently with Keynes throughout the war on aspects of war finance, including the principles underlying the gap approach. In its simple form, and abstracting from external flows of income and expenditure, the 'gap' methodology was commonly expressed as follows: from expected war expenditure, deduct current taxation receipts and loan revenues. The residual was the measure of the 'gap' which would have to be funded either by new taxation, new loans, or borrowings from the banking system (including the central bank), or by some combination of these three sources.

There were, in effect, four policy choices that faced the government.

One was simply to allow inflation. This would transfer resources from consumption to war-related activities, since wages lagged behind price increases and taxes on profits and progressive rates of income tax would divert income from employers to the government.

A second was rationing and price control. But the F&E hesitated to recommend direct controls, particularly rationing. [33] Several members of the F&E did, however, think rationing was inevitable. Certainly, Copland was sanguine about the efficacy and practicality of controls. Although he still took the view that the best way to drain purchasing power from the community was through taxation, he was far from confident that the rate of taxation necessary to maintain the war effort and ward off inflation would be politically acceptable. Hence he lent his support to a limited scheme of rationing covering a restricted range of goods. [34]

---

[33] At the outbreak of war Giblin said it 'should be a matter of general policy to go slow with wartime controls which check and frighten business. The control of exchange, investment, imports, exports and prices should all be brought in gently. The fascination of safeguarding the future must be restrained by the issues of the present' (NAA LFG to PS 17 October 1939, 571/1/39/3799).

[34] By the time it met at the end of August 1941, the F&E had moved some distance toward Copland's position, concluding that: 'If new taxation ... cannot be obtained, then ... the only way to avoid an excessive rise in prices is to impose restrictive measures sufficient to ensure that the required amount of savings is made'. In fact, it concluded that, even if its recommended tax increases (including the

The third device was borrowing from the private sector. But there were limits to which individuals and institutions would respond to war loans without the incentive of higher interest rates.

The fourth device – and that preferred by Giblin and the F&E as a whole – was taxation. Keynes had proposed a useful variant of this device: that orthodox taxes be supplemented by what he initially called 'deferred pay', and later 'post-war credits'. Here a certain proportion of revenue levied from taxation – or from a compulsory loan – would be earmarked for repayment to taxpayers after the war. Keynes was concerned that steep rates of taxation might create disincentives to work, whereas a system of deferred pay would not, since the revenue would be returned later to those from whom it had been collected. Moreover, it could be repaid after the war, when it was expected that a slump would occur after an immediate post-war boom; tax refunds in these circumstances would provide a boost to effective demand when they were spent upon goods and services.

As early as its meeting on 16 December 1939, the F&E had discussed for the first time the possibility of introducing a system of compulsory loans ('post-war credits') along the lines of the scheme proposed by Keynes. The committee concluded, however, the compulsory loans scheme should be kept in reserve.[35]

By July 1940, and with war expenditure accelerating rapidly, the F&E was adamant that taxation would have to rise, and that meant taxing lower-income groups, in spite of critics arguing that there remained considerable spare capacity, and so excessive taxation could be avoided. The F&E proposed that the government consider imposing a consumption tax at the point of retail sales of 1d on every shilling spent. It was Wilson who suggested this idea, allowing for the possible exemption of bread and milk.

It was at this point that Giblin raised once more the idea of the compulsory loan scheme, but now in the context of a national program of uniform taxation. The Commonwealth should levy a uniform national income tax, he argued, and the difference between the levy and income taxes already imposed by the Commonwealth and the states should be collected as a compulsory loan. The compulsory loan component would be greater for taxpayers in wealthier, low-taxing states, such as Victoria and New South Wales, than in other states.

National Contribution) were introduced, and the amount of loan revenues it was suggesting was secured, 'it might still be necessary to impose certain real restrictions'. Even so, the committee felt that 'the more the rationing method was considered the more desirable appeared the alternative of taxation, and suggested that, in presenting the problem to Cabinet, the difficulties of rationing be strongly emphasised' (AWM August 1941, SJB/118, 29/30).

[35] NAA 16 December 1939, M 70/117.

Not only would this bring in additional revenue, but it would help to make the sharing of the cost of the war more equitable across the states.[36] By October 1940, Giblin had further refined his proposal for a uniform income tax via a compulsory loan. The Commonwealth would introduce a uniform income tax on personal and company income, and from the amount assessed, income tax payable to the states would be deducted on the basis of existing state income tax. The residual would constitute federal tax. Of the residual, a part would be taken in the form of current or future federal income tax; the surplus would be regarded as a compulsory loan. The amount taken as a compulsory loan would be relatively small in high-taxing states, and relatively large in low-taxing states.[37]

The Treasurer, now Arthur Fadden, was said to have been impressed with Giblin's scheme but considered that it was too late to be introduced in the 1940/41 financial year.[38]

Therefore, the F&E was left with the problem of how to raise taxation upon lower incomes without creating political difficulties. It was clear that the magnitude of the resources needed for the war effort could not be realised simply by taxing upper and middle incomes; it would have to reach down to lower incomes. But the Labor Party and its trade union affiliates were opposed to any such attempt. The decision to introduce child endowment, suggested initially by Dick Downing, who worked for Copland in the Office of the Economic Consultant to the Prime Minister, and supported strongly by Wilson, was intended in part to dampen criticism from low-income groups.

Giblin's contribution to the impasse was to draft a major paper, 'Prospects for 1941–42', in which he suggested how 'the political opposition' to expanding taxation 'could be overcome'. He suggested, as a bargaining strategy, even heavier taxation on high incomes; a 90 per cent excess profits tax; and a levy on wealth of perhaps $3\frac{1}{2}$ per cent. The committee gave its tentative approval to each of these recommendations, going further on excess profits tax (to 100 per cent), and less on the wealth tax (no more than two per cent a year).[39]

Shortly after submitting his paper to the F&E, Giblin wrote to Fadden saying that the 'key to the financial situation is taxation. With taxation equitably distributed over all incomes, there is a fair chance of avoiding any drastic all-round rationing control.' He acknowledged that, while there was likely to

---

[36] In a note to the Treasurer, Giblin said that the committee favoured the uniform income tax idea on equity grounds, but recognised that it would be difficult politically, and therefore it might not be possible to implement (NAA LFG 30 June 1941, 'Taxation and post-war credits', CP 184/5/23[2]).

[37] NAA LFG 7 October 1940, 'War finance at 5.10.40', CP 5/1/Bundle XV11, File CCLX111.

[38] NAA AWF to Cabinet, 'Can prices be controlled?', CP 184/8/13.1

[39] AWM LFG 18 and 19 February 1941, 'Prospects for 1941/42', SJB 117.

be some immediate hostility from low-income groups to any proposal for increased taxation, he did not believe that it would prove to be very deep. 'It could give way', he said, 'to a good statement of the case for taxation, addressed to them by their leaders. But it must be their leaders who do the job.' He added that 'it is largely regarded as good Labor policy to resist'. Giblin proposed that Labor's representatives on the Advisory War Council be counselled. [40]

There was a drift back in interest to a compulsory loan. In June 1941, Giblin prepared a detailed paper on a system of post-war credits. What Giblin now proposed was a 'National Contribution', from which Commonwealth and state income taxes would be deducted, leaving a special war contribution in the form of a compulsory loan, for which a post-war credit would be given. [41]

It was clear that by July 1941 a crisis in war finance had been reached. Fadden wrote to Menzies on 1 July 1941 saying that 'we face the biggest budget problem in the history of the Commonwealth'. [42]

In the Budget of September 1941 the government proposed a borrowing requirement of £122m, compared with £60m the previous year. It was acknowledged that borrowing of this magnitude would be difficult to achieve. In the budget Fadden announced the government's intention to introduce a compulsory loan scheme along similar lines to that proposed by Giblin (and similar to the one that Keynes had proposed in the United Kingdom). A 'National Contribution' was to be assessed on every income earned in Australia (exempting incomes below £100); after the deduction of state and Commonwealth income taxes, the remainder was to be collected as a compulsory loan (or as post-war credits), which would attract an interest rate of two per cent a year, to be repaid after the war. [43]

In the Budget of September 1941 the influence of Giblin and the F&E committee had reached its high watermark.

Labor opposed the budget, largely because of the National Contribution, on the grounds that low-income groups were to be taxed and because the lighter-taxing states would be the greatest beneficiaries of the post-war credits. The Opposition successfully moved a motion of no confidence in the budget and it was defeated in House of Representatives on 3 October 1941 when two independent members of the parliament crossed the floor and voted with Labor to defeat the budget.

---

[40] NAA LFG to AWF n/d but March 1941, CP 13/1, C File LXV.

[41] NAA LFG 28 May 1941, 'Restriction of public expenditure. The immediate problem', CP 184/5/23(2).

[42] NAA AWF to RGM, July 1941, 571/1/41/2868.

[43] It was announced also that 20 per cent of company depreciation funds would be collected as a compulsory loan.

The government resigned, and a Labor Government took office the same day. Curtin was sworn into office as Prime Minister with Chifley as Treasurer.

The inability to implement a politically acceptable policy of war finance was the principal reason for the failure of the Menzies and Fadden Governments. The dependence of the government on two independent members of the House of Representatives encouraged a degree of timidity in the formulation and application of economic policy, and hesitation over the advice of the F&E. In particular, the resort to taxation was clearly inadequate, given the extent to which resources had to be transferred from civilian to war activities in conditions of full employment. Menzies and Fadden were also unable to convince the states of the need to transfer some of their taxing powers (particularly in the field of income tax) to the Commonwealth; and they took a somewhat pusillanimous attitude toward the credit expansion of the private trading banks. Labor attacked the Menzies and Fadden Governments unmercifully on the grounds that their financial and economic policies – including the compulsory loan – were inequitable.

Controls

With the arrival of the Labor Government a marked shift in economic policy began, as market-oriented instruments of policy were replaced by direct controls. The new Treasurer, J. B. Chifley, quickly introduced a revised budget (on 29 October 1941) to replace the one that had been presented by Fadden: the National Contribution was jettisoned; heavier taxation was imposed on higher-income groups; and taxation was reduced on lower incomes.

With the entry of Japan into the war it was clear that a significant increase in taxation and voluntary borrowing from the public would be required. Shortly after the beginning of the war Giblin had predicted an annual war expenditure of about £100m in current prices, with 'the possibility but not probability of it rising to £200m per annum (still at present prices) at a later period of the war.' But after Pearl Harbour this was utterly outmoded. Defence spending was, in fact, to reach £500m, and absorb not one-fourth of GDP, but about 40 per cent of it. Some increases in taxation were introduced, and loan programs of a considerably greater scale than hitherto entertained were foreshadowed. But these policies failed to match the real resources that were needed to meet the demands of the armed services and war industries, such as munitions. [44]

By the early months of 1942, prices were beginning to accelerate at a rapid rate. As a consequence, on 10 February 1942 Curtin announced a dramatic change of economic policy. A National Economic Plan was to be introduced based on a

---

[44] NAA LFG 26 October 1939, 'War finance', 1968/391/139.

powerful set of direct controls, which were to be promulgated under the National Security (Economic Organisation) Regulations.

The principal elements of the plan were the pegging of wages and profits; private spending was to be curtailed by direct controls on production, consumption and trade; price rises were to be reduced by tighter price controls; profit margins were to be squeezed; and spending by state governments was to be limited by the introduction of a uniform system of income taxation. The rationing of basic consumer goods was introduced from the middle of 1942. The administration of capital issues control similarly underwent a transformation aimed at tightening non-essential private investment. Credit creation was also used, on the basis of Labor's claims that reserves of labour still existed, but stringent National Security (Wartime Banking Control) Regulations were introduced. These tightened government control of the private banks and required increases in bank assets from a designated date (August 1941) to be lodged with the Commonwealth Bank 'as special deposits', both as a means of controlling credit expansion and limiting bank profits.

This system of direct controls marked a decisive shift in the nature of Australian economic policy. The war economy henceforth was shaped in large measure by direct controls and other policies associated with the National Economic Plan. The F&E and the Treasury were now to take back seats as new government agencies, such as War Organisation of Industry, the Production Executive and the Manpower Directorate took the leading roles as providers of policy advice.

Even so, the F&E continued to advise the government on war finance after October 1941. Giblin remained in 'daily touch' with Chifley, the Treasurer (Day 2001, p. 148), including on the subject of uniform taxation. 'Luckily I have a thoroughly good understanding with Curtin, and also Chifley', Giblin told Keynes on Labor's accession. 'But they have some very difficult colleagues, and their independent "majority" is quite crazy on finance'.[45] Giblin noted with alarm the burgeoning of central bank credit following the introduction of the National Economic Plan. The F&E – particularly Giblin – warned the government that suppressed inflation was building up for the post-war era, as extensive direct controls placed a lid on inflationary pressures. But the government's requirements shifted to the efficient 'administration' of the war economy and planning for post-war reconstruction, and new administrative agencies began to recruit their own economists. The need for the F&E's expertise was reduced. Its influence diminished, and it scarcely met after 1942.[46]

---

[45] PRO LFG T236/548 5/10/41.

[46] NAA LFG n/d but mid-1942, 'Excess spending power: present and future', 571/1/42/2568 Pt 1. NAA LGM 31 August 1942, 'The budget and inflation', CP 6/2B, File XXV.

'The ordeal of 42'

With the advent of the Labor Government, 'The time had come, some thought, for ousting [Essington] Lewis' (Blainey 1971). Instead, it was Brigden who was ousted.

The key figure in this manoeuvre was Norman Makin, now forgotten, but then a senior member of the Labor government.[47] When the ALP formed government in 1941, Curtin had offered him the department of Social Services and Repatriation, a backwater position in wartime. Upon Makin's protest, Curtin instead made him Minister for the Navy, and Minister for Munitions, positions he held throughout the war.

The new minister quickly felt a painful lack of rapport with the permanent head, J. B. Brigden. Makin was a Methodist preacher. He was emphatic and glib. Brigden was the economist and lawyer. He was 'subtle', 'reticent' and 'pertinacious'.

Makin has told his side of the story several times. The first occasion came in 1961 in his collection of cameo memoirs, *Federal Labor leaders*:

> It was quite evident that the start in the expanded war effort was all too long delayed ... The blame could not be attached to executives or workmen ... Two things were principally responsible for this state of affairs, firstly, the hesitation with which policy decisions were made and, secondly, the unsatisfactory set up in the administration of the Munitions Department by having an Economist as the Head of staff ... The Economist was a man of high integrity, and likeable, but totally unable to administer a Department like that of Munitions. (Makin 1961, p. 114).

On this occasion Brigden is spared identification. He is 'The Economist'. And he is 'totally unable to administer a department'.

By the time of a 1974 interview of Makin, the Economist has become Professor Brigden:

> When I came to Munitions, I found that Professor Brigden, an economist, was the head of a department for the manufacturing of munitions and he knew nothing whatever about any of the procedures ... A genial, kindly, a gracious man but totally unfitted for the position of head of a Munitions Department. Even in peacetime, I would never have thought of appointing him to that position. So the first thing I've got to do is to

---

[47] Norman Makin (1889–1982), MP for the South Australian seat of Hindmarsh since 1919, the Speaker in the Scullin Labor Government, candidate for ALP leadership, member of the Advisory War Council.

make a change in the head of the Department of Munitions, if we are to get production, we've got to do that because I'm satisfied that the present head is bottlenecking all of the things that are requiring to get decisions upon, and unfortunately delays are taking place that we cannot afford to have at this time, and therefore we've got to make a change … and I must ask for a change in the head of my department. (Makin 1974).

Brigden is now 'bottlenecking'.

In his posthumously produced *Memoirs* of 1982 Makin repeats the story, but adds a psychological dimension.

> Almost immediately upon examining the set-up of the Munitions Department, I became convinced that a change in the Head of Department was essential. Professor J. B. Brigden was a man of excellent personal qualifications as an Economist, a delightful and pleasing man in his staff relationships, but totally out of place in a technical department. He was, I feel sure, conscious of this. The second in charge, Mr J. K. Jenson … was one of the brilliant minds of the Department. Professor Brigden knew this, and was no doubt anxious to counter with extreme caution in all decisions. This had the effect of creating delays and, at times, indecision … I was therefore determined that a change was essential if a free flow of decision making was to be possible. (Makin 1982, p. 80).

The tale has thickened; a vein of jealousy has been added to Brigden's incapacity. Brigden wished to thwart the 'brilliant mind' of his deputy J.K. Jensen.

Makin's suggestion of a general incapacity may be dismissed. Essington Lewis, praised by Makin, wrote of Brigden's role in the Department:

> His ripe experience as an administrator was of the greatest value in placing the new and complex organisation upon a satisfactory basis … I shall always be grateful to him for relieving me of all responsibility for political matters arising out of the Department's activities, and for shielding me from the minor tribulations inseparable from the Public Service Act. (Quoted in Wilson 1951).

Jensen, too, had explicitly defended Brigden on this score (Ross 1995).

The accusation of 'bottlenecking' can also be dismissed. Any lack of momentum can be traced to political leadership. In 1973 Melville recalled Menzies' wartime prime-ministership:

> We had a great deal of difficulty in getting decisions from Menzies. He would study his brief over a very long time. Whether he studied it, I'm never sure, but at any rate it remained on his desk for a very long time, and he would discuss the matter in cabinet, and we just didn't get decisions. Things went very slowly. (Melville 1973).

In fact, it was Brigden who did some unplugging of bottlenecks created by political vacillation. A case in point was a decision over investment in railways to facilitate the transport of military hardware. The overwhelming case in favour of this investment was met with incomprehension and indecision. Melville again:

> Finally, Brigden, who was a pretty choleric sort of man, I believe burst in on the meeting of the Defence Council[48] and we did finally get approval.

But if Brigden was neither bottlenecking nor maladministering, why was he eliminated? Political circumstances created a context favourable to it. The Labor Party had campaigned throughout 1941 against the lack of energy in the government's prosecution of the war. Makin was now minister for munitions when munitions were in short supply in the face of a Japanese invasion. He had to be seen to be doing something. 'Off with his head!' But whose head? Not Jensen's. He had Chifley's backing. Lewis was one obvious target. But Brigden made a better scapegoat. Brigden was something of a marked man.

There was also evidently a personal tension. Makin's posy of compliments – 'high integrity, likeable, genial, kindly gracious, delightful, pleasing' – appears to be the bouquet laid sanctimoniously by the assailant on the victim's graveside. He is more truthful when he noted waspishly later in an interview that, having removed Brigden, the two were to cross paths once more, in Washington: 'I put up again with him when I became Ambassador, you see'.

But how to purge the Department of him? 'Permanent Heads' were meant to be permanent. A suitable means of elimination would be some call of patriotic duty to another front. At this point Brigden's old boss Richard Casey, now Minister to the United States, came unwittingly and serendipitously into service.

Since April 1941 Casey had been imploring the appointment to the Legation in Washington of a 'first-class economist', 'as early as possible' – 'a high-grade professional economist with prestige in his profession, to follow along, to argue and dispute'. Menzies took the counsel of Giblin, Copland and Wilson on this matter, who variously proposed Gerald Firth, John La Nauze and Keith Isles, Roland Wilson's old classmate and sparring partner. Casey took these names to Keynes, but their lack of seniority left Casey dissatisfied. Giblin then proposed Coombs, 'who has been a tower of strength at the Treasury since September 1939', but Chifley refused to let him go. Wilson, observed Giblin, 'has been badly over-worked, at a pace that cannot be safely continued', and therefore expressed the hope that his release for Washington was possible. 'I feel it terribly

---

[48] The membership of the Defence Council generally consists of the Minister for Defence, the Secretary of the Department of Defence, the Chief of the Defence Force and the three service chiefs.

important to have the best possible representation in America, if anything is to be saved from the impending wreck' (NAA LFG to Casey, 10 October 1941).

But the elimination of Bridgen presented itself as a convenient means to finally meet Casey's repeated 'very persistent' request for an economist 'of standing with wide knowledge of Australia and experience of the business of government'.

The blow was crushing to Brigden, and seemingly unexpected. One of the very few surviving personal letters of Brigden conveys his state of mind on the eve of his embarkation for the United States.

> Sunday 11.1.42
>
> Dear Leslie [49]
>
> Today is a pause before my ship's delayed departure tomorrow. How sudden things happen. I really thought that Wilson or someone else would go to Washington, but the PM and govt would have no one else. It was a blow of course …
>
> Now and then I'll speak a small prayer for you and yours, until the ordeal of 42 passes. (NAA JBB).

'He arrived [in Washington]', Wilson later recalled, a sick and exhausted man' (Wilson 1951).

The full employment approach

Brigden's destination – Washington – reflected the widening of the war.

During the remaining years of the Second World War the four devoted themselves to trying to shape as best they could the architecture of post-war international economic arrangements. In particular, they sought an international agreement to promote full-employment in the post-war period.

The immediate occasion of this struggle lay in the seemingly arcane matter of Article VII of the 'Mutual Aid Agreement'. This agreement amounted to a commitment by the United States to assist other allied powers economically. The United States was determined that this aid be conditional on the beneficiary country removing discrimination against its imports in the post-war period. The substance of Article VII was the 'consideration', whereby Britain pledged itself to support the elimination of impediments to world trade in return for American military aid through the process of Lend-Lease. The Empire Preferences agreed at Ottawa in 1932 appeared to be the most irksome to the Americans. Keynes had spent many months in the United States during the second half of 1941 negotiating with his American counterparts on the conditions that Britain and other allied countries would have to meet in return for Lend-Lease.

---

[49] Leslie Melville? Possibly.

Late in 1941 the Inter-departmental Committee on Economic Relations (the ICER) was established to formulate an Australian response to the American conditions. The F&E economists, under Giblin's direction, concluded that Australia should support the American proposals, since the alternative to international economic cooperation – comprehensive restrictions on the international flow of goods, services and capital – would constitute a greater threat to Australia's post-war prosperity than the non-discriminatory, multilateral approach that was foreshadowed in Article VII. This was the position adopted by the ICER in its recommendations to the government early in 1942.

By the middle of 1942, detailed work had commenced to identify what the signing of Article VII might mean for Australia. Again, the F&E took the initiative. And once more it was Giblin who commenced discussion. He prepared recommendations that were distributed to ministers in August.

The essence of Giblin's report was a description of the difficulties associated with reconciling internal and external balance, when domestic policy was directed at maintaining high levels of aggregate demand. At the same time Australia was expected to fulfil its commitments in relation to Article VII. These commitments called for the dismantling of the Empire trade preferences and a general relaxation in trade, capital and exchange controls. Were Australia to adopt unilaterally a policy of full employment, imports would rise as domestic demand expanded, and exports would decline as local costs rose and resources flowed out of export industries into those catering to domestic demand. Consequently, Australia's international economic policy should be to promote the full employment objective amongst the major world powers, above all, the United States. If countries such as the United States failed to pursue expansionary domestic policies, then Australia would have a good case for the adoption of restrictive international policies, such as import and exchange controls and exchange rate adjustment, as a means to preserve full employment at home.

Giblin's report proposed that nations should enter into international agreements committing them to full employment. The agreements were to contain specific targets in relation to employment and unemployment, and penalties (import controls, exchange controls, devaluation, and the like) were to be imposed if the commitments were not met. Integral to these recommendations was the argument, devised by Firth and taken up by Giblin, Coombs and Melville, that the welfare gain arising from free trade was likely to be minor compared with the benefits that would arise from full employment. More especially, and in contrast to the view adopted by American officials, the report highlighted the claim that it would be difficult to achieve free trade unless domestic full employment was maintained (the American view, in contrast, was the exact reverse, that free trade would lead to full employment). [50]

Giblin, strongly supported by Melville and Coombs, was responsible for formulating the 'positive approach', or the 'full employment approach'. In a lecture he gave in mid-1943, Giblin set out the basis of the 'positive approach' as follows:

> If we could get effective international agreement to keep up employment, we need not fear any external repercussions from ourselves pursuing a policy of maintaining employment at the highest level. If we cannot get agreement on this point and we maintain employment on a much higher level than other countries, then we shall probably be faced with a serious adverse balance of trade. If we were resolute to maintain employment and refuse deflation, we should have to cut down imports, either by direct restriction of imports, or indirectly by depreciations of the currency. Either way would be bad for us, and would tend to lower our standards of living. Besides, either way would invite retaliation from other countries and lead to a cumulative reduction in world trade, such as we got in the 1930s. (Giblin 1943, p. 20).

The 'positive approach' was clearly aimed at the United States, the most powerful economy in the world. If Australia could induce the Americans to maintain full employment in their domestic economy, there might be a good chance of avoiding an economic crisis of the kind experienced in the early 1930s. In his *Report on economic conditions in the United Kingdom, United States and Canada* to the government following his visit to these countries in 1944–45, Copland emphasised this point, declaring that the:

> … most significant influence determining general world economic prosperity will be the economic policy pursued by the United States. If that policy is one of high employment and increasing international investment, the total demand by the United States … will provide a basis for an expanding world economy and a general increase in the volume of international trade. (Copland 1945, p. 6).

Australian delegates to all of the major international conferences from 1943 onwards sought to have commitments to full employment inserted in international agreements. [51]

---

[50] NAA LFG 19 January 1943, 'Report on Australia's position in relation to article VII', CP 13/1/ii, File LXXXIII.

[51] The Food and Agriculture Conference at Hot Springs, Virginia, in May–June 1943, the International Labour Organisation Conference at Philadelphia in April 1944, the International Economic and Monetary Conference at Bretton Woods, New Hampshire in July 1944, the United Nations Conference

Roland Wilson had attended, as the sole Australian representative, the first international conference called to discuss post-war economic planning.[52] This was a conference of officials from the British Commonwealth and India held in London in October and November 1942. Wilson was expressly instructed by Curtin and Chifley not to raise the 'positive approach', on the grounds that it had not yet been approved by ministers. But it is possible that he raised the full employment approach unofficially with Keynes, who had taken him to Cambridge during the conference for a ceremony at the Marshall Library to mark the centenary of Alfred Marshall's birth. Giblin had briefed Keynes on Wilson: he was 'the man who has the most complete confidence of Chifley and Curtin' (KCLA LFG 3 October 1942).[53] He added: 'Wilson, I should say, on first contact is inwardly nervous, and apt to be frivolous or flippant, defensively'. Keynes was to write later to Giblin in glowing terms about Wilson's performance at the conference, saying that he 'took a prominent, indeed a leading part through all the discussions and played a major role in them with the greatest success. We had a great gathering of Whitehall officials, who came to feel the greatest respect for both his wisdom and for his pertinacity' (quoted in Cornish 2002, p. 24).

Wilson was fortunate to survive the return journey. 'Dr Wilson spent some time sitting on a reef off the coast of Fiji, clutching his dispatch case and his documents'. One engine of his plane 'had caught fire and the aircraft had landed rather hazardously in shallow water on the reef, where the offending engine immediately dropped off' (Hasluck 1954, p. 144).

He eventually arrived in Sydney feeling sceptical about the possibility of the United States endorsing an international treaty that would tie its hands in relation to domestic economic policy. He considered, correctly as it turned out, that it was most unlikely that the United States would ever agree to surrender its sovereignty in this way. Even if the United States Government were persuaded to do so, he doubted that any agreement of this nature would be ratified by the United States Senate. Wilson reported to the F&E that, while the Atlantic Charter and Article VII entailed general commitments to expansionary economic policies after the war, he very much doubted that the United States would sign an agreement that bound itself to particular domestic policies. Giblin, Melville and Coombs were more optimistic.[54]

---

at San Francisco in April–June 1945, and the various international trade conferences, leading up to the Havana Conference held between November 1947 and April 1948.

[52] Giblin: 'I have been pressing that Wilson be sent as he is in every way our best representative and I am very pleased it has come off' (KCLA LFG 3 October 1942 KCL/A).

[53] KC LA/56.

[54] NAA RW, 'Post-war economic talks, London, October–November 1942', A989/43/735/56/1.

The first international arena in which the 'positive approach' was aired was the Food and Agricultural Conference at Hot Springs in June 1943 (Hasluck 1980, p. 9). This conference was a somewhat Wavian affair. Its provenance was mysterious, and seemingly lay in the fact that President Roosevelt 'was anxious to have a conference although he found it hard to know what to have a conference about' (Brigden 1948). The topic of food was chosen as suitably uncontroversial. 600 delegates duly arrived at Hot Springs, 'a luxurious spa on the border of West Virginia', and were surrounded by 200 military police. The Ethiopian delegate came bearing three boxes of gold. Iraq was represented by a 'judge' from Utah.

The Australian delegates were Brigden and Coombs. ('No delegate excelled Coombs in exposition of the practical', Brigden reported). The peg on which to hang their advocacy of the full-employment approach centred on discussions over the future International Monetary Fund (IMF). Brigden pushed the Australian position that a pledge to maintain full employment be incorporated into the Fund's articles.

> The proposal is for a kind of watch dog, to protect us all. The Fund is the dog. But we are not sure that the dog … may not bite the children. You [the US] know that the dog won't bite us, but does the dog know … we ask that the full employment criterion be stated.

But the climax of the 'full employment approach' came not with the creation of the IMF at Bretton Woods but with the establishment of the United Nations at San Francisco. In long-running infighting at San Francisco in 1945 the delegates finally agreed to insert a 'pledge' to 'joint action' to achieve 'full-employment' into the UN's Charter. In repeated sub-committee sorties Wilson and Brigden maintained the drive for the inclusion of the full-employment pledge in the face of the rearguard action by the United States delegation.

That both Wilson and Brigden were at San Francisco arose from the fact that the Australian delegation was a 'freak show of a calf with two heads' (Hasluck 1980, p. 191). It had two principals: the Deputy Prime Minister, Frank Forde, and the External Affairs Minister, H. V. Evatt. Evatt took a collection of negotiators/advisors from his Department, including Brigden. Forde declared to Curtin that he needed 'a first class brain' at San Francisco, and Wilson was supplied (Hasluck 1980, p. 153). The double-headed delegation stayed at the Sir Francis Drake Hotel: Forde's half on the 10th floor and Evatt's on the 17th. (Hasluck 1980, p. 153). They were there for the next 10 weeks, working 80 hours a week.

Before the conference, Chifley as Treasurer had briefed Wilson to be 'in no doubt' of the importance of 'full employment' in the Charter. In San Francisco, Brigden 'backed Wilson strongly' on this (Crisp 1965, p. 8). Brigden argued that 'the time and circumstances were ripe to push the full-employment approach forward'. Roosevelt's Fourth Inaugural Addresshad promoted full employment, and he (Brigden) 'felt that three years of Australian propaganda in conference after conference had not been without effect' (Crisp 1965, p. 8).

Wilson proposed the Australian delegation present the drafting committee these words:

> PLEDGE:
>
> Each member of the United Nations pledges itself to take, singly and in concert with other members, such measures as may be necessary and practicable to secure for its own people and the people of other lands –
>
> (a) economic advancement and improved living standards
>
> (b) useful employment or work for all who seek it, at fair wages or returns under conditions which will satisfy the conscience of mankind
>
> (c) social security
>
> (d) the maintenance of an expanding world economy free from disturbing fluctuations. (Crisp 1965, pp. 8–9).

Evatt took Wilson's carefully worded draft and reduced it to a more speech-like phraseology:

> All members of the United Nations pledge themselves to take action both national and international for the purpose of securing for all people, including their own, improved labour standards, economic advancement, social security and employment for all who seek it. (Crisp 1965, p. 10).

Peculiar, unstable, and partly crazed, Evatt was sometimes liked, sometimes hated. But 'Wilson himself was better equipped to handle a difficult minister than any minister was equipped to handle him. Wilson was quietly the master' (Hasluck 1980, p. 193). He was indeed 'the one public servant that could not be stared down by Evatt' (Hudson 1993, p. 128). Wilson redrafted Evatt's phrasing as: 'All members pledge themselves to take separate and joint action and to cooperate with the organisation, and with each other, to achieve these purposes' (Crisp 1965, p. 14).

But these evolutions deliberately let pass the sticking point - the word 'pledge'. This word seemed to irk the US delegation. Perhaps its aversion was rooted in the fact that 'pledge' - unlike 'to undertake' (that is, 'to take upon oneself') - can be synonymous with 'vow' and 'oath'.

Figure 9.2. Wilson at the time of the United Nations San Francisco conference

Whatever the case, the dispute was not treated casually. John Foster Dulles warned Wilson that to insist on a pledge would wreck the charter (Crisp 1965, p. 16). Dulles appeared with Nelson Rockerfeller, the Assistant Secretary of State for Latin America, and gave 'two speeches with overtones and even explicit statements highly offensive to Australia and not all strictly true. His manner and much of the substance of his speech were overbearing and even offensive in his overweening assertions of American superiority in wisdom and virtue ... Wilson maintained perfect control of himself and in a cold, factual comment, once again insisted that the American proposal meant changes of substance'. This same witness recalled that one of his 'most vivid conference memories is of the swollen, pulsing veins on Roland Wilson's neck and temple as he strove to maintain composure during Dulles' intemperate outburst'(Crisp 1965, p. 16).

Dulles had the relevant committee reverse its earlier approval of Wilson's draft. Wilson refused to recognise the legitimacy of this procedure. Ultimately, it was Wilson's doggedness that triumphed over Dulles' bluster. The relevant article finally appeared in the Charter barely different from the one Wilson had drafted on May 22, and with the word 'pledge' intact.

> Article 55
>
> [...] the Organisation shall promote: (a) higher standards of living, full employment, and conditions of economic and social progress [...]
>
> Article 56
>
> All members pledge themselves to take separate and joint action in cooperation with the Organisation, to achieve these purposes set forth in Article 55. (Crisp 1965, p. 18).

The 'pertinacity' of Wilson that Keynes had noted in London in 1942 had been discovered by Dulles in 1945. [55]

---

[55] Evatt claimed Article 56 as his triumph. Curiously enough, so did the American delegate, Deane Gildersleeve (Crisp 1965, p. 18).

10. The last ridge

'The curious thing is that in my mind he was so "indestructible" that his physical passing makes little difference.'
Ronald Wilson

Introduction

The Second World War did not bring the four the culmination of their careers that might have been hoped or expected. At the war's close three were over 50 years old, and perhaps none would have been buoyed by any marked sense of the completeness of their accomplishments. Brigden had been dismissed from the inner counsels of government not long after he reached them. Copland's ambition for a preeminent place in academia had been crushed in 1938, and he had spent the war in a government position more imposing than powerful. In 1946 Wilson was returned to the position he had first been awarded 10 years before – Treasury 'adviser' and Commonwealth Statistician – to endure, heavy with expectation, a 'seat of government' that brought him to despair. And Giblin? Now an old man, in bad health – where was his monument? He had produced a profusion of reports, pamphlets, lectures, reviews, columns. But nothing more.

For Giblin it was, obviously, the last act, the last stage of the ascent. But it was an ascent which he was to climb until the last moment, and make his most memorable. In the same years, Copland's academic aspirations were to be handsomely consummated, and Wilson was to achieve his own acme of ambition.

These accomplishments were realised amidst, and coloured by, the contradictions of post-war Australia: an unexpected prosperity co-existent with vexatious shortages and accelerating inflation; and full-employment concurrent with bitter economic tensions. But it was a third incongruity that most specifically absorbed the four: the restoration of fundamental military security coincident with a renewed anxiety about Australia's 'independence'. This incongruity was seen sharpest in the controversies over Australia's place in the post-war international economic order, and it was there that the four for the last time as a group offered their guidance.

The road to Savannah

With the advent of peace Australia found itself excluded from the leading vehicle of economic cooperation of the post-war world: the International Monetary Fund. It had been excluded by its own choice – its own hesitant choice. For the next two years a decision to join or not join the Fund foundered on divisions within the Chifley Labor Government. The four, from Canberra, Washington,

New York and Chunking,[1] added their wary approval to voices supporting joining.

The current of hostility to the Fund that the four sought to moderate was impelled by three considerations.

First, it was widely held that the success of full-employment policies would be obstructed by a commitment to rigidly fixing the value of the Australian pound (except in the face of 'fundamental disequilibrium'), as membership of the IMF would require.

Secondly, any commitment to a financial agreement triggered unpleasant associations on the Left. 'To many Labor stalwarts it smelt of international financiers, Wall Street, 'the Money Power' – the ultimate forces of capitalistic evil which Labor had felt itself to be fighting down the years' (Crisp 1960, p. 201). This resonance provoked crazed responses from maverick MPs, Eddie Ward and Jack Lang.[2]

Finally, the treaty brought out tensions between economic autonomy and economic internationalism; or 'independence versus dependence' as nationalists would put it.

The four were not immune to the tug of the first and last of these three, and during the war they had sought, as supporters of the Australian Government's policy, to obtain a more acceptable agreement.

During the war the four – like other Australian policy-makers and advisors – had more sympathy with Keynes' Clearing Union than the Stabilisation Fund proposal of the US Treasury. Keynes' plan was an attempt to contrive a system of stable rates that made unnecessary the deflationary policies that a commitment to fixed exchange rates had formerly entailed. It essentially amounted to granting a large pool of credit to deficit countries, thus giving these countries room to pursue full-employment policies while avoiding balance of payments crises. The plan manifested a concern to avoid full employment being sacrificed for the sake of maintaining fixed exchange rates. This sentiment was one that the four strongly shared.

---

[1] Until 1947 Giblin continued to occupy his room in the Treasury in Canberra, and was available to undertake special projects for the government. In 1946 Copland was appointed Minister to China, surely another diagonal move. His impatience for the Nationalist government and his trustful regard for Mao were evident. In August 1946 Copland 'wrote to Canberra describing the Nationalists as inept and incapable of pulling the country together … Early in 1951 Copland publicly reproved the Liberal Party for having failed to recognise China' (Albinski 1964, pp. 12, 68).

[2] Ward was Minister for Labour and National Service from 1941–43, the department of which Roland Wilson was Secretary.

The Assistant Secretary to the US Treasury, Harry Dexter White, advocated an alternative scheme, a Stabilisation Fund, which more strongly resembled the IMF that was to eventuate. The Stabilisation Fund emphasised exchange rate stability, rather than full employment, and consisted of a pool of a number of currencies and gold, accumulated from contributions by member nations, which would be deployed towards maintaining the relative values of member country currencies. As the US dollar would be pegged to gold, and as other currencies were pegged to the $US, the Stabilisation Fund would in some measure be a revival of the old gold standard, the difference being that each member country would be committing part of its gold and currency reserves to any other member country endeavouring to maintain its exchange rate.

As early as January of 1943, Wilson, fresh from consultations in the United Kingdom and the United States, had expressed his doubts to Curtin about the White scheme:

> One of the more important weaknesses of the American scheme is the fact that … the United States would be the greatest subscriber to any scheme of this kind, and even with what might be regarded as generous concessions in the matter of control, the United States would still remain the dominant partner. With South American voting strength added, other countries and even the British Empire as a unit would find it difficult to exercise much control over operations of the Fund. (DFATHP RW 18 January 1943).

Another 'unpalatable' feature of the US proposals, he reported, is 'the exalted position given to gold'. Finally, 'a country's rate of exchange would be much more under the control of the Stabilisation Fund than would be under the International Clearing Union'. As a consequence, Wilson believed that 'the most useful approach from our point of view appears to be to press the British proposals in regard to the International Clearing Union as strongly as possible'.

At the Hot Springs conference of May 1943 Brigden pressed the same warning against the restoration of a gold standard, and the same support for the Clearing Union. In Brigden's view (Brigden 1943b), the 'C[learing]U[nion] has a more vivid sense of the realities of the post-war world'. He explained: 'There must be an expansionist outlook, and some credit creation'. Predictably, Brigden was on guard against the 'dangers' of credit expansion. 'It will come somehow and it will be dangerous. It will come better if planned and controlled'. He also complained that the draft articles of the putative Fund gave its board no guidance on policy. White sought to deflect this criticism by promising that full employment would be mentioned in the Fund's preamble (Brigden 1943b, p. 2).

The United States had every wish to placate its allies in these discussions, but had no intention of conceding. Brigden was sensitive to how the American sense of resolution could shade into presumption.[3] In 'Discussions on the S[tabilisation] F[und]', he complained of the habit of the American negotiators to treat the US Congress 'as though it were recognised to be in fact a super-national authority. … Latin American countries and the Canadians accept it from habit. Europeans accept it with varying moods, from a state of chronic indignation among the Norwegians, to fatalistic resignation among the Continentals. The UK attitude is … quietly watchful for opportunities to escape the oppression' (Brigden 1943b, p. 1). He added that the Canadians 'never feel safe' with the United States. To H.V. Evatt, the Australian External Affairs Minister, he grumbled about the 'puppet states' (mainly Latin American) that voted according to the United States' say so. To his 'horror' this remark was passed on to White.[4]

Other Australian advisers – above all Melville – were also critical of the proposed Stabilisation Fund. Reinforced by this doubt, on 8 June 1944, Curtin told the Australian Legation in Washington that no ministers were to attend the crucial 'monetary conference' that was to be held at Bretton Woods in the first three weeks of July. Australia's presence was to be limited solely to officials. Curtin seems to have initially proposed that Brigden alone attend. In the event, four officials went: one from the Commonwealth Bank (Melville, the delegation leader), one from Treasury (F. H. Wheeler), one from the Department Post-War Reconstruction (A. H. Tange), plus 'in practice' Brigden. At the end of the conference the Australian delegation merely indicated its presence at the proceedings, and declined to sign the Articles of Agreement. A decision to join was put off.

For the next 20 months Brigden's task was to keep Australia at the card table, without ever playing its hand. In the hottest summer in Washington for 70 years, Brigden coped with shingles, and met Keynes for a 'depressing' discussion about Lend-Lease. This meeting was a reminder that Australia had more than one international alliance to cope with, and Brigden tried to convey to Keynes Australia's ambivalent attitude to any reliance on the traditional Imperial link:

> The answer may be 'Trust London'. Many of us whose spiritual homes are in England, are always inclined to do so. But we should be neglecting

---

[3] 'The outlook is perhaps no more infected with the mammon of self-righteousness than was that of mid-Victorian England. That it is much more insular is natural enough. It is natural, too, that the people should attribute their success to their own efforts rather than the gifts of nature, and an important virtue in their minds is that of minding their own business. The idea of international co-operation leaves them cold' (Brigden 1943a).

[4] 'One cannot but remark that there is more sense and stability in the American scene than appears on the surface … The Americans may be comically and excessively vain about their political and constitutional "way of life", as they are … But their way has historical roots and probably suits them better than any other' (Brigden 1943c, p. 3).

our duty if we did not at this stage question this policy. In another connection, we remember Singapore. We remember not only that Singapore fell, that the UK could do nothing to help Australia, and that we had to appeal to the USA (all that might have been inevitable), but that for many months previously we had been given repeated assurances. We poured out our men and our munitions on the basis of these assurances, and were left destitute. Now, and for similar reasons, we have poured our dollars into your pool. We want to trust the judgment behind the advice from London, but should we?[5]

By the time of the inaugural meeting of the IMF (and World Bank) in March 1946 (in Savannah, Georgia) Australia was still a non-member and still undecided. Nevertheless, the United States wished Australia to join, and invited Australia to send a delegation in any case. Melville and Brigden were the two Australians amongst the 600 delegates. It was at Savannah that there perished any lingering hopes that the Fund might bear Keynes' imprint. The US pushed through its wishes with barely a consoling concession. As Brigden told Giblin '... when Keynes went through the ordeal (to him) of Savannah he found it very distressing. The way in which the International Monetary Fund and [World] Bank were launched was anything but propitious and the whole atmosphere of the occasion must have been very disappointing indeed to Keynes' (RWA JBB to LFG, 21 November 1946). Keynes, to put the matter starkly, went home and died.[6]

Brigden, too, found much to 'dislike and disapprove' at Savannah. It confirmed his 'fears', and 'did nothing to reduce my general scepticism' (DFTHP JBB 8 April 1946). But where could Australia turn?, Brigden asked. The old imperial connection was derelict: 'whoever won the war', he wrote, 'it was not the British'. The imperial power was now itself the supplicant of the United States. The December 1945 loan agreement between the United Kingdom and the United States, imposed, in Brigden's judgement, 'preposterous burdens on the UK people'. Keynes, Brigden felt, did not deal 'frankly' with the British public.

And total isolation was not an advisable choice either, for 'we can defend ourselves better inside an organisation than outside'. He concluded: 'I see no real alternative to our membership of the Monetary Fund'.

From the discomfort of Chunking, Copland read the post-Savannah reports of Brigden and Melville and sent his own analysis to Chifley (DFTHP DBC 2 July 1946). He noted that the traumatic events of Australia in 1930 would seem to argue against joining the Fund; a fixed exchange rate had then prevented Australia from depreciating in the face of the slump in its export prices. The prospect of a the exchange rate being fixed – except in the case of 'fundamental

---

[5] JBB Australian Joint Copying Project T247/62 folio 15.

[6] Keynes died in April 1946 from a progressive heart condition that first manifested itself in 1937.

disequilibrium' – was intimidating. The spectre of 1930 hung heavily: 'it is ever present in the minds of all of us who have to consider the course Australia should pursue'. Copland and Giblin had, in the inter-war period, pressed hard against the gold standard, and to their minds it was – in attenuated form – being revived as a piece of 'post-war reconstruction'. Giblin was pessimistic about Australia's balance of payments if full employment was to prevail. How could a stable rate of exchange be preserved under full employment? [7]

But on the other hand, Copland suggested Australia would not receive a capital inflow from the UK in the post-war period, so its vulnerability to external shocks was reduced. There was no 'flow' to 'dry up'. Finally, Britain had abdicated from international leadership.

By 1946 the Chifley Government was quietly in favour of joining the IMF, but was still delaying this difficult decision. More than two years after Australia's initial decision to stay out, Brigden was instructed to go to the September 1946 meeting of the Fund and keep alive Australian membership (DFATHP G.P.N. Watts 12 September 1946). Not long after, on 31 December 1946, the official deadline (already once extended) for any joining country to be deemed an 'original' member passed. And Australia was still outside. Finally, on 5 March 1947, not quite three years after Bretton Woods, Chifley manoeuvred his party into agreeing to Australia's membership.

In the same month Wilson visited Washington, having been appointed to a United Nations committee of experts. [8] He discovered that Brigden was suffering high and uncontrollable blood pressure, which threatened a heart attack. He told Giblin that there was 'a probability of trouble increasing at a rate of 10 per cent per annum as long as he continues at his present work'. And Brigden was hesitating to take the obvious course of action. 'At one moment he contemplates retirement on the 30th June with his return spread out over a period of months ... and at other moments he mumbles somewhat incoherently about this, that and the other, which might keep [him] in the harness for another year or two.' Wilson hinted that Giblin should intervene. 'It would seem to me that somebody should make up his mind for him' (RWA RW 10 March 1947).

Whether Giblin made up Brigden's mind for him is not known. But Brigden resigned in the middle of 1947, with the intention of totally withdrawing from active life. He wrote to Eggleston: 'My intentions are to retire entirely and live quietly somewhere on the outskirts of Melbourne'. His last duty was to attend

---

[7] In 1946 Giblin asked student examinees at Canberra University College to give a 'critical account of the provisions against changes in exchange rates, contained in the Articles of Agreement in the International Monetary Fund'.

[8] In 1948 Wilson was appointed Chairman of the UN Employment Commission in place of Professor Ragnar Frisch, the first Nobel laureate in economics.

the annual meeting of the IMF in London in September 1947, *en route* to Australia. He noted with satisfaction: 'the F[oreign]O[ffice] has had to accept economics as a really serious influence' (NLA JBB 20 August 1947). Wilson filled Brigden's place as Financial Counsellor to the Australian Embassy in Washington, and as Australia's Alternate Executive Director at the International Monetary Fund and World Bank. [9]

On his return Brigden retreated into a retirement that was rarely interrupted. On one occasion he spoke to University of Melbourne students; a witness recalls him leaving the podium several times in mid-speech. The problems were physiological, not mental. But a watchful custody of the mind was a necessary part of the appropriate care of the body. Wilson later commented to Giblin: 'There was never any hope, following his return from the United States, that he would be able to do serious intellectual work without undue danger …' (RBA RW 2 November 1950). In Brigden's world the problems of the compost heap had replaced the problems of finance. How well he faced up to the empty spaces of an enforced retirement is not clear. Giblin made sure he visited whenever possible. He pressed Eilean to at least make a phone call; such a call, he said, was always a tonic to persons 'feeling they have been forgotten' (NLA LFG).

'Above all, to know the nature of things'

In 1948 Copland returned to Australia from Chunking. He was to now refight – and this time win – a contest for Vice-Chancellorship.

Ten years earlier Copland had been defeated in his pursuit of the Vice-Chancellorship of the University of Melbourne. This was a major trauma in an unquiet life.

A full-time Vice-Chancellor's position had only been created in 1933, and the first holder of the new office, Raymond Priestly, was presented with an institution that was 'small, woefully understaffed and financially starved' (Serle 1993, p. 19). Consequently a struggle between modernisers and the old guard began; or, alternatively, between 'professionals' versus 'amateurs'. The 'amateurs' were concentrated in Council. The Professorial Board was the base of the 'professionals'. And Copland was chairman of the Board. The outcome of this wrestling was undecided in 1938 when Priestly suddenly resigned over the refusal of the Victorian Government to fund his expansion proposals. [10]

---

[9] Brigden chaired the Contributions Committee of the United Nations, which was responsible for working out the contribution of each member state to the UN budget. Wilson was later to replace Brigden on this committee.

[10] Priestly recorded that 'the Coplands have been a tower of strength'. 'Copland is a strong man and we may not always see eye to eye in the future' (Priestly 2002, p. 23).

The choice of his replacement as vice-chancellor would constitute a test of strength of the rival parties. Copland was the choice of the modernisers. His victory seemed assured. He was already Acting Vice-Chancellor. And there were no other candidates: Clunies Ross and a swathe of economists, including J. B. Brigden, R. C. Mills and Herbert Heaton, were out of the running. Who else but Copland? But the vehemence of the 'amateurs' bred an 'anybody but Copland' movement. Sir Alan Newton, a foundation fellow of the Royal Australasian College of Surgeons, produced the name of John ('Jack') Medley.

The son of a Glasgow professor, Medley had obtained a First in 'Greats' at Oxford, where he befriended Ronald Knox and Harold Macmillan. In 1914 he was granted a grace and favour fellowship at Corpus Christi, Cambridge, on the expectation that he would expose 'the damnable heresies of Lowes Dickinson'. Instead he joined up. With the help of his cousin Viscountess Milner he secured a commission and spent the war in a series of staff jobs that a frontline solder might describe as 'cushy'. Demobbed and footloose, he accepted an uncle's offer of a commercial position in Australia. He slipped easily into the local social network (including the Melbourne Club), but his excursion into the antipodean world of business was miserable and abortive. Relief came in his appointment of Headmaster of Tudor House preparatory school, the alma mater of Patrick White and Malcolm Fraser.

Medley became, in K. H. Bailey's words, 'the favourite candidate of those who opposed Copland'. A bitter brawl ensued.

The Professorial Board unanimously carried a motion saying that university experience was a necessary qualification. (The Council replied that it was none of the Board's business.) The *Age* and the *Herald* were brought in to provide editorial support for Copland. Scuttlebutts were disposed of. 'Some of the reports of Copland's unpopularity in the business world were in particular cruelly damaging, and we spent a good deal of time gathering comments in rebuttal' (UMA KHB 4 June 1938). Sir Colin Fraser of Collins House mining declared his confidence in Copland. Priestly 'strongly advised' a vote for Copland over Medley (Priestley 2002, p. 430).

On 21 March 1938 there came the day when the 30 Council members were to make a decision. Priestly was 'convinced' that the vote would fall 19:10 in favour of Copland. K. H. Bailey, not long after, wrote that 'on a repeated scrutiny of the Council list I had come to the conclusion that the worst possible result would be 15 to 14 in Copland's favour' (UMA KHB 4 June 1938).

In the debate of Council Copland's supporters dismissed alleged 'rough angles and edges to his personality'; one spoke 'at very considerable length and some heat – unfortunate heat' (Priestly 2002, p. 436). One of them slighted Medley's personal capacity in insulting terms. For their part, the Medley faction's Sir James Darling – head of Geelong Grammar – announced: '[I] would rather choose a man who knew what a university ought to be than one who knew what this one actually was'.

The voting was by ballot. Bailey told Giblin: 'I myself was dumbfounded when the voting went 15 to 14 in favour of Medley'. [11]

The decision was, indeed, extraordinary. The candidate who was prolific in publication, dedicated in teaching, massively experienced in university administration, honoured by invitations to lecture at Cambridge and Harvard, and with extensive academic contacts (Keynes, Schumpeter, Einaudi), had been refused in favour of a prep school head who had not stepped inside a university in 24 years. As Medley put it: 'There can certainly never have been a previous case of a Headmaster of a Preparatory School being promoted to the Vice-Chancellorship of a University' (quoted in Serle 1993).

Copland's failure has been ascribed to his personality. Some economist colleagues allowed that he was 'difficult to work with' (Hytten 1971). But this is not entirely unusual among successful administrators. An even-handed historian later summarised several of Copland's positive personal qualities: 'He had the courage of a lion, inexhaustible energy, extraordinary patience with staff, and a better mind and more fineness of sentiment than he was usually credited with' (Foster and Varghese 1996).

It would be truer to say that Copland lost in a clash of social formations, which might be variously described as classics versus moderns; culture versus trade; gentlemen versus players; the man from New College, Oxford versus the man from the University of New Zealand, Timaru. [12]

Copland's supporter, Bailey, put what was at stake in more precise terms: 'It is tempting to explain the whole contest in terms of a struggle for power between the academic and lay members of Council'. Bailey explained the perversity of the outcome: 'In that view, it was Copland's own impressive record of achievement and his tried strength of character which caused his defeat'.

It has been suggested that Copland had only himself to blame. This was the view of the outgoing Vice-Chancellor, Priestly. 'If Copland had been clubbed by someone two months ago he would have awaked after one month to have found himself Vice Chancellor! Unfortunately, no one thought of doing it' (quoted in Serle 1993, p. 24). Priestley's claim may be true, and yet be irrelevant. A candidate may cause his own failure, without deserving to fail. The decision to prefer Medley over Copland was a marvel.

---

[11] Giblin had assumed the position was in Copland's lap. 'It looks as if DBC could be offered V-C, within the next week or two, if it has not been done already.'

[12] 'Copland was basically defeated by Council's old guard, hanging on to power … the bourgeois revolution failed' (Serle 1993).

Whether it was, in retrospect, a bad decision is another question. Medley did have 'what is called "charm"' (Bailey). With his charm he balmed and bound the torn flesh of the University. In the following decade his playful nonchalance proved a useful opiate to ideological aches that wracked the University. He is fondly remembered, especially by one section of political opinion (Cain and Hewitt 2004).

Copland assured Giblin that he had not been taken aback by his defeat. 'I feared that the enemy would triumph and would have withdrawn my name had I had my own way a few days before the meeting' (UMA DBC 29 March 1938). But Bailey believed Copland had been confident of victory. Bailey reported to Giblin (then in Cambridge): 'The whole thing has hit Copland exceedingly hard … His first reactions were quite magnificent, but he has not been able to maintain the nonchalance with which he met the first blow' (UMA KHB 4 June 1938). Copland felt so badly humiliated he did not attend Commencement, and 'his absence was very obvious' (Priestley 2002, p. 453). Copland wrote to Giblin: 'It is a thousand pities that you were not here and that your steadying hand is not available at the moment' (UMA DBC 19 March 1938).

To the alarm of his supporters, Copland began to plan a devastating counter-attack. 'He would have liked, himself, to see us all lead an attack, not only on the actual decision itself, but on the whole University administration, and what I think he had in mind was an eventual government enquiry which would result in the complete discredit of the existing regime' (UMA KHB 4 June 1938). Copland also planned to mimeograph copies of the proceedings of the selection committee and the relevant Council meeting, and send them to his professorial peers overseas.

Presumably thwarted in these desperate moves, Copland resolved to leave the University, and on 7 April 1938 cabled Giblin in Cambridge:

> Would Cambridge offer me position statistical economics 1000 pounds Sterling with possible College Fellowship (stop).

But Cambridge, it seemed, would not offer a position.

By his own choice, Copland's academic career appeared to be over. 'I feel my future here [in Australia] does not lie in academic work at all' (UMA DBC 29 March 1938). He took leave, and in 1940 presented his resignation. [13]

Copland's academic career was revived 10 years later by one of the quixotic visions of Australian 'nation building': the Australian National University.

The original plan for Canberra had called for a national university, seated at the foot of Black Mountain. In June 1926, with the translation of the 'seat of

---

[13] Copland was 'persuaded to withdraw' (Serle 1993, p. 46), but he remained on leave.

government' to Canberra imminent, a committee was gathered to report on a provision of university facilities for residents in the new capital. The committee was composed of what Giblin later described as stars of the first magnitude: Mungo Macallum (Challis Professor of Literature at Sydney University) and R. S. Wallace (Professor of English Language and Literature at the University of Melbourne, and Chief Film Censor). 'I was added as a twinkle', said Giblin. The report recommended the establishment of a small teaching university in Canberra, instructing introductory students in Arts, Law and Commerce. The proposal was in essence accepted. A modestly named University College crept silently and unnoticed into the world, an outpost of the University of Melbourne.

But with the advent of war a more sweeping project gripped imaginations. Australia would have a research university in her national capital, to enlighten her citizens and government.

Giblin was dead against the project (Giblin 1941). Where were the students for such a venture? He pointed out the slender student base of the existing University College. 'Canberra University College has no full time students', and the existing (part-time) enrolments were the equivalent of only 50–60 full-timers. And who would be the staff? Why should anyone want to come to Canberra?' Melbourne University, he observed, 'cannot now attract first-class people … You might offer 50 per cent more salary and still he won't come'. He disallowed any significance of the location of the proposed university. 'It is suggested that Canberra can contribute something. Canberra cannot contribute very much.' [14] And he disputed the viability of a pure research institution. 'In general, research is built around and grows out of a teaching organisation. Few things are better for research than stating difficulties for students and seeing how to overcome them. Research and teaching mutually help one another.'

He concluded that the project is 'extraordinarily difficult', 'pretty hopeless', 'verging on the impossible'. The 'policy of Canberra should not be at this time to push for a national university, but to go on developing the Canberra University College, expanding facilities, until the Govt. really means to make Canberra a go'. Giblin was much more attracted to prodding Cambridge to be more accommodating to Australian students seeking to study there.

But Giblin's nay-saying was without influence. An Act was passed in 1946. Four 'Advisers' – Howard Florey, Marcus Oliphant, Keith Hancock and Raymond Firth – were to advise the Interim Council on the selection of a Vice-Chancellor.

---

[14] There is a resemblance between Giblin's posture on the creation of the Australian National University, and Brigden's leadership, as a member of the Senate of the University of Queensland, of the opposition to the relocation of that University from the centre of Brisbane to the new St Lucia site (see Brigden 1937b). On this opposition the historian of the University comments: 'in a sense' the move to St Lucia did 'throw the University back a generation' (Thomis 1985, p. 166).

The clear favourite for the position of Vice-Chancellor had been H. C. Coombs, then Director-General of the Department of Postwar Reconstruction. But he was soon to become the Governor of the Commonwealth Bank, and Coombs declined the position.

It was David Rivett, a professorial colleague of Copland at Melbourne in the 1920s, who suggested Copland. This suggestion caused some consternation. 'Copland was known to everyone – and that was his major problem' (Foster and Varghese 1996). Copland's 'rather beefy, beery and in some ways brash outlook' was 'very uncongenial' to the 'Adviser' who had responsibility for economic studies, W. K. Hancock. Thanks to Hancock, the name of Copland became problematic to some who were not acquainted with Copland. Florey, who had never met Copland, acquired the belief that he was not a 'gentleman'. Did Copland perhaps recall that the bitterest opposition to his appointment as Vice-Chancellor in Melbourne had come from the medicos?

Coombs presented another difficulty for Copland. Coombs claimed to 'like' Copland, despite considering him 'pompous'. But he keenly backed his former boss at the Commonwealth Bank, Leslie Melville, for the vice-chancellorship. Unable to attend the critical meeting of Council, he cablegrammed the Registrar: 'When Question of Vice-Chancellor is discussed at December meeting glad if you would inform Council that I strongly urge appointment of Melville'.[15]

Was Melville now to play Medley? He was an infinitely more plausible candidate than the prep school head. But Council contained more strong allies of Copland (Rivett; Bailey; Eggleston) than adversaries. The Advisors might have the prestige, but they didn't have the power. Most of the Interim Council wanted Copland, and it was finally he who was offered the job. He accepted with alacrity. In March 1948 he commenced as first Vice-Chancellor of the Australian National University.

In retrospect, it is clear that Copland was the correct choice for the task of establishing a new university. His energy, entrepreneurial skills, and extensive contacts in academia, in business and government, both in Australia and worldwide, were to prove indispensable in the transformation of some acres of scrub and a few wooden huts into what was later to be recognised as Australia's pre-eminent university.[16]

---

[15] Giblin: 'Coombs ... is supposed to be very opposed to Copland's appointment' (NLA LFG 11 February 1948).

[16] Judgements on Copland's performance as Vice Chancellor are, inevitably, not unanimous. Sir Walter Crocker, Copland's first professorial colleague at the ANU, writes in his memoirs that 'despite some notable merits, including courage', Copland lacked a sense of quality, and had 'early lost interest' in the University (Crocker 1981, p. 174).

Figure 10.1. Copland (centre) in charge at the Australian National University.

Source: ANU: UA 2000/15, Envelope 1, CU457/9

Figure 10.2. Copland and Medley (at left) as friends on the Council of the Australian National University

Source: ANU: UA2000/15, Envelope 2, UN193/2

But the victory of Copland's appointment did not mean the end of his struggles. A new difficulty arose involving one of the advisers who had been doubtful of his appointment, Keith Hancock. The object of the struggle was the guiding philosophy of the new Research School of Social Sciences. A question arose which was absent in Physical Sciences or the Medical School. Would the inspiration to research be specific (and local), or universal (and global)? Briefly, would it be Australian or internationalist? It was not surprising that Copland and Hancock would fall on different sides of this question. Hancock was an Australian native who had been captivated by Oxford. He had assimilated himself to the English environment, and shed the Australian accent that so pained his ears. [17] He now shuddered at the blatancy of the patriotism in the name of the infant institution: the Australian National University. Localism was parochialism in Hancock's reckoning, and when it came to senior appointments, he would seek the best in the world.

These differences crystallised over the appointment of the inaugural chair in economics. Hancock insisted on making the appointment, and in order to keep control over it, refused Copland's wish to advertise the position. Instead he sounded out some of the best talents worldwide: Paul Samuelson, Nicholas Kaldor, A. E. G. Robinson, James Meade, Brian Reddaway. In reaction to Hancock's strategy, Eggleston in January 1949 complained to Copland that Hancock was 'trying to get brilliant specialists'. Copland replied, saying: 'I agree very fully with you that we do not want who you call an "all-star cast"'. Copland wished to reverse the 'bias' Hancock was imparting 'in favour of examining the Australian environment'.

There was, however, no call for anxiety about the arrival of an 'all-star cast' of 'brilliant specialists'. The best in the world had no interest in applying for the chair at the Australian National University. Indeed, on many occasions they had no interest in replying to Hancock's nudging letters. 'One of the disheartening things in this search is the number of people who are not sufficiently interested to answer letters' (ANUA KH to DBC 4 April 1949). Arthur Smithies told Hancock: 'I have been completely at a loss to think of anyone who would be willing to go to Australia and whom I would recommend' (quoted in ANUA WKH 21 March 1949). Copland must have been reminded of his trials in seeking an overseas economist to fill the Ritchie chair in 1928.

In the face of this failure, Copland did in 1948 what he had done in 1928: he turned to champion his own local candidate. 'Do you know Roland Wilson at

---

[17] 'I must confess that it is harder for Australians to speak well than it is for most other users of the English language, because, for some reason or other, Australians are shy of opening their mouths, which means their tongues have too little room for moving about and their vowels tend to get mixed up with one another' (Hancock 1954, p. 61).

all well?' he asked Hancock (ANUA DBC 18 November 1948). But Hancock was not interested. 'We discussed him here, but I doubted [the] wisdom of trying to steal from the Commonwealth Government one of its most senior servants' (ANUA WKH 27 November 1948). Copland sought to persuade Hancock that the Commonwealth Government would be no obstruction to Wilson's appointment. 'I had the opportunity of talking to the Prime Minister ... the Prime Minister said that if Wilson preferred to go over to the national University he would in no way oppose the move' (ANUA DBC 21 December 1948). Hancock procrastinated. 'There will be, I am afraid, a delay at the approach of Roland Wilson'. For Hancock had found a potential taker in G. D. MacDougall, now best remembered for empirical studies of comparative advantage. But there Hancock had no success either; MacDougall was angling for a Fellowship at Balliol.

The fundamental problem was that while Hancock knew well what he wanted, he was hopelessly unaware of what he could get.[18] This is illustrated by how he – unable to supply a professor – instead turned on Copland over the 'old point of domestic service'. Oblivious to the acute labour shortages in post-war Canberra, he chided Copland: 'It is no private fancy of my own to insist that good professors will not long continue to do their best work unless they are reinforced by good charwomen ... Experience convinces me that the charwoman is the bottleneck. Everywhere good people are frittering away their possibilities by doing many chores'. Copland responded patiently: 'You will be aware of the fact that a matter of this kind requires very careful handling under present circumstances' (ANUA DBC 18 August 1948).

So the approach to Wilson was finally made. It was the tenth offer made.[19] It was to receive the tenth rejection. Wilson was in low spirits at this time. He had written to Giblin in 1947: 'As to my future movements, God only knows at the present stage. There are a lot of possibilities ahead but none of them sound attractive as lazing away the days at Seven Mile Beach or some other sylvan retreat' (RWA RW 10 March 1947). Not long before the offer came Giblin told his wife that 'Roland [was] very gloomy'. 'Roland seems almost nauseated by Canberra – general inefficiency, short of all goods and services ... much worse than other capitals, much worse than Canberra in 1945. Everyone returning to Canberra from US – or even from the UK – feels it a drop into barbarism' (NLA

---

[18] Copland: 'I must say that I have found it extremely difficult to get Hancock's mind on the basic organisation of the School'.

[19] ANUA WKH 21 March 1949.

LFG 27 October 1949). 'I think he has also fallen out with most people or is suspicious of them'. [20]

With Wilson's rejection, there seemed nothing left. As Giblin said to Wilson: 'Copland has no alternative. He has a sticky job at present to get anything going' (RWA LFG 19 March 1949). It was perhaps Wilson who gave impetus to the notion of appointing Trevor Swan. Hancock granted it was 'even conceivable' that Swan 'might a few years hence be ready for a chair'. Swan was, in fact, appointed in June 1950. Hancock, in Giblin's summarising words, had not turned out to be an asset.

But Hancock managed to settle the scores. In his memoirs of 1954 he managed to convey to his readers that it was Copland's fault that Australia had forfeited his involvement in the ANU. Wilson dismissed the relevant passages as 'unwise, mischievous and childish' (Foster and Varghese 1996, p. 128). But the newspaper headlines shouted: 'Canberra Lost a Brilliant Brain': 'Who Froze Out This Brilliant Australian?'. [21] These journalist champions of academic standards need not have lamented: in 1957 Hancock returned to the ANU as director of the Research School of Social Sciences.

Economic policy

With the ANU human coordinates in place, Copland began to write copiously on the Australian economy, and became a regular public affairs commentator on ABC radio (Copland 1951).

By 1949, with several other economists, Copland had become disheartened by the direction of Australian economic policy, and with the failure of the government to deal with the manifold difficulties that faced it. These problems were to some degree the result of failures by the economists themselves. They had failed to identify the major problem that would beset the post-war economy: an excess of aggregate demand rather than a deficiency of aggregate demand, which they had predicted would recur once the immediate post-war reconstruction boom had run its course. The economists (with one or two exceptions) had also failed to emphasise sufficiently the problems of a full-employment economy, including wage pressures, price inflation, exchange rate instability and current account deficits.

---

[20] Copland, as noteful as ever of these things, pointed out that Wilson would take a salary cut in being professor.

[21] Sir Walter Crocker, a supporter of Hancock, recorded in an interview: 'He [Hancock] was one of the academics who do not quite grow up, they're sheltered from the hard cruel world in a way that people that go into business or even into the bureaucracy, let alone politics, have to face ... He was unfair to Copland' (Crocker 1991).

Worst of all, they had failed to educate the public – and ministers – of one of the fundamentals of the new (Keynesian) economics, that when excess demand manifested itself, it was necessary to curtail demand. The public welfare required tax increases, or reduced government expenditure, or higher interest rates, or the appreciation of the exchange rate, or some combination of these and other policies. This was a problem that the economists had first encountered in the early stages of the war when attempting to apply Keynes' policy blueprint for an economy experiencing excess demand. At this time the politicians had been reluctant to adopt measures involving steep rises in taxation and severe limitations on credit expansion. They were equally reluctant to do so in the late 1940s, with Chifley – now Prime Minister as well as Treasurer – hoping to stop the inflationary pressures by clinging to direct controls.

In a veritable flood of publications, most of them written after he returned to Canberra, Copland pursued this line of argument.[22] His critical stance on the problems besetting the economy, and his recommendations for change in economic policy, were robustly stated. There was an excess of aggregate demand in relation to aggregate supply. Domestic shortages, fuelled by a backlog of demand and an accumulation of savings manifested in high levels of liquid reserves held by the banking system, were being augmented by a strong demand for Australian exports. Supplies of coal, steel, electricity, transport and housing were in critical short supply, while output was booming for many inessential consumer goods. Australia, Copland asserted, had the hallmarks of a 'milk bar economy': basic industries, such as iron and steel, power and housing, were starved of resources, while consumer goods industries were attracting an over-abundance of essential resources to them.

According to Copland, there 'had been a tendency to concentrate on "full employment" as a goal, regardless of the costs and difficulties that may follow … Our economic thinking as well as our political outlook has been too much pre-occupied with depression psychology' (Copland 1948, pp. 42–3).[23] What he believed was required was a refocusing of economic policy, so that the emphasis was placed less on preserving aggregate demand for the purpose of achieving full employment (or, more accurately, over-full employment) and more on augmenting aggregate supply for the purpose of alleviating wage and price pressures. In later publications he developed his criticism of post-war economic policy further, arguing that direct controls, and government

---

[22] Several of Copland's articles were reprinted in Copland (1951).

[23] This small booklet is the first publication by an author employed by the ANU.

intervention generally, were adversely affecting productivity, and hence the capacity of the economy to generate increased supply. [24]

Much of the blame, he asserted, should be directed at the younger economists who had formulated Australia's full-employment policy and who had actively promoted it in Australia and overseas. They had been altogether too pessimistic about the state of the post-war economy, both in its international and domestic contexts. Rather than experiencing balance of payments difficulties, the excessive buoyancy of the Australian economy was a consequence of the vigorous demand for its exports.

The seeds of this disagreement lay in the White Paper on Full Employment in Australia (Commonwealth of Australia 1945). The authors of the official history of the war economy state that 'Coombs was not as closely involved as Giblin and others in the early formulation of the employment approach' (Butlin and Schedvin 1977, p. 648). But as the White Paper [25] progressed through its various drafts, Giblin's influence became fainter. He became apprehensive about the inflationary pressures that would arise from the increased wage bargaining strength of labour in conditions of full employment. He was much more optimistic than many others that buoyant levels of demand would continue for many years. Overall, he thought that somewhat greater attention should be placed in the White Paper on the problems of excess demand, rather than being devoted almost exclusively to problems associated with a deficiency of aggregate demand. He doubted whether, when demand was excessive, politicians would be able to discriminate sufficiently between different investment projects, and would probably allow the economy to run at dangerously high levels of domestic demand.

In the same vein, Copland was critical of the idea that public works could be turned on and off at short notice, as public works programs provided basic services. He believed that the White Paper should have given greater emphasis to the stabilisation of private investment expenditure, rather than public works, as the chief mechanism for stabilising aggregate demand.

---

[24] Appreciation of the Australian pound might serve to dampen the demand for the country's exports, but Copland did not favour this, since he thought it would adversely affect some of the weaker export industries, and cheaper imports would jeopardise the profitability of many manufacturing industries. Rather than appreciation, he preferred to see some of the exporters' income attracted into stabilisation funds, the proceeds of which could be released at times when activity was less exuberant.

[25] The principal draftsman in the early stages of the paper's preparation was a Giblin protégé, Gerald Firth, who had arrived from the United Kingdom to take the position of Ritchie Research Fellow at Melbourne University, a post funded from Giblin's Commonwealth Bank director's fees. In 1947 he was, with Giblin's benefaction, appointed Professor of Economics at the University of Tasmania.

Copland had lost sight of this difference of opinion during his venture to China. But four years after his return he told Melville: 'Since I have been back to Australia and have come more into contact with the economists, both official and non-official, I am greatly impressed by the fact that the generation to which you and I belong are [sic] really talking a different language from that used by the generation that came after the depression … I need not dwell too intimately on this but it is extraordinary how far apart we are in our approach to the basic problem'.[26] He told a friend: 'I'm sure he [Keynes] would disown Coombs and his school if he was with us now' (Millmow 2005b, p. 1).

Earlier, Brigden had expressed his own distance from the new Keynesian consensus to J. M. Garland, a former pupil of Giblin who was to become the Economic Adviser at the Commonwealth Bank: 'Personally I have always been a sceptic on that theme [of full employment], in any sort of "free society" … in fact I may be classed as no longer progressive'.[27]

In this disagreement, Giblin played the peace maker, in spite of his own views: 'The Economics Winter School went off very harmoniously last weekend leaving me nothing to do in reconciling the combatants' he told Eilean. He added: 'Coombs was unexpectedly chastened in his outlook – to everyone's disappointment' (NLA LFG 8 May 1948). For Coombs, the chief architect of the 1945 White Paper, had also expressed publicly his disillusionment with the trend of economic policy in Australia, that was, in his view, an abdication of the government's earlier commitment to the policy of maintaining aggregate demand within the limits of aggregate supply (Coombs 1948).

The problem of industrial relations is another illustration of the distance between the four and more commonly held views. Before peace had been reached, Giblin had grown concerned about the possibility of aggressive trade unions pressing for wage increases and shorter hours, the deterioration in productivity as unskilled labour was engaged in conditions of supply shortages, and disrupted production through industrial turbulence. The chaos of the late 1940s – the weeks of rationed electricity and gas, and consequent factory closures – was the cause of the deep, bitter pessimism of his unpublished memorandum, 'Crisis in democracy'. His thesis was that the wage earner was threatening to halt and even reverse Australia's already slow growth in productivity. 'This crisis has been looming in the distance for the last, perhaps, sixty years [=1890]'. But he refused to accept that there was any simple economic solution for this militancy.

> It is difficult to know what the world really needs. It thinks it wants peace and prosperity but that is an obvious delusion. It would be worse than Milton's heaven before the angels fell. The world would be bored

[26] ANUA DBC to LM 18 June 1952, Melville Box 2.
[27] RBA JBB to Garland 13 December 1949, RBA GJG-51-1.

to death in twenty years – literally to death like the Jesuit communities in Paraguay. Human activity must be kept alive by conflict. (RBA LFG 'Why the Empire?').

In brief, man 'needs a fight at intervals'. 'The problem is to provide conflict in other terms than high explosive' – or strikes. 'The government might establish a National Theatre to provide catharsis. "Hamlet" on the coal fields might well step up the production of coal'. [28] More conventionally, 'the continuing degradation of our economy' might also be stemmed by a research effort. He nominated Copland, Wilson, Coombs and Melville. This effort could be under the auspices of the Commonwealth Bank or the ANU.

A related initiative was the Dyason Foundation Psychology of Conflict run by 'old Australian friends': Giblin, Bailey and Rivett, and funded by Dyason. For this venture they turned to the exotic figure of Kurt Singer: disciple of Stefan George and Martin Buber, refugee from Nazism, nipponophile and economist (Arndt 2000). Deprived of an academic post in Hitler's Germany, he established himself in Japan. Perhaps it was there that Dyason met Singer, on one of his hopeful, 'bridge building' trips to Japan before the outbreak of war. In any case, Singer arrived in Australia – in disputed circumstances – only to be interned as an 'enemy alien'. Upon his release in 1943, the Dyason Foundation gave him a modest stipend for three years as Research Fellow to write the book, *The idea of conflict*, an 'immense amount of work', which was published by Melbourne University Press in 1949. [29]

Chronicling a central bank

But Giblin was now absorbed in his own book: *The growth of a central bank: the development of the Commonwealth Bank of Australia 1924–1945*.

He had been invited to write this history by the Bank, was granted full access to its archives, and paid £15 per week. Giblin declined to be paid any royalties.

Giblin embarked on this project at the age of seventy-five and in precarious health. His bronchial condition could give him 30-minute coughing fits (NLA LFG 10 July 1947). Midway through writing, he was hospitalised from a suspected heart attack (NLA LFG 8 April 1948). A few months later he was (NLA

---

[28] This was not a casual remark. In the mid 1940s Giblin and Copland actively aired the establishment of an Australian National Theatre that would be a 'rational entertainment, the entertainment of the people' (Hytten 1951). Curtin was supportive – only his death stilled the project – but he wanted the Director to be an Australian. Keynes advised that more attention be paid to getting the right building than the right Director. Sharing the same concern for rationally entertaining 'the people', Brigden was excited by the English 'Little Theatres' movement, fostered by the Village Drama Society, that was a vehicle for the inter-war vogue of 'modern' and 'authentic' one-act plays.

[29] Mention may be made of Giblin's role in Bertrand Russell's tour of Australia in 1950.

LFG 2 Sept 1948) in hospital again, with suppurating ankles, a legacy of his time in the trenches 30 years before.

There were other obstacles. The archival material was 'very scanty' for earlier times. And for the later decades there was too much. The 1937 Royal Commission into the Monetary and Banking Systems was – 'a mine of information' – but a 'low grade ore' (NLA LFG 27 July 1948).

A greater difficulty lay in the sharp and sometimes painful difference in the opinions with his professional peers over what had happened, and why it had happened. Even with such a kindred spirit as Roland Wilson, parts of his manuscript were unsympathetically received. Giblin at one point expressed himself 'amazed' at Wilson's 'fantastic' comments on a draft chapter (RBA LFG 28 December 1949). 'The difference in our impressions of various happenings is rather disturbing' and he implied that a further exchange of the points at question would be unhelpful.

The root of the trouble here was that, if Giblin was to understand the history of the Bank, he would have to excavate past rivalries between Treasury and the Bank, and surmount the different standpoints of these institutions. Midway through preparation Wilson complained to Giblin:

> You have written the history as [the Commonwealth Bank Board Chairman Sir Claude] Reading or Melville would have written it. What your Commonwealth Bank records would not have shown was the extremely strong aversion to Reading and all his works, and Melville and some of his works, on the part of the trading banks. In the case of the Government, aversion would be too strong a word but exasperation was frequently felt. (RBA RW 22 October 1949). [30]

It was not only Treasury who were irked. These draft chapters were read with mixed pleasure by members of the Bank of England. Raymond Kershaw (1898–1981), the Australian-born Bank of England aide of Niemeyer on his 1930 visit, protested: 'If you will allow me to be a frank critic, I should say that it seems rather too wise after the event' (RBA RK 15 November 1949). Melville explained to Giblin: 'What may be irritating Kershaw is a certain levity in these pages. In your references to the Bank of England you do not "pay the deference due to a man of pedigree" … it could be argued that since in speaking of the tabernacle your tones are not sufficiently hushed there is an implication that you are in some way critical' (RBA LGM 10 December 1949).

---

[30] There were also rivalries between personalities, especially between Wilson and Leslie Melville. As Wilson put it: 'files do not cover the whole story in a matter where personal relationships were more than usually important' (RBA RW 7 December 1949, GLG-51-5).

Not only Bank outsiders had difficulties. At the beginning of 1949 Giblin told Eilean of 'new trouble over bank history. It has to be discussed with three or four people here [the Bank] both for accuracy on certain doubtful matters and for propriety in making public certain matters of policy and certain criticism of persons' (NLA LFG 21 February 1949). Six months later Giblin was still not in the clear. 'History is rather in trouble over a difficult part. I think I mentioned it as open to criticism. I thought I had fairly met this when I found the critics strongly disagreed, and the memoranda go to and fro' (NLA LFG 8 August 1949). A revised draft appeared in October 1949. But there still one hurdle to leap: the Prime Minister. Gladly Giblin could report to Eilean: 'Coombs talked it over with Chifley who is happy about it'.

Giblin's *Growth of a central bank* is an authoritative account of the development of the Bank and major economic events experienced in Australia between 1924 and 1945. It is also an insider's account: 'it is with a sense of witnessing the lifting of a veil that one reads part of the narrative' (Wilson 1952). [31]

Its theme is one familiar to Giblin: the birth and growth of an Australian institution. Its thesis is that the development was slow, fitful, and difficult.

Giblin's history taught that this development could not be hastened by importing a replica of the Bank of England. Giblin records the meagre fruit of the much anticipated visit to the Commonwealth Bank in 1927 of Sir Ernest Harvey, Comptroller of the Bank of England and later Deputy Governor. Commonwealth Bank members considered it 'a compliment to us that one so high up in the Bank of England should take the trouble to come out and have a look at what we were doing … All Directors were intensely interested in Sir Ernest Harvey, and what he had to say generally' (RBA D. B. Murdoch to LFG 8 April 1947). [32] Twenty years later Giblin found little memory of what Sir Ernest actually did say, except for a list of 14 points purporting to be an epitome of the principles of central banking. In *Growth* Giblin does not sew fig leaves to cover their nakedness; he reprints them in their feeble entirety.

In truth, the Bank of England's example was somewhat worse than useless. Giblin complains of 'the shibboleths, promulgated too lightly from the Bank of England from a special experience and accepted too easily by other banking

---

[31] Giblin had been appointed to a seven-year term on the Bank Board in 1935, and proposed to take leave from Melbourne University. There was a revolt on the University Council: 'the real objection arises from Giblin's political and economic opinions which are suspect to a good many people' (Priestly 2002, p. 135).

[32] Murdoch, the Secretary to the Commonwealth Bank Board at the time, added: 'I am sure that Sir Ernest personally was our good friend and anxious to help us but it was a great disappointment that the Bank of England did not come to our rescue in better effect in 1930 when Australia got into a bad squeeze in London'.

systems; which were a serious obstacle to any rational consideration of the central banking problem in Australia' (Giblin 1951, p. 111). He faulted the 'very cold' response of the Bank of England to Australia's request during the Depression of a loan of a 'comparatively trifling' sum. He scorned as a 'fatuous inference from Bank of England experience' the notion that private ownership of a central bank amounts to political independence of a central bank. Giblin's estimation of the benefit of the Bank of England connection would hardly be encouraged by the hearsay, investigated by Giblin in researches, that Casey had sought advice from Niemeyer over the 1938 banking legislation. [33]

Unable to import a ready-made central bank in kit form, neither could a central bank be 'improvised' from materials made for another purpose. In particular, a cadre of experts could only develop with the passage of time. This poverty of proficiency in central banking was exacerbated by legislators' lack of any sincere concern for this proficiency. Earl Page, the author of the 1924 Commonwealth Bank Act, announced he would leave decision-making 'to the experts' on the Bank Board. 'No doubt he was perfectly well aware that there were no real "experts" available, and that, if there were, he would not appoint them'. In the event, Page's appointments to the Bank Board were wholly premised on the assumption that 'successful businessmen and farmers were obviously competent to make all necessary decisions' (Giblin 1951, p. 352).

The benefit that experience would slowly confer on the Bank over time was to some extent counter-weighed by the mythologisation of the Bank's experience. The tribulations of the Bank's Board were illustrative. The Labor Government of 1911 established the Commonwealth Bank without a board. The Board was added by a Nationalist government in 1924, and filled with friends of that government. In consequence, the Labor opposition inferred a board was obviously a bad thing. When that opposition became the government in 1941, 'Now was clearly the time to remedy this disaster and restore the pristine knight-errantry of a single Governor with a horse and lance of Sir Denison Miller' (p. 343). The Board was abolished. *Growth* closes with an entreaty that the merits of a Board not be overlooked by future legislators.

The development of the power and competency of the central bank was also stymied by the interests of the commercial banks. Genuine compacts between the Bank and the commercial banks were resisted, since commercial banks were possessed of 'a natural longing for binding agreements which will not in fact bind' (Giblin 1951, p. 284). A show of alarm by the commercial banks greeted

---

[33] Giblin recorded in 1938 of Montague Norman: 'The Governor likes to play grandfather to anyone connected with Dominion Central banks and had been very hospitable'. He added 'Every now and then the Old Man gives a very interesting glimpse of his outlook – and the essential hostility between him and Keynes becomes very understandable (RBA LFG 30 April 1938).

Roland Wilson's proposal that statistics on foreign currency reserves be made generally available. 'This was heady and dangerous information for the public.' Throughout *Growth*, the banks make a hypocrites' chorus, which combined noisy professions of conventional morality with a steady-eyed devotion to their own advantage.

These theses are minutely researched. In many instances this does not make for laborious reading; Giblin's great blocks of factual granite are gilded with his gossamer webs of irony. ('Sir Robert [Gibson] had a clear and confident but somewhat imperfect vision of Central banking problems in Australia' (p. 353)). But the density of the material is often excessive. Perhaps Giblin saw himself as writing an official history. The great example of Australian official history in the later 1940s was Charles Bean's *The official history of Australia in the War of 1914–1918*.[34] This was ultimately a 12-volume effort. The last of the six volumes that Bean had written himself had only appeared in 1942. The official history is a minutely crowded canvas, without broad strokes. The Australian War Memorial states that the *Official history* was 'warmly acclaimed', but 'it is unlikely that Bean's massive history of the war was widely read'. Something similar may be said of *Growth of a central bank*.[35]

A portrait of the author

One reviewer of *Growth of a central bank* wrote: 'I found myself increasingly absorbed by Giblin at the expense of interest in the Commonwealth Bank of Australia' (Bopp 1952). The book's author had already been the subject of numerous newspaper profiles, but the most elaborate attempt to convey what Giblin was all about was soon to be undertaken in oil and pointed sable brushes.[36]

It was Copland who had conceived the project of a portrait of Giblin. Copland in his devotion to Giblin was sometimes undiscerning, and always forgiving. Giblin could receive Copland's tributes ironically: 'I'd a very appreciative audience last-night, though my performance was very mediocre. DBC was there throwing bouquets with great fervour.' (NLA LFG 7 December 1948). But it was this unmeditated urge of Copland to honour Giblin that manifested itself lastingly

---

[34] Giblin had assisted Bean in his research.

[35] *Growth of a central bank* was widely and well reviewed. *The Economist*, however, complained 'The honest liberal must admit that some passages in his book suggest that he was the wrong sort of adviser – for example, he does not seem to recognise that a disinflationary monetary policy and pegged low interest rates cannot ride together' (*The Economist* 29 October 1951).

[36] Unless otherwise stated the correspondence and quotes in this section are drawn from Reserve Bank Archives, GJG-46-1

in his successful effort in 1945–46 to have Giblin's portrait painted. A committee to achieve this end was formed in 1945, with Copland as the Chairman.

An artist was selected: William Dobell. An interesting choice! Dobell had been embroiled in 1944 in one of the boisterous controversies that punctuate Australian cultural life. He had caused a 'sensational' break with 'academic tradition' by winning the Archibald Prize for his portrait of Joshua Smith. Defenders of tradition had succeeded in taking the decision to court on the grounds that it was not a portrait but only a 'caricature'.

How Dobell came to be asked to paint Giblin is not specifically known, except that Copland was not involved. But the controversy of 1944 had kindled a general interest in Dobell; the painter later claimed that, in its aftermath, 'everybody was clamouring for pictures'. How Dobell came to accept the commission is also unclear, as in later years he would have it understood – falsely – that he had ceased painting portraits in the aftermath of *Joshua Smith*: 'I was afraid of flooding the market and then, on the other hand, I was afraid to touch portraiture in case similar things happened and I didn't want to go through that experience again'.

But a commission of £200 and five shillings was agreed upon. Subscribers were sought, with an upper limit of 200: Curtin, Chifley, Menzies, Ian Potter, Sir John Clapham, Keynes. It appears that Keynes accepted – three colour copies of the portrait were dispatched to him, as to all acceptors.

But some of those approached 'were not altogether happy about our choice of artist'. Sir William Massey-Greene (Assistant Treasurer during the Lyons Government) replied to Copland:

> I want a portrait, not a caricature ... Dobell can paint and do good work, but if he allows his ideas to produce Giblin in the same guise as Joshua Smith I could conceive of no greater disservice that we could do Giblin than let the artist loose on the old chap ... Dobell is the last man I would have selected to paint Giblin, because Giblin's fine face wants a kind of understanding that I do not think Dobell is capable of ... I do not want my stomach to roll over every time I look at the result.

Another Depression colleague of Giblin's, Sir Alfred Davidson, the General Manager of the Bank of New South Wales, refused to subscribe: 'I do not approve of the work of William Dobell. I have seen all his recent portraits, so called, but with all diffidence I suggest they would be more appropriately described as caricatures'.

Giblin appeared unperturbed. He minuted himself at the time: 'Chief anxiety – I would offer him a subject totally obstructive to artistic endeavour'.

After Copland had departed for China, Melville took over the task of managing the artist. Copland told Melville: 'Dobell must be a real artist because he has not answered my official letter written to him a month ago'. Melville also had to cope with the artist's wishes. Melville informed Copland that Dobell wanted brushes of sable hair that were pointed. 'He is prepared to do the best he can with his fingers', Melville added. Copland replied: 'I know nothing about sable brushes, but I have asked the Deputy Prices Commissioner in Melbourne to make some enquiries as to whether any such things exist in Melbourne'.

The completed portrait did not invoke enthusiasm among subscribers. Melville complained: 'I do not feel it is quite so satisfactory ... I feel that a few minor adjustments would probably achieve an accurate rather than an approximate likeness' (February 1946). Copland advised Melville to discuss with Dobell 'adjustments in the face'. But Giblin responded: 'I should be sorry if he was pressed'.

The finished work was first displayed in the Commonwealth Bank building in Sydney, and then at 'a little ceremony' in Canberra before the unveiling at the University of Melbourne on 6 April 1946.

But this was not an academic portrait, in any sense. Medley, a humourist and versist, thought these lines fitting:

> *Inscription For A Portrait in the Union*
> Pan with his pipe, a leer upon his face
> Recalls in rosy mist
> The economic nymphs he used to chase
> But ah! So seldom kissed (Serle 1993).

Vance Palmer, less facetiously but in the same vein, wrote that it 'hinted at qualities that were earthy, impish, humorously derisive of ordinary social conventions' (Palmer 1954, p. 221).

Giblin was not happy with the portrait. He told his sister Edith:'Dobell was a little perverse. His painting was quite different from his sketch. [This is correct.] It was of course his imagination of how I might look ... For its personal verisimilitude, I am of all people the worst possible judge. After careful consideration I told William [Dobell] that I thought it was "fair comment". And I leave it at that'.[37] Eilean thought the portrait a 'horror'. Wilson called it an 'indignity'.

It was entered for the Archibald Prize. The judges' final choice came down to a choice between Dobell's Giblin, and a portrait of L. C. Robson (the headmaster of Sydney Church of England Grammar School) by William Dargie, a young artist who had won the prize three times in the previous four years. Dargie's

---

[37] RBA LFG January 1948.

Figure 10.3. The Dobell Giblin was expecting

Source: nla.pc-an5418395

precise and opulent portraits represented the traditionalism enraged by *Joshua Smith*. [38] Giblin, who was a trustee of the Gallery of New South Wales, absented himself from the judges' deliberations. Dobell received five votes, Dargie seven.

The Giblin portrait made little lasting impression on art critics. It was forgotten by Dobell experts, some of whom have accepted at face value Dobell's claim that for several years he stopped painting portraits after the court case.

The most memorable comment came when the portrait was exhibited in Sydney. 'The first day, an elderly waitress bustled up' and said to Giblin,

'That your photo?'

'Yes'

'Very good, I think it is, *very* good' (NLA LFG12 November 1949).

Death

On 12 October 1950, Brigden, aged 63 years, died from a heart attack. Wilson wrote to Giblin a few weeks later: 'I am sure he would have enjoyed a yarn about the old days. This was about the only thing he was hanging on for' (RBA RW to LFG 2 November 1950).

A haphazard and unnoticed assortment of memorials was instituted. His widow, 'being desirous of perpetuating his memory', endowed the University of Tasmania with the J. B. Brigden Memorial Prize of £1000. The Brigden gate, that he had left the University of Tasmania on his departure, was respectfully transferred to the University's new campus at Sandy Bay. In 1987 a circling street in a new Canberra locality was christened Brigden Crescent. It nestles in the suburb of Theodore, a neighbourhood named in memory of the Treasurer whose policies he abhorred. [39]

Immediately upon Brigden's death, Giblin took upon himself the task of writing Brigden's obituary. But he never finished it. Giblin was dying. A cancer of the bowel had spread to his liver, and he would be dead in just over four months. [40]

---

[38] 'A good portrait painter never paints character', Dargie believed. 'People who really like what is called "modern art" are like people who have lost the taste for healthy food.'

[39] The planners of the national capital deemed that the 'theme' of street names in Theodore would be civilian service in the world wars. Elsewhere Canberra includes a Giblin Place, a Giblin Street, and a Copland Drive. In addition, Copland College (a government secondary college in Canberra) and the Copland Building, housing the Faculty of Economics and Commerce at the ANU, are named after D. B. Copland. The Sir Roland Wilson Building in Canberra is the home of the National Graduate School of Management.

[40] It was completed by Wilson.

In these last months he forced himself to complete his labour on the still unfinished *Growth of a central bank*. Late in October he obtained a large file of papers from Wilson 'which I must now tackle'. But, 'I'm so slow in getting about and getting things done' (NLA LFG 25 October 1950). In February 1951 he wrote to his sister, Edith: 'energy gone very low in the last few weeks, and I cannot keep up even with the most urgent business, writing or reading or thinking … I doubt if you can read this, though it leaves me knocked out with the effort'. Gladly, on 22 February, in the last full week of his life, he was able to tell Coombs that the 'printer started on Monday to print, cuff and bind'.

In that last week he managed to pen notes to those to whom he was closest. One, written on 24 February read:

> Dear Roland
>
> Your letter of 22nd Feb came just as I was going to write asking you to cut me out of *all* mailing lists. Everything is moving to zero: use of legs, arms, fingers, voice & mind. I have no interest now except to finish off with the least possible trouble to other people. I shall leave some messages. I shall probably have to go into hospital next week and give up. Everything is very slow. A brief note like this is very difficult and slow. There's a lot I would like to say but cannot write it and could not speak it.
>
> Yours LFG. [41]

Epilogue

The Bulletin truthfully noted that 'Giblin died bravely, as he lived'. More widely registered 'was a general feeling that the country had lost a fabulous old man' (Palmer 1954, p. 221).

Over the next 10 years his former colleagues and friends took pains to give a permanent record to his feats. [42] 'Certain friends of the late Lyndhurst Falkiner Giblin' endowed a prize in Sociology. Giblin Libraries appeared at the University of Melbourne and the University of Tasmania. An annual Giblin Memorial

---

[41] Copland: 'In his closing days he wrote to say farewell to a few intimate friends, to express regret that his powers were failing and say a word of encouragement to the honoured recipient. I have rarely been so emotionally affected as on receipt of one of these letters, almost the last he wrote.' (Copland 1960).

[42] There is a Mt Giblin and a Giblin River in the south west wilderness of Tasmania that Giblin did much to explore and popularise.

Lecture was commenced in 1958: Copland was the inaugural speaker, and Giblin was his subject. [43]

Rex Ingamells expressed an interest in writing Giblin's biography, but his sudden and premature death in 1955 extinguished that interesting possibility. A committee that gathered to devise appropriate memorials did consider a volume of essays in Giblin's memory. But it dismissed such a book as likely to have only a very small readership, and concerned itself instead with erecting buildings named in Giblin's honour. Ironically, the buildings never appeared but the volume of essays did, and has weathered the years very well. It was published in 1960 under Copland's editorship: *Giblin: The scholar and the man: papers in memory of Lyndhurst Falkiner Giblin.* [44] This volume furnished a deep fund of fact, research and appreciation about the man. But it has defects. One is its omnibus character (18 authors and 35 segments). Giblin's tale is fragmented almost beyond recognition to the casual reader. Another defect is that it misses out on the sheer strangeness of Giblin; it implicitly presents Giblin as a normal person who did extraordinary things; as a person of ordinary silhouette who was uniformly expanded in all directions. [45] But Giblin was not a normal person.

Perhaps the most general way of expressing this was that his pleasures were different. Giblin greatly enjoyed life – if he did not he could not have achieved what he did. But he enjoyed different things. [46] Giblin took pleasure, for example, in physical toil. After his death Hytten observed that Giblin 'had deliberately chosen a hard life' (Hytten 1951). It was certainly hard, but the point is it was chosen. The passive, comforting entertainment that pleases the millions was insipid to him. One evening he recalled to Eilean: 'I had arranged to see [Chairman] Boyer (ABC) on Tuesday at 3 pm when the [Melbourne] Cup

---

[43] For over 30 years the leading lights of Australian economics were lecturers. They included Richard Blandy (1985), Geoffrey Brennan (1984), H. C. Coombs (1969), Peter B. Dixon (1990), Fred Gruen (1982), Austin Holmes (1980), Joseph Isaacs (1977), Peter Karmel (1975), Allan Lloyd (1987), Leslie Melville (1967), John Nevile (1993), G. A. Rattigan (1971), Brian Reddaway (1965), Richard Snape (1983), Trevor Swan (1972), Sir Ronald Walker (1964), and Sir Roland Wilson (1976). The lecture perished in the late 1990s. Another annual Giblin Lecture was established at the University of Tasmania in 1996.

[44] Copland, knighted in 1950, left the ANU in 1953 to become Australia's High Commissioner to Canada. When he returned to Australia he was appointed foundation Principal of the Administrative Staff College at Mt Eliza, and displayed there once more his outstanding abilities as an academic entrepreneur. In 1960 he founded the Committee of Economic Development of Australia. He died in Melbourne in 1971.

[45] The publication of Giblin's letter to E. M. Foster (see Chapter 8) is one significant exception.

[46] 'He had a habit of reticence, and was always on guard against self-revelation' (Garland in Copland 1960 p. 222).

is run. He had the wireless on and said "Do you want to hear this?" I said "No"'. [47]

Giblin enjoyed a terrain of human relations different from the ordinary adult. His values were so exclusively masculine – 'mental stamina, endurance … fortitude, self-reliance, stability, courage' as Wilson summarised them – that he had little toleration for the purely womanly. For all his formidable maturity, his mental landscape remained a pre-adolescent one, of boyish of adventure and comradeship. As Sibyl Giblin told Edith: 'His 78 years made no difference – he was a boy at heart … I don't know what religious beliefs he held, but I am sure he saw the kingdom of heaven in children'. [48] One journalist, interviewing Eilean after Giblin's death, recorded the 'extraordinary number of children's books' that Giblin owned, the most numerous being titles by Arthur Ransome, the author of school-holiday adventures that were first published when Giblin was aged fifty-eight. [49]

Giblin's longing for comradeship was sustained in adult life by a suite of fatherly relations with those a generation younger. The soldiers he commanded on the Western Front knew him as 'Dad'. He very plainly took a paternal care of Wilson. Copland frankly accepted him as a father figure, defender and guide. [50]

Giblin's dedication to guiding youth induced Hytten in his funeral oration to shoot much higher, and invoke Socrates. [51] Peter Pan or Socrates? Whatever the answer, there was in Giblin some differentness that left him amongst but apart; amidst but above; that gave him a holiness without saintliness; that made him a Puck and a pilgrim in our foolish, unhallowed times.

---

[47] NLA LFG 4 November 1949. He wrote shortly after: 'Much cheered by the news – failure of the favourite for Melbourne cup and win by an outsider'.

[48] They were not aware that the only person allowed in Giblin's will apart from Eilean was Nicholas Gardley, whose education was funded by Giblin.

[49] 'Many a boy and girl owe their introduction to the delights of reading to this old man, who seemed to have time to revel with them in the simple virtues of an adventure well told' (*The Bulletin*, 7 March 1951).

[50] Upon Giblin's death, Wilson wrote to Eilean: 'The curious thing is that in my mind he was so 'indestructible' that his physical passing makes little difference'. A few weeks after Giblin's death, Wilson, at the age of forty-seven, became Secretary to the Treasury, the first economist to hold the position. Holding this post for 15 years, he remains the longest serving Secretary to the Australian Treasury. Knighted in 1955, and for a second time in 1965, he died in Canberra in 1996.

[51] Assuming Hytten's obituary (1951) is substantially the same as his oration.

References

Albinski, Henry Stephen 1964, *Australia and the China problem during the Korean War period*, Department of International Relations, Research School of Pacific Studies, ANU, Canberra.

Anderson, Karl. L. 1970, 'Protection and the Historical Situation: Australia', *Quarterly Journal of Economics*, vol. 53, no. 1, pp. 68–104.

Andrews, E. M. 1970, *Isolationism and appeasement in Australia: reactions to the European crises, 1935–1939*, Australian National University Press, Canberra.

Anonymous 1930, 'Escape to prosperity', *Australian Quarterly*, vol. 2, no. 3, pp. 106–9.

Anonymous 1951,'L.F. Giblin', *Annual Report of the Council of King's College*, Cambridge.

Anonymous 1952, 'L. F. Giblin: An Appreciation', *Economic Record*, vol. 28, pp. 189–203.

Arndt, H. W. 2000, 'Kurt Singer: wandering Jewish scholar', *History of Economics Review*, no. 32, pp. 72–6.

Austin, Ronald J. 1997, *Black and gold: the history of the 29th battalion, 1915–1918*, Slouch Hat Publications, Victoria.

Bach, John 1976, *A maritime history of Australia*, Thomas Nelson, Melbourne.

Barrett, John 1979, *Falling in: Australians and 'boy conscription', 1911–1915*, Hale & Iremonger, Sydney.

Bastable, C. F. 1903, *The theory of international trade: with some of its applications to economic policy*, 4th ed., Macmillan, London.

Beaumont, Joan & Joshi, Vijaya 2001, '*Australian defence: sources and statistics'*, *The Australian centenary history of defence,* vol. 6, Oxford University Press, Melbourne.

Benham, F. C. 1926, '"The Australian tariff and the standard of living": a reply', *Economic Record*, vol. 2, no. 2.

—— 1935, 'Taxation and the Relative Prices of the Factors of Production' *Economica,* vol. 2, no. 6, pp. 198-203.

Bennett, Bruce 1988, *The Penguin new literary history of Australia,* Penguin, Vic.

Bennett, Scott & Bennett, Barbara 1986, *Tasmanian electoral handbook, 1851–1982*, History Project Incorporated, NSW.

Blainey, Geoffrey 1954, *The peaks of Lyell*, Melbourne University Press, Melbourne.

—— 1957, *A centenary history of the University of Melbourne*, Melbourne University Press, Melbourne.

—— 1971, *The steel master: a life of Essington Lewis*, Macmillan, Melbourne.

Blakely, Arthur 1929, 'Another weapon against the workers', *The Worker*, vol. 24 May.

Bopp, Karl R. 1952, 'The growth of a central bank: the development of the Commonwealth Bank of Australia, 1924–1945', *Journal of Economic History*, vol. 12, no. 3, p. 303.

Bosenrup, Mogens 1969, 'A note on the prehistory of the Kahn Multiplier', *Economic Journal*, vol. 79, no. 315, pp. 667–9.

Brigden, J. B. 1912, 'The Tragedy', *Labor Call*.

—— 1922, *The economics of Lyell: an introduction to a year's work in local tutorial classes, illustrating the sources of income and the forces governing its value and distribution*, University of Tasmania, Hobart.

—— 1924, 'The definition of money', unpublished manuscript, NAA JBB.

—— 1924, *The first British labour government*, World Printery, Hobart.

—— 1925, 'The Australian tariff and the standard of living', *The Economic Record*, vol. 1, no. 1, pp. 29–46.

—— 1926, 'Obituary: F. Y. Edgeworth, late Emeritus Professor of Political Economy at the University of Oxford', *Economic Record*, vol. 2, no. 2, pp. 143–4.

—— 1927a, 'The Australian tariff and the standard of living: a rejoinder', *Economic Record*, vol. 3, no. 1, pp. 102–116.

—— 1927b, 'Comment on Mr Benham's restatement', *Economic Record*, vol. 3, no. 2, pp. 249–51.

—— 1928, 'Economic outlook of Australia', *Mining Standard*, 27 September.

—— 1929, 'Notes on the economic position of Australia', NLA JBB.

—— 1930a, *Escape to prosperity*, Macmillan, Melbourne.

—— 1930b, 'Notes on monetary policy', 3 December 1930, NLA JBB.

—— 1931a, *P. P.: on purchasing power and the pound Australian*, Government Printer, Brisbane.

—— 1931b, 'Federal assistance to the states', *Economic Record*, vol. 7, no. 2, pp. 292–6.

—— 1931c, *Railway economics*, Government Printer, Brisbane.

—— 1932a, *Credit*, Government Printer, Brisbane.

—— 1932b, *The story of sugar*, Government Printer, Brisbane.

—— 1934, 'Grants to the states: the report of the Commonwealth Grants Commission and some its implications' *Economic Record*, vol. 10, no. 19, pp. 230–42.

—— 1937a, 'Tides in Australian history', NLA JBB, Canberra.

—— 1937b, *A private letter to the members of the Senate of the University of Queensland from J. B. Brigden on buildings for the university*.

—— 1939a, 'The credit theory of full employment', *Economic Record*, vol. 15, no. 2, pp. 236–7.

—— 1939b, *Social services in Australia*, ed W. G. K. Duncan, Angus & Robertson, Sydney.

—— 1942, 'Notes on Australian war administration', NAA A981/4.

—— 1943a, 'A visit to a western US farm bureau', NAA A981/1.

—— 1943b, 'Discussions on the S. F.', NAA A981/1.

—— 1943c, 'Economic trends in the USA no. 4', NAA A981/1.

—— 1948, 'British Commonwealth Relations', NLA JBB, Canberra.

Brigden, J. B. & Giblin, L. F. 1928, *The Australian tariff: its unequal effects upon the states*, Economic Society of Australia and New Zealand, Hobart.

Brigden, J. B., Copland, D. B., Dyason, E. C., Giblin, L. F. & Wickens, C. H. 1929, *The Australian tariff: an economic inquiry*, Melbourne University Press, Melbourne.

Brigden, J. B., Hytten, T. & Shann, E. O. G. 1931, 'Draft of report prepared for the consideration of committee appointed to investigate the position and prepare information for consideration by the conference', NLA JBB, item no 15.

Brown, Jethro 1927, 'Economic welfare and racial vitality', *Economic Record*, vol. 3, no. 1, pp. 15–34.

Butlin, N. G. 1962, *Australian domestic product, investment and foreign borrowing 1861–1938/39*, Cambridge University Press, Cambridge.

—— 1985, 'Australian national accounts 1788–1983', *Source Papers in Economic History*, no. 6, Australian National University, Canberra.

Butlin, S. J. 1955, *War economy 1939–41*, Australian War Memorial, Canberra.

Butlin, S. J. & Schedvin, C. B. 1977, *War economy 1942–1945*, Australian War Memorial, Canberra.

Cain, John & Hewitt, John 2004, *Off course: from public place to market place at Melbourne University*, Scribe, Melbourne.

Cain, Neville 1973, 'Political economy and the tariff: Australia in the 1920s', *Australian Economic Papers*, vol. 12, no. 2, pp. 1–20.

—— 1979, 'Cambridge and its revolution: a perspective on the multiplier and effective demand', *Economic Record*, vol. 55, no. 149, pp. 108–117.

—— 1983, 'Recovery Policy in Australia 1930–33: certain native wisdom', *Australian Economic History Review*, vol. 23, no. 2, pp. 193–218.

—— 1985, 'Keynes and Australian policy in 1932', *Working Papers in Economic History,* no. 58, Australian National University, Canberra.

—— 1987, 'The Australian economists and controversy over depression policy 1930–early 1931', *Working Papers in Economic History*, no. 79, Australian National University, Canberra.

Cairncross, Alec 1998, *Living with the century*, Lynx, Fife.

Camsell, Charles 1960, 'Giblin in North British Columbia', in *Giblin: the scholar and the man*, ed. D. B. Copland, Cheshire, Melbourne.

Castles, Ian 1998, 'Vice-president's note', *Dialogue*, 4/1998.

Colebatch, Hal 1926, 'Australian credit as viewed from London', *Economic Record*, vol. 2, no. 2, pp. 217–27.

Coleman, William 1992, *Salisbury Review*, 'Keynes and Communism', vol. 11, no. 2, pp. 10–13

—— 2001a, 'The Strange Laissez Faire of Alfred Russel Wallace: The Connection Between Natural Selection and Political Economy Reconsidered', in *Darwinism and evolutionary economics*, eds John Laurent and John Nightingale, Edward Elgar, Cheltenham.

—— 2001b, 'Is it possible that an independent central bank is impossible?', *Journal of Money, Credit and Banking*, vol. 33, no. 3, pp. 729–38.

—— 2004, *Economics and its Enemies*, Palgrave Macmillan, New York.

Commonwealth of Australia 1945, *Full employment in Australia*.

Commonwealth Grants Commission 1995, *Equality in diversity: history of the Commonwealth Grants Commission*, AGPS, Canberra.

—— 1999, *Report on general revenue grant relativities* 1999, vol. 1, CanPrint Communications Pty Ltd, Canberra.

Coombs, H. C. 1981, *Trial balance*, Macmillan, Melbourne.

—— 1948, 'Australia's ability to avoid booms and depressions', *Economic Papers*, no. 8, pp. 36–53.

Copland, D. B. 1920, 'Currency inflation and price movements in Australia', *Economic Journal*, vol. 30, no. 120, pp. 484–505.

—— 1930a, 'The economic outlook', *The Argus,* June 19, 20, 21.

—— 1930b, 'The economic and financial outlook', *Australian Quarterly*, vol. 2, no. 3, pp. 17–28.

—— 1931a, 'Financial and currency proposals', *Australian Quarterly*, vol. 3, no. 1, pp. 17–27.

—— 1931b, 'A neglected phase of tariff controversy', *Quarterly Journal of Economics*, vol. 45, no. 2, pp. 289–308.

—— 1934, *Australia in the world crisis, 1929–1933*, Cambridge, University Press Cambridge.

—— 1937a, 'Some problems in Australian banking', *Economic Journal*, vol. 47, no. 188, pp. 686–96.

—— 1937b, 'Problems of federal finance and federal grants in Australia', *Quarterly Journal of Economics*, vol. 51, no. 3, pp. 497–508.

—— 1945, *Report on economic conditions in the United Kingdom, United States of America and Canada by professor D. B. Copland, CMG, economic consultant to the Prime Minister, Commonwealth Parliamentary Papers*, session 1945–46, vol. IV.

—— 1948, *Back to earth in economics: Australia, 1948,* Angus and Robertson, Sydney.

—— 1950, 'Culture versus power in international relations', in *Liberty and learning: essays in honour of Sir James Hight*, ed. R.S. Allan, Whitcombe and Tombs, Christchurch.

—— 1951, *Essays on the Australian economy,* F.W. Cheshire, Melbourne.

—— 1952, 'Economic study and public opinion in Australia: the role of the economist', *The Australian Highway*, vol. 34, no. 2, pp. 30–32.

—— 1960, *Giblin: the scholar and the man*, ed. Douglas Copland, F. W. Cheshire, Melbourne.

—— 1968, 'Interview with Sir Douglas Copland' by Eric Waite, National Library of Australia.

Cornish, Selwyn 2002, *Sir Roland Wilson: a biographical essay,* The Australian National University, Canberra.

Crisp, L.F., 1960, *Ben Chifley: a biography,* Longmans, London.

—— 1965, 'The Australian full employment pledge at San Francisco', *The Australian Outlook*, vol. 19, no. 1, pp. 5–19.

Crocker, Walter 1981, *Travelling back: the memoirs of Sir Walter Crocker*, Macmillan, Melbourne.

—— 1991, 'Sir Walter Crocker, interviewed by Stephen Foster', 9 August 1991. Australian National University Oral History Archive, UA2001/20 Box 1 Interview 24.

Crozier, Michael 2002, 'Society economised: T. R. Ashworth and the history of social sciences in Australia', *Australian Historical Studies*, no. 119, pp. 125–42.

Davis, E. G. 1980, 'The correspondence between R. G. Hawtrey and J. M. Keynes on the *Treatise*: the genesis of output adjustment models', *Canadian Journal of Economics*, vol. 13, no. 4, pp. 716–24.

Davis, Richard. P. 1975, 'Tasmania', in *Labor in politics, the state labor parties in Australia 1880–1920*, ed. D. J. Murphy, University Queensland Press.

—— 1990, *Open to talent: the centenary history of the University of Tasmania 1890–1990*, University of Tasmania, Hobart.

Day, David 2001, *Chifley*, Harper Collins, Sydney.

—— 2003, *The politics of war*, Harper Collins, Sydney.

De Lissa, Alfred 1890, 'The Law of Incomes', *Australian Economist*, vol. 1, no. 27, pp. 6–17.

—— 1896, *Production distribution and Quesnay's Tableau Économique*, privately printed, Sydney.

—— 1898, 'The practical application of economics', *Report of the seventh meeting of the Australasian Association of the Advancement of Science*, Sydney.

Dimand, Robert W. 1988, *The origins of the Keynesian revolution*, Edward Elgar, Cheltenham.

Dollery, Brian & Whitten, Stuart 1998, 'An empirical analysis of tariff endogeneity in Australia, 1904–1974', *Economic Analysis and Policy*, vol. 28, no 2, pp. 213–30.

Downing, R. I. 1971, 'Sir Douglas Copland: a personal memory', *Economic Record*, vol. 47, no. 120.pp.465–9.

Dunn, Leonard James & Pratt, James Denis 1990, *The Faculty of Commerce 1919 to the Faculty of Economics and Commerce in 1990 in the University of Tasmania*, unpublished manuscript.

Earp, F. R. 1960, 'Giblin at Cambridge', in *Giblin: the scholar and the man*, ed. D. B. Copland, F. W. Cheshire, Melbourne.

Edgeworth, F. Y. 1897, review of 'The theory of international trade' (second edition) by C. F. Bastable, *Economic Journal,* vol. 7, no. 27, p. 257.

—— 1900, review of 'The theory of international trade' (third edition) by C. F. Bastable, *Economic Journal*, vol. 10, no. 39, pp. 389–93.

—— 1901, 'Disputed points in the theory of international trade', *Economic Journal*, vol. 11, no. 44, pp. 582–95.

Farrell, John Joseph, 1997, 'Opting out and opting in: secession and the new state movements', *Armidale and District Historical Society Journal and Proceedings*, vol. 40, pp. 139–48.

Fitzpatrick, Brian 1921, 'Student life: the twenties', *Melbourne University Magazine*, pp. 10–16.

Forster, Colin & Hazlehurst, Cameron 1988, *Australian statisticians and the development of official statistics*, Australian Bureau of Statistics, Canberra.

Foster, S. G. & Varghese, Margaret M. 1996, *The making of the Australian National University*, Allen and Unwin, Sydney.

Garnett, David 1953, *The golden echo*, Chatto & Windus, London.

—— 1955, *The flowers of the forest*, Chatto & Windus, London.

Giblin, L. F. [1923] 1960, 'The Icelandic sagas', in *Giblin: the scholar and the man*, ed. D. B. Copland, F.W. Cheshire, Melbourne.

—— 1924, *The taxable capacity of Australian states*, Government Printer, Hobart.

—— 1926, 'Federation and finance', *Economic Record*, vol. 2, no. 2, pp. 145–60.

—— 1927a, 'The Australian tariff and standard of living – a note on Mr Benham's statistics', *The Economic Record*, vol. 34, no. 1, pp. 148–56.

—— 1927b, 'The national dividend', *Economic Record*, vol. 3, no. 2, pp. 189–96.

—— 1929, 'The recruiting of the public service', *Papers and proceedings of the Victorian regional group, The Institute of Public Administration*, vol. 1, no 2, pp. 17–19.

—— 1930a, 'Australia agonistes', *Australian Quarterly*, vol. 2, no. 4, pp. 7–16.

—— 1930b, *Australia, 1930*, Melbourne University Press, Melbourne.

—— 1930c, 'Appendix J: state disabilities – with special reference to Tasmania' in *The case for Tasmania, 1930: statement of a claim for an increased special grant from the Commonwealth*, Government Printer, Hobart.

—— 1930d, *Letters to John Smith*, Herald, Melbourne.

—— 1933a, review of 'The means to prosperity', *Economic Record*, vol. 9, no. 1, pp. 141–3.

—— 1933b, 'Australia in the shadows', NLA LFG.

—— 1935, 'Foreword', *Gumtops*, by Rex Ingamells, F.W. Preece & Sons, Adelaide.

—— 1941, 'A university for Canberra', RBA LFG.

—— 1942, 'The premiers plan myth. The myth. The facts', NLA LFG, Canberra.

—— 1943, *The Australian problem of maintaining full employment*, Melbourne, University Press Melbourne.

—— 1946, 'John Maynard Keynes, some personal notes', *Economic Record*, vol. 22, no. 42, pp. 1–3.

—— 1947, 'The *Record* and its editors', *Economic Record*, vol. 23, no. 1, pp. 1–4.

—— 1951, *The growth of a central bank: the development of the Commonwealth Bank of Australia*, Melbourne University Press, Melbourne.

Giblin, L. F, Brigden J. B., Lewis, E., Ashbolt, A. Strutt, P. J. & Woods, W. A. 1925, *Report of committee appointed to inquire into Tasmanian disabilities*, Government Printer, Hobart.

Giblin L .F., Copland D. B. et al. 1937, 'Australia's policy – peace or war', *Herald*, 16 April 1937.

Giblin, L. F., Copland D. B. & Dyason A. E., 1930, 'A Plan for economic readjustment', NLA LFG MS366/9/227.

Giblin, R. W. 1939, *The early history of Tasmania*, Melbourne University Press, Melbourne.

Giblin, Wilfrid W. 1945, *Kith and kin: Some notes on our branch of the family*, privately printed,Hobart.

Gilbert, R. S. 1973, *The Australian Loan Council in Federal Fiscal Adjustments, 1890–1965*, Australian National University Press, Canberra.

Glezer, Leon 1982, *Tariff politics: Australian policy making 1960-1980*, Melbourne University Press, Melbourne.

Goodwin, C. D. 1962, 'Alfred de Lissa and the birth of the multiplier', *Economic Record,*vol. 38, no. 81, pp. 74–93.

Green F.C.1956, *A century of responsible government 1856-1956*, Government Printer, Hobart.

—— 1959, 'Hydro-electric development in Australia', *Papers and proceedings of the Tasmanian Historical Research Association*, vol. 8, no. 1, pp. 3–11.

—— 1960, 'Giblin in politics and war', in *Giblin: the scholar and the man*, ed. D.B. Copland, F.W. Cheshire, Melbourne.

Gregory, R. G. & Butlin N. G. 1988, *Recovery from the Depression: Australia in the world economy in the 1930s*, Cambridge University Press, Cambridge.

Gregory, R. G. 1976, 'Some implications of the growth of the mineral sector', *Australian Journal of Agricultural Economics*, vol. 20, no. 2, pp. 92–102.

Groenewegen, P. D. and McFarlane, Bruce 1990, *A history of Australian economic thought*, Routledge, London.

Haig, Bryan 2001, 'New estimates of Australian GDP, 1861–1948/49', *Australian Economic History Review*, vol. 41, no. 1, pp. 1–34.

Hall, Allan Ross 1963, *The London capital market and Australia, 1870–1914*, Social Science Monograph no. 21, Australian National University, Canberra.

Hancock, W. K. 1954, *Country and calling*, Faber and Faber, London.

Hancock, Jim & Smith, Julie 2001, *Financing the Federation*, South Australian Centre for Economic Studies, Adelaide.

Harper, Marjorie 1984, 'Douglas Copland – applied economist: some issues raised by the Copland papers', Economic History Joint Seminar, Australian National University, Canberra.

—— 1989, 'The writing of the Brigden Report', *Working Paper no. 151*, Department of Economic History, University of Melbourne.

Hasluck, Paul 1952, *The government and the people, 1939–1941*, Australian War Memorial, Canberra.

—— 1954, 'Australia and the formation of the United Nations', *Journal and Proceedings of the Royal Australian Historical Society*, vol. 60, pp. 133–78.

—— 1980, *Diplomatic witness: Australian foreign affairs 1941–1947*, Melbourne University Press, Melbourne.

—— 1997, *The chance of politics*, ed. Nicholas Hasluck, Text, Melbourne.

Healy, Derek T. & McFarlane, Bruce J. 1989, 'Colin Clark reminisces: an unscripted discussion with Bruce McFarlane and Derek Healy', Department of Economics Working Paper 89-12, University of Adelaide.

Hegeland, Hugo 1954, *The multiplier theory*, C. W. K. Gleerup, Lund.

Hergenhan, Laurie 1988, *The Penguin new literary history of Australia*, Penguin, Melbourne.

Hirst, John 1999, 'Labor and the Great War', in *The Australian century: political struggle in the building of a nation*, ed. Robert Manne, Text, Melbourne.

Hodgart, Alan W. 1975, *Faculty of economics and commerce: a history 1925–1975*, Faculty of Economics and Commerce, University of Melbourne.

Holder, R. F. 1970, *Bank of New South Wales: a history*, vol. 2, Angus and Robertson, Sydney.

Hudson, W. J. 1986, *Casey*, Melbourne University Press, Melbourne.

—— 1993, *Australia and the New World Order: Evatt at San Francisco, 1945,* Australian National University, Canberra.

Hytten, T. 1951, 'Lyndhurst Giblin', *Australian Quarterly*, vol. 33, no. 2, pp. 7–10.

—— 1960, 'Giblin as an economist' in *Giblin: the scholar and the man*, ed. D. B. Copland, F. W. Cheshire, Melbourne.

—— 1971, *To Australia with thanks – reminiscences of an immigrant*, unpublished manuscript, University of Tasmania Archives.

Hytten, T., Giblin, L. F., McPhee, J.C., James, Claude, Soundy, J., Cummins, H. H., Cummins, W. H., Strutt, P. J., Batt, F. J., McPhee, E. T. & Murphy, W. T. 1930, *The Case for Tasmania, 1930: statement of a claim for an increased special grant from the Commonwealth*, Government Printer, Hobart.

Irwin, Douglas A. 1996, 'The Australian case for protection', in *Against the tide: an intellectual history of free trade*, Princeton University Press, Princeton.

Isles, K. 1931, 'Australian monetary policy', *Economic Record*, vol. 7, no. 1, pp. 1–17.

—— 1932, 'Australian monetary policy reconsidered', *Economic Record*, vol. 8, no. 2, pp. 199–205.

Kahn, Richard 1984, *The making of Keynes's general theory*, Cambridge University Press, Cambridge.

Karmel, P. H. 1960, 'Giblin and the Multiplier', in *Giblin: the scholar and the man*, ed. D.B. Copland, F. W. Cheshire, Melbourne.

Kewley, T. H. 1965, *Social security in Australia: The development of social security and health benefits from 1900 to the present*, Sydney University Press, Sydney.

Keynes, John Maynard 1933 [1972], 'The means to prosperity', *Collected Writings of John Maynard Keynes*, ed. Donald Moggridge, vol. 9, Macmillan, London.

—— 1936, *The General theory of employment interest and money*, Macmillan, London.

—— 1939, 'How to pay for the war', *The Times*, 14 and 15 November 1939.

—— 1940, *How to pay for the war*, Macmillan, London.

King, John 1998, 'From Giblin to Kalecki: the export multiplier and the balance of payments constraint on economic growth, 1930–1933', *History of Economics Review*, no. 28, pp. 62–71.

Lake, Marilyn 1975, *A divided society: Tasmania during World War I*, Melbourne University Press, Melbourne.

Lang, J. T. 1980, *The great bust: the Depression of the thirties*, McNamara's Books, Sydney.

Loveday, A. 1931, 'The Australian tariff: a criticism', *Economic Record*, vol. 6, no. 2, pp. 272–8.

McDougall, F. L & Bruce, S. M. 1986, *Letters from a 'secret service agent': F. L. McDougall to S. M. Bruce*, eds W. J. Hudson & Wendy Way, AGPS, Canberra.

McLachlan, A. J. 1948, *McLachlan: an F.A.Q. Australian*, Lothian, Melbourne.

Maddock, Rodney & Penny, Janet 1983, 'Economists at war: the financial and economic committee 1939–44', *Australian Economic History Review,* vol. 23, no. 1, pp. 28–49.

Makin, Norman 1961, *Federal labor leaders,* privately printed,Sydney.

—— 1974, *Monologue and interview with the Hon. Norman Makin,* interviewed by Suzanne Walker, National Library of Australia, Canberra.

—— c.1982, *Memoirs of Norman John Oswald Makin*, facsimile NLA, Canberra.

Manger, Gary J. 1981, 'The Australian case for protection reconsidered', *Australian Economic Papers*, vol. 20, no. 37, pp. 193–204.

—— 1981, 'Summing up on the Australian case for protection: comment', *Quarterly Journal of Economics,* vol. 96, no. 1, pp. 161–8.

Mansbridge, Albert 1920, *An adventure in working class education: being the story of the Workers' Educational Association 1903–1915*, Longmans, Green and Co., London.

May, R. J. 1971, *Financing the small states in Australian federalism*, Oxford University Press, Melbourne.

Melville, L.G.1929, 'The Australian tariff: a review of the report of the committee appointed by the Prime Minister', *Australian Quarterly*, vol. 1, no. 3, pp. 54–63.

—— 1973, *Interview with Sir Leslie Melville*, interviewed by Alan Hodgart, National Library of Australia, Canberra.

Menzies, R.G. 1993, *Dark and hurrying days: Menzies 1941 diary*, edited by A.W. Martin and Patsy Hardy, National Library of Australia, Canberra.

Millmow, Alex 2000, 'Revisiting Giblin: Australia's first Proto-Keynesian economist?', *History of Economics Review*, no. 31, pp. 48–67.

—— 2003, 'W. Brian Reddaway – Keynes' emissary to Australia 1913–2002' *Economic Record*, vol. 79, no. 244, p. 136–9.

―― 2004a, 'Niemeyer, Scullin and the Australian economists', *Australian Economic History Review*, vol. 44, no. 2, pp. 142–6.

―― 2004b, The power of economic ideas: the origins of macroeconomic management in interwar Australia, PhD thesis, School of Economics, The Australian National University, Canberra.

―― 2005a, 'Searching for a "first-class man": the first occupant of the Ritchie Research Chair', *History of Economics Review, vol. 41*.

―― 2005b, 'D.B. Copland and the aftershocks of the Premiers' plan: 1931-1939', *unpublished manuscript*.

Miyaki, Taro & Tani, Yakio 1906, *The game of ju-jitsu,* ed. L. F. Giblin & M. A. Grainger, Hazell, Watson and Viney, London.

Moggridge, D. E. 1993, *Maynard Keynes: an economist's biography*, Routledge, London.

Mowle, P. C. 1943, *A genealogical history of pioneer families of Australia,* John Sands, Sydney.

Myrdal, Gunnar 1944, *An American dilemma: the Negro problem and modern democracy,* Harper Brothers, New York.

Nicholson, J. Shield 1901, *Principles of political economy*, Black, London.

―― 1917, 'Statistical aspects of inflation', *Journal of the Royal Statistical Society,* vol. 80, no. 4, pp. 467–520.

Ogilvy, A. J. 1892, *Is capital the result of abstinence?,* Australasian Association for the Advancement of Science, Hobart.

―― 1896, *Saving and spending*, Australian Science Association, Hobart.

Ohlin, B. 1933, *Interregional and international trade*, Harvard University Press, Cambridge, MA.

Page, Earle 1963, *Truant surgeon,* Angus and Robertson, Sydney.

Palmer, Vance 1954, *National portraits*, Melbourne University Press, Melbourne.

Patinkin, Don 1993, 'On the chronology of the general theory', *Economic Journal*, vol. 103, no. 418, pp. 647–63.

Pigou, A. C. 1932, 'The effect of reparations on the ratio of international interchange', *Economic Journal*, vol. 42, no. 168., pp. 532–43.

Plumptre, A. F. W. 1940, *Central banking in the British dominions*, University of Toronto Press, Canada.

Priestley, Raymond 2002, *The diary of a Vice-Chancellor. University of Melbourne 1935–1936*, ed. Ronald Ridley, Melbourne University Press, Melbourne.

Reynolds, John c.1951, *L. F. Giblin: a plea for an adequate biography and some Tasmanian incidents*, The Ingamells Collection, Flinders University Library.

Richmond, S. M. 1983, 'S. M. Bruce and Australian economic policy 1923–9', *Australian Economic History Review*, vol. 23, no. 2, pp. 238–57.

Robson, Lloyd 1983, *A history of Tasmania*, Oxford University Press, Melbourne.

Roe, Michael 1991, 'The best and most practical mind: J. B. Brigden as an educator and economist, 1921–30', *Journal of Australian Studies, no. 30*.

——1984, *Nine Australian progressives: vitalism in bourgeois social thought, 1890–1960*, University of Queensland Press, St. Lucia, Qld.

Ross, A. T. 1995, *Armed and ready: the industrial development and defence of Australia, 1900–1945*, Turton and Armstrong, Sydney.

Ross, Lloyd 1983, *John Curtin: a biography*, Sun Books, Melbourne.

Salter, W. E. G. 1959, 'Internal and external balance: the role of price and external expenditure effects', *Economic Record*, vol. 35, no. 2, pp. 226–38.

Samuelson, Marion Crawford 1939, 'The Australian case for protection reexamined', *Quarterly Journal of Economics*, vol. 54, no. 1, pp. 143–51.

Samuelson, Paul A. 1981, 'Summing up on the Australian case for protection', *Quarterly Journal of Economics*, vol. 96, no. 1, pp. 147–60.

—— 1987, 'Joint authorship in science: serendipity with Wolfgang Stolper', *Journal of Institutional and Theoretical Economics*, vol. 143, no. 2, pp. 235–43.

—— 1994, 'Tribute to Wolfgang Stolper on the fiftieth anniversary of the Stolper-Samuelson Theorem', in *The Stolper-Samuelson theorem: A golden jubilee*, eds Alan V. Deardoff & Robert M. Stern, University of Michigan Press, Ann Arbor.

Sawer, Geoffrey, 1963, *Australian federal politics and law, 1929-1949*, Melbourne University Press, Melbourne.

Scarrow, Herbert A. 1957, *The higher public service of the Commonwealth of Australia*, Duke University Press, Durham, NC.

Schedvin, C. B. 1970, *Australia and the Great Depression: a study of economic development and policy in the 1920s and 1930s*, revised edition 1988, Sydney University Press, Sydney.

Schwoner, Alfred 1930, 'Die Anstosswirkung der Gütervermehrung auf die Konjunktur', *Archiv für Sozailwissenschaft und Sozial Politik*, pp. 43–63.

Scott, R. H. 1988, *The economic society of Australia: its history 1925–1985*, The Economic Society of Australia, East Ivanhoe.

Selleck, R. J. W. 2003, *The shop: the University of Melbourne 1850–1939*, Melbourne University Press, Melbourne.

Serle, Geoffrey 1993, *Sir John Medley: a memoir*, Melbourne University Press, Melbourne.

—— 1973, *From deserts prophets come: the creative spirit in Australia 1788–1972*, Heinemann, Melbourne.

Shann, E. O. G. 1938, *An economic history of Australia,* Cambridge University Press, Cambridge.

Shann, E. O. G. & Copland, D. B. 1931, *The crisis in Australian finance: 1929 to 1931,* Angus and Robertson, Sydney.

Sidgwick, Henry 1887, *The principles of political economy,* London, Macmillan.

Smithies, A. 1942, 'The behavior of money national income under inflationary conditions', *Quarterly Journal of Economics*, vol. 57, no. 1, pp. 113–28.

Spender, Percy 1972, *Politics and a man,* Collins, Sydney.

Stolper, Wolfgang F. & Samuelson, P. A. 1941, 'Protection and real wages', *Review of Economic Studies*, vol. 9, no. 1, pp. 58–73.

Stone, John 1997, 'Sir Roland Wilson', *Economic Round-up, Department of the Treasury,* AGPS, Canberra.

Sutcliffe, J. T. 1926, *The national dividend: an enquiry into the amount of the national dividend of Australia and the manner of its distribution*, Melbourne University Press, Melbourne.

Sutherlin, Kim 1980, *The struggle for central banking in Australia: The Royal Commission of 1935–1937 on the monetary and banking systems*, Honours thesis, Department of Economic History, Australian National University, Canberra.

Swan, T. 1955 [1963], 'Longer run problems of the balance of payments', paper delivered to ANZAAS, reprinted in *The Australian economy: a volume of readings,* ed. by H.W. Arndt & W.M. Corden. F.W. Cheshire, Melbourne.

—— 1972, 'Overseas investment in Australia: "Treasury Economic Paper, no. 1"', *Economic Record*, vol. 48, no. 122, pp. 282–5.

Thomis, Malcolm I. 1985, *A place of light and learning: the University of Queensland's first seventy-five years*, University of Queensland Press, St Lucia, Qld.

Torrens, Robert 1821, *An essay on the production of wealth*, reprinted 1965, A. M. Kelley, New York.

Viner, Jacob 1929, 'The Australian tariff', *Economic Record*, vol. 5, no. 2, pp. 306–15.

Walker, E. Ronald 1933, *Australia in the world depression*, P. S. King & Son, London.

—— 1947, *The Australian economy in war and reconstruction*, Oxford University Press, New York.

Walker, James Backhouse 1976, *Prelude to Federation 1884–1898: extracts from the journal of James Backhouse Walker, FRGS, legal practitioner, historian, author*, ed. Peter Benson Walker, O.B.M. Publishing, Hobart.

Watts, Robert William 1983, '*The light on the hill: the origins of the Australian welfare state 1935–1945*', PhD thesis, University of Melbourne.

—— 1987, *The foundations of the national welfare state*, Allen & Unwin, Sydney.

Webb, Sidney 1899, *Facts for socialists: from the political economists and statisticians*, Fabian tract no. 5, Fabian Society, London.

White, Kate 1987, *A political love story: Joe and Enid Lyons*, Penguin, Ringwood.

Whitwell, Greg 1986, *The Treasury line*, Allen and Unwin, Sydney.

Wilkinson, L. P. 1981, *Kingsmen of a century 1873–1972*, King's College, Cambridge.

Wilson, Andrew 2001, 'Forest exploration, assessment and mapping in the Weld Valley, Tasmania 1925', *Tasforests*, vol. 13, no. 1, pp. 9–21.

Wilson, J. S. G. 1952, review of 'The growth of a central bank – the development of the Commonwealth Bank of Australia, 1924–1945', *Economica*, vol. 19, no. 76, pp. 447–8.

Wilson, Roland 1931a, 'Australian monetary policy reviewed', *Economic Record*, vol. 7, no. 2, pp. 195–215.

—— 1931b, *Capital imports and the terms of trade, examined in the light of sixty years of Australian borrowings*, Melbourne University Press, Melbourne.

—— 1932, 'Unemployment in Australia', *Revista di Assicurazioni Sociali*, vol. 1.

—— 1951, 'James Bristock Brigden: a tribute', *Economic Record*, vol. 27, no. 1, pp. 1–10.

—— 1976, 'L. F. Giblin: a man for all seasons', *Search*, vol. 7, no. 7, pp. 307–14.

—— 1984, 'Interview with Sir Roland Wilson', interviewed by Cameron Hazlehurst & Colin Forster, National Library of Australia, Canberra.

Working, Holbrook 1923, 'Prices and the quantity of circulating medium, 1890–1921', *Quarterly Journal of Economics*, vol. 37, no. 2, pp. 228–56.

Wright, A. L. 1956, 'The genesis of the multiplier theory', *Oxford Economic Papers*, vol. 8, no. 2, pp. 181–93.

Index

Advisory War Council, 192
Aircraft Production, Department of, 179
Alexander, D., 139
Anderson, Karl, 70
Archibald Prize, 233
armament program. See Munitions, Department of
art, 133, 142–4
Atlantic Charter, 201
Australia. See also economic policy; Federation
　1872 compared to 1951, 1
　in 1930, 111–12
Australia, 1930 (Giblin), 85, 89, 92, 94, 95, 97, 99n28, 125, 127
Australian Imperial Force (AIF), 16
Australian Labor Party (ALP), 22, 121
　and Copland, 182
　and the Economic Research Act, 74
　Giblin joins, 14–16
　and the IMF, 208
　and national insurance, 170
　and public administration, 162
　and spending cuts, 126
　and the Second World War, 197
　and war financing, 191, 192
Australian National University (ANU), 56, 216–23
Australian Tariff: an Economic Enquiry, 65–8, 103
　significance for Australian economics, 71–3
　theoretical significance of, 68–71
'Australian tariff and the standard of living' (Brigden), 64, 63–5, 70
Austria, 49
autarky, 65

Bailey, K. H., 214, 215, 216
Bank of England, 228, 229–30
Bank of New South Wales, 117
banking, 149, 164, 187
Bastable, Charles, 64, 70, 71
Bean, Charles, 231

Beasley, J. A., 182
Bell, Vanessa, 8, 18
Belshaw, Horace, 79

Benham, F. C., 63, 72, 90
Blake, J. D. 139
Blakely, Arthur, 74n17, 120
Blanc, Louis, 154
Blatchford, Robert, 133–4
Bloomsbury group, 8–9, 18, 85
borrowing, 53, 54, 56
　during the Second World War, 186–8, 190, 192, 193
Brave New World (A. Huxley), 141–2
Brigden, James Bristock, 22–6, 313-2, 226. See also Australian Tariff; economics
　'The Australian tariff and the standard of living', 64, 63–5, 70
　and Bureau of Economic Research, 78–9
　and central bank borrowing, 186–7
　and 'child endowment', 76
　and Copland, 67
　Credit, 138
　death of, 235
　and economic policy, 226
　The Economics of Lyell, 36
　Escape to prosperity, 118n20, 135
　and the F&E Committee, 178
　on federalism, 160
　and Giblin, 23n43, 58n22, 90, 213
　and the Great Depression, 108–11, 117–19, 127
　and the writing of Depression history, 129–30
　and grants to states, 151–3
　and the IMF, 209–13
　and international agreements, 202–3
　and Keynes, 129, 210
　and the multiplier, 88, 89–90
　and national insurance, 164–73
　personal attributes, 38, 108
　'Population supported by 1,000 pounds by new export production', 88, 89
　and the Quantity Theory, 50
　in Queenstown, 36–7
　as radio communicator, 135

Railway economics, 137–8
retirement of, 212–13
and the Second World War, 177–82, 195–8
The Story of sugar, 137
and the Tasmanian University, 37
and the 'Theodore Plan', 119
and Wilson, 42
Brigden Report. See Australian Tariff: an Economic Enquiry
Brigden, Dorothy (née James), 26, 37
Britain, 176, 209, 211, 212. See also Bank of England; Niemeyer, Sir Otto
British Economic Mission of 1928, 73, 161
Bruce, Sir Wallace, 121, 122, 123
Bruce, Stanley Melbourne, 59, 61n2, 66, 67, 72, 73, 78, 123
Bulletin, 24, 142n23, 175
Bullock, C. J., 66
'Bunny'. See Garnett, David
Bureau of Census and Statistics, 161
Bureau of Economic Research, 73–9, 120
Burton, Eilean, 19. See also Giblin, Eilean

Cain senior, John, 130
Cairncross, A. K., 94n21
Calwell, Arthur, 182
Canada, 9–11
Canberra, 178–9
Canberra University College, 212n7, 217
Cannan, Professor Edwin, 25, 46, 49, 50, 68n7, 90
Capital imports and the terms of trade examined in the light of sixty years of Australian borrowing (Wilson), 53–7
capitalism, 22, 24, 132
Carruthers, Reverend George, 138
Case for Tasmania, 1930, (Giblin), 154, 156
Casey, Richard G., 141, 163–73, 186, 197–8, 230
censorship, 133, 140–2
Central Council of the Economic Society, 61, 73
Chifley, Joseph Benedict ('Ben'), 74, 197, 201. See also Labor Governments
and the Commonwealth Bank, 229
and economic policy, 193, 194, 224
and full employment, 202
and the IMF, 212
'child endowment', 76–8, 191
Churchill, Winston, 45, 48, 177
Clapham, Sir John, 18, 124
Clarke, Inglis, 32, 70n10, 150
Clay, Henry, 26
Clearing Union, 208, 209
Cobbett, William, 37
commercial banks, 116, 230
Commonwealth Bank of Australia, 113, 114, 116, 119, 161, 164
Board, 100, 165, 230
history of, 227–31
and war financing, 186, 187, 188
Commonwealth Grants Commission, 152, 153–4, 157–60
Commonwealth Public Service, 161, 164. See also public administration
Commonwealth Public Service Act 1933, 162
Commonwealth Statistician
Giblin (Acting), 96, 120, 161
C. H. Wickens, 66, 120
Wilson, 163, 207
Communist Party of Australia, 139–40, 170
Condliffe, J. B., 79
Conrad, Joseph, 13n22
Coombs, H. C., 56, 175n3, 197
and the ANU, 218
and economic policy, 187, 188, 226
and the F&E Committee, 178, 187
and full employment, 225
and international agreements, 201, 202
Copland, Douglas Berry, 26–8, 165–70, 208n1, 237n44. See also Australian Tariff; economics.
and the ANU, 218–23
and Brigden, 67
and the Brigden Report, 66–8, 72
and the Bureau of Economic Research, 73, 78
and 'child endowment', 76–8
and economic policy, 223–6
Facts and fallacies of Douglas Credit, 138

and the F&E Committee, 178
and Giblin, 33–5, 91, 231–3, 238
Giblin: The scholar and the man (ed.), 237
and the Great Depression, 108–9, 110n8, 112, 116, 117, 122, 127, 128–9
health collapses, 33, 121–2
and the IMF, 211–12
and Keynes, 48, 51, 102n34, 107
'Melbourne Report', 67
and Melbourne University, 59, 60–3, 66, 90–2, 213–16
and the multiplier, 87–8
and Niemeyer, 113
A Plan for economic readjustment (with Giblin and Dyason), 115
personal attributes, 26–7, 33, 34, 38, 108, 215
and Quantity Theory, 51–2
during the Second World War, 174n3, 176, 177–8, 182
and University of Tasmania, 32–5
and the Theodore Plan, 119
and the United States, 48, 200
and wage cuts, 130
and war financing, 188, 189
and Wilson, 38, 41, 238
Copland Plan, 120–1, 126. See also Premiers' Plan
Council for Scientific and Industrial Research (CSIR), 66, 73
Credit (Brigden), 138
credit expansion, 110, 117, 118, 119, 188, 193, 209, 224
Curtin, John, 14, 121, 158, 210
and the Bureau of Economic Research, 74, 75–6
and 'child endowment', 77, 78
and Giblin, 135–6, 194
and the Second World War, 175, 182
and Wilson, 201

Dargie, William, 233–5
Darling, Sir James, 6n12, 214
Davidson, Sir Alfred, 117–18, 232
De Lissa, Alfred, 86–7
defence, 14

defence spending, 184, 193
deficits, relief for, 153–4
'deflation', 115, 128n33
democracy, 131, 149
Depression of 1930s. See Great Depression
devaluation, 118
Dickinson, G. Lowes, 8n18, 18, 214
direct controls, 189, 193–4, 224
Dobell, William, 232–5
Douglas, Paul, 46
Downing, Dick, 191
Dulles, John Foster, 205
'Dutch Disease', 45, 55
Dyason Foundation Psychology of Conflict, 227
Dyason, E. C., 66, 115, 117, 227

Eccles, J. C., 46n2
economic policy, 109, 185, 193, 194, 199, 223–27
Economic Record, 52, 59, 61–4, 75, 132
economic reform, 149
Economic Research Act, 73, 78
Economic Society of Australia and New Zealand, 59, 61, 73, 75
economics, 91n14, 132–3, 135
study of, 32–3, 45–6, 59–64
Economics of Lyell, (Brigden), 36
economists, 10, 48, 49, 120, 226. See also economics
and Curtin, 75, 76
in public life, 41, 59, 71–2, 73, 79, 107–8, 114
and wage cuts, 125
Edgeworth, Professor F. Y., 25, 64
Eggleston, F. W., 152, 157, 221
Escape to prosperity (Brigden), 118n20, 135
Europe, 48, 177
Evatt, H. V., 182, 202, 203
expansionary policy, 96, 97, 108, 117, 118, 124, 130
Eyeless in Gaza (A. Huxley), 141–2

Facts and fallacies of Douglas Credit (Copland), 138
Fadden, Arthur, 191, 192, 193

federalism, 154, 160
Federation, 149, 150–60
Financial and Economic Committee (F&E), 178, 185–91, 192–4, 199, 201
financial relations of the states, 150
'First Manifesto', 112, 114
Firth, Gerald, 197, 199, 225n25
Firth, Raymond, 217
fiscal equalisation, 154–60
Fisher, Irving, 49, 50
Fitzgerald, T. M., 126
Florey, Howard, 217, 218
Food and Agricultural Conference at Hot Springs (1943), 200n51, 202, 209
Forde, Frank M., 74, 182, 202
Forster, E. M., 148, 237n45
free trade, 68, 69, 72, 199–200. See also protectionism
full employment, 125–6, 187, 198–205, 224, 225, 226
  and Brigden, 129
  and lead-up to IMF, 208, 209, 212

Galton, Francis, 6, 144n26
'gap' methodology, 189
Garland, J. M., 226
Garnett, David ('Bunny'), 8–9, 18, 102n33, 103, 143
Garnett, Edward, 8, 143n24
General theory of employment, interest and money (Keynes), 93, 94–6, 98, 99n29, 103
  and Giblin, 100, 101
Germany, 49, 176
Giblin, Lyndhurst Falkiner. See also Australian Tariff; Financial and Economic Committee
  and the ANU, 217, 222–3
  Australia, 1930, 85, 89, 92, 94, 95, 97, 99n28, 125, 127
  birth of, 1
  and the Bureau of Economic Research, 73, 78, 79
  and Brigden, 23n43, 58n22, 90, 213
  and the Brigden Report, 68, 72
  The Case for Tasmania, 1930, 154, 156
  and censorship, 133, 140–2

  and the Commonwealth Bank, 227–31
  and Commonwealth Grants Commission, 152, 153–4, 157–60
  and Copland, 33–5, 91, 238
  death of, 1, 235–7
  and economic policy, 226–7
  education of, 5–8
  and full employment, 225
  and the gold standard, 52
  and the Great Depression, 108–9, 111, 114–26, 127n31
  and the writing of Depression history, 130
  The Growth of a central bank, 227, 229, 230, 231, 235
  illness, 21n37, 121, 207, 235
  and international agreements, 199–200
  and the IMF, 212
  and Keynes, 39, 96–103
  'Letters to John Smith', 112, 119, 133–5, 140
  and letter-writing, 145–8
  and Melbourne University, 90, 100, 121
  and the multiplier, 85–90, 92, 93–6, 98–9
  and national insurance, 165–70
  'New farms and population', 88–9, 96n23
  and Niemeyer, 113–14
  personal attributes, 8–11, 18, 34, 39–40, 85, 108, 140, 237–8
  A Plan for economic readjustment (with Copland and Dyason), 115
  political outlook, 13–16, 40
  portrait of, 231–5
  'The Recruiting of the public service', 162
  and religion, 1, 4–5
  as Tasmanian Government Statistician, 33–4
  during the Second World War, 174n3, 176–7, 178–9
  outlook on war, 21
  and war finance, 183–5, 186, 187, 188, 191–2, 193, 194
  and Wilson, 38–41, 188, 233, 236, 238
  interest in youth, 8n18, 147–8, 238
Giblin, Edith (Mrs Hall), 145–7
Giblin, Edward Owen, 2
Giblin, Eilean (wife of LFG), 19, 77n21, 145–7, 151, 178, 233

Giblin, Robert Wilkins, 3–4
Giblin, William Robert (father of LFG), 3–4, 6, 150
Giblin: The scholar and the man: papers in memory of Lyndhurst Falkiner Giblin (ed. Copland), 237
Gibson, Sir Robert, 61, 114, 118, 135, 231
gold standard, 45, 49, 50, 51, 52, 113, 209, 212
Grainger, Martin, 9, 10, 11, 13
Grant, Duncan, 8, 18, 101
Great Depression, 37, 72, 97, 109–11, 149
  and economists, 108–9, 116–19
  and the 'First Manifesto', 112
  and the quest for inflation, 114–16
  and the Premiers' Plan, 120–8
  and the Theodore Plan, 119–20
  writing the history of, 128–30
Green, H. C., 165
Greenwood, John, 139
'Gregory Thesis', 45, 54, 55, 57
Gregory, Professor T. E., 98, 113
Gregory, R. G., 57
Gregory, T. E., 163
Growth of a central bank: the development of the Commonwealth Bank of Australia 1924–1945, (Giblin), 227, 229, 230, 231, 235

Hall, Allan Ross, 56
Hancock, W. K. ('Keith') , 72, 217, 218, 221–3
Harrod, Roy, 42, 46, 54–5, 99n29
Harvey, Sir Ernest, 229
Hasluck, Paul, 179
Hawtrey, Ralph, 69, 85n2, 99n29
Heaton, Herbert, 27–8
Heckscher-Ohlin-Samuelson model, 69
Henderson, Arthur, 25
Hight, Professor (Sir) James, 27, 28, 47, 79
Holt, Harold, 141, 178
Hoover, Herbert, 48
Hot Springs conference. See Food and Agricultural Conference
Hutchins School, 6, 145
Huxley, Aldous, 141–2

Hytten, Torlieve, 78, 88, 117, 154, 157n7, 237

industrial relations, 226
inflation, 110, 114–16, 185–8, 189, 194
Ingamells, Rex, 142–4, 237
Inter-departmental Committee on Economic Relations (the ICER), 199
international agreements, 198–205
International Monetary Fund (IMF), 202, 207–213
international trade theory, 63. See also 'modern international trade theory'
Isles, Keith, 52, 197

Jensen, J. K., 181, 196, 197
Jindyworobaks, 142–4
Johnston, R. M., 34
Ju-Jitsu, 11–13

Kahn, Richard, 93, 97n25, 99
Kaldor, Nicholas, 56
Kalecki, Michal, 56, 94
Kershaw, Raymond, 228
Keynes, John Maynard, 18, 56, 140
  invitation to Australia, 123
  and the Brigden Report, 69
  and Copland, 48, 51, 107
  death of, 103, 211
  General theory of employment, interest and money, 93, 94–6, 98, 99n29, 100, 101, 103
  and Giblin, 19–21, 22, 96–103, 107, 189
  and the IMF, 208, 211
  and Lend-Lease, 198, 210
  The Means to prosperity, 99
  and the multiplier, 85, 93, 94–6, 99
  and post-war planning, 201
  and the Ritchie Chair, 90, 91
  and taxation, 190
  Tract on monetary reform, 50
  Treatise on money, 48, 85n2, 97–8, 116n14, 136
  and the Wallace Bruce Report, 124
  and Wilson, 201
Keynes, Lydia Lopokova, 48, 102

Keynesianism, 97, 108, 110–11, 125, 127, 129–30, 183
King's College, Cambridge, 7–9, 99, 101, 102, 103, 143, 148
King's School, Hobart, 11
Klondike gold rush, 9, 10
Knight, Frank, 102

La Nauze, John, 56, 197
Labour and National Service, Department of, 178
Labor Governments
  Chifley, 207, 212
  Curtin, 182, 188, 193, 195
  Fisher, 16
laissez-faire, 63
Lang Government, 108
Lang, Jack (John Thomas), 107, 114n12, 119, 124, 162, 208
  and Giblin, 124–5
League of Nations mandates, 176
Lend-Lease, 198, 210
'Letters to John Smith' (Giblin), 112, 119, 133–5, 140
letter-writing, 145
Lewis, Essington, 181, 182, 195, 196, 197
Lewis, Sir Neil, 22
Liberal Democratic League, 13–14
liberalism, 63
loans, compulsory, 190–1, 192, 193
Lucas, E. V., 8
Lyons, Joseph A., 14, 23n39, 76n18, 96, 98, 114–16, 121, 123. See also UAP Government
  Giblin as advisor to, 16
  and national insurance, 173
  and the Second World War, 175, 176

Macallum, Mungo, 217
MacFarlane, S. G., 183n13, 186
Makin, Norman, 121n25, 182, 195–7
Malinowski, Bronislaw, 48
Mansbridge, Albert, 26, 27
Marschak, Jacob, 102
Marshall, Alfred, 7–8
Masefield, John, 142, 143n24

Massey-Greene, Sir William, 232
maternity allowance, 16
Meade, James E., 46, 56
means test, 171
Means to prosperity, (Keynes), 99
Medley, John ('Jack'), 214–16, 233
Melbourne Chamber of Commerce, 59, 60–1
'Melbourne Report' (Copland), 67
Meldrum, Max, 139
Melville, Leslie, 161, 199, 218, 228n30
  and the ANU, 218
  and Australian Tariff, 70
  and Casey, 163
  and the Commonwealth Bank, 114, 228
  and the F&E Committee, 178, 188
  and Giblin portrait, 232–3
  and the IMF, 210, 211
  and Mutual Aid Agreement, 201
  and monetary policy, 116, 117
  and the Premiers' Plan, 120, 122, 123
Menzies, Robert G., 78, 102, 173, 197
  and the Copland Plan, 121
  and the Second World War, 175, 177, 181, 184, 193, 196
Menzies' Government, 181, 193
Mill, J. S., 15, 53, 54, 55
Miller, Sir Denison, 230
Mills, R. C., 56, 61, 72, 122
'modern international trade theory', 68–9, 71
monetary reform, 49–52
monopoly, 63
Mount Lyell, 35–6
multiplier concept, 31, 94–6, 97, 98–9, 127
  and Cambridge University, 93–4
  and Giblin, 85–90, 92, 93–6, 98–9
  and the Great Depression, 108
  and wage cuts, 126
Munich agreement, 175, 176
Munitions, Department of, 179, 181, 182, 195, 196
Murdoch, Keith, 123
'Mutual Aid Agreement' (Article VII), 198, 199, 201

National Economic Plan, 193–4
national income, 36–7, 109, 112, 127, 184

national insurance, 164–73, 182
national product, 107, 126
National Theatre proposition, 103, 227
Needham, Abraham, 14
New England, 152
'New farms and population' (Giblin), 88–9, 96n23
New South Wales, 155–6, 158, 159
New Zealand, 122
New Zealand Expeditionary Force, 27
Niemeyer, Sir Otto, 112–14, 230
Norman, Montague, 34n11, 230n33
Northern Territory, 158

Ogden, James, 19, 22n39
Ogilvy, A. J., 86
Ohlin, Bertil, 69
old age pensions, 164–5, 173
Oliphant, Marcus, 217
Oriel College, Oxford, 25, 46
Overseas Shipping Representatives Association, 79

Pacific Islands Company, 13
Page, Earl, 152, 173, 230
Palmer, Vance, 233
Passchendaele, Battle of, 18
Pearson, Karl, 6, 7
Pigou, A. C., 55, 98, 99
Pitt Cobbett, William, 37
Plan for economic readjustment, A (Giblin, Copland and Dyason), 115
poetry, 142–4
politics, 132–3
'Population supported by 1,000 pounds by new export production' (Brigden), 88, 89
'post-quantity theorising', 50
Premiers' Plan, 120–30, 182. See also Copland Plan
price control, 189
Priestly, Raymond, 107n3, 213, 214, 215
protectionism, 31, 65, 72. See also Australian Tariff
public administration, 149, 160–4
public opinion, 112, 133, 136, 181
public works, 86, 98, 122–3, 225
purchasing power parity, 77

Quantity Theory, 31, 49–52, 77
Queenstown, 35–6

radicalism, 23
Railway economics (Brigden), 137–8
rationing, 189
Reading, Sir Claude, 228
'Recruiting of the public service' (Giblin), 162
Reddaway, Brian, 100–1, 128
reflation, 116, 117, 118, 185–8
Research School of Social Sciences, ANU, 221
returns-to-labour argument, 64, 70
Reynolds, John, 39
Rhodes Scholarship, 40–1, 144
Ritchie Chair, 90–2, 221
Ritchie, R. B., 90
Rivett, David, 218, 227
Robertson, D. H., 98, 99, 102
Robinson, E. A. G., 100, 102
Robinson, Joan, 98, 100n30
Rockefeller, Nelson, 205
Roosevelt, President F. D., 202
Royal Commission on Banking and Monetary Policy (January 1936–July 1937), 164
Russell, Bertrand, 19, 227n29
Russia, 49, 139–40

Salter, Wilfred, 56
Samuelson, Marion Crawford, 70–1
Samuelson, Paul, 68–9, 70–1
Schumpeter, Joseph Alois, 48, 57
Scullin Labor Government, 79, 112, 121, 130
Scullin, James Henry, 74, 112, 114, 116, 119, 126
Shann, Edward Owen Giblin, 2, 70, 116, 117, 120, 122, 163
Sheehan, Sir Harry, 161, 165
'Sidgwick Assumption', 65, 71
Sidgwick, Henry, 64, 70, 71
Singapore, 211
Singer, Kurt, 227
Smithies, Arthur, 56, 57, 221

social reform, 149
socialism, 14, 23, 63, 139
South Australia, 159
Soviet Union. See Russia
Spender, Percy, 183, 184
spending cuts, 126–8
Stabilisation Fund, 208–10
standard of living, 65, 68, 72, 109. See also 'The Australian tariff and the standard of living'
states. See Federation
Stephensen, P. R., 46n2, 143
Stolper, Wolfgang, 69, 70
Stolper-Samuelson theorem, 69, 71
Story of sugar, The (Brigden), 137
sugar, 136–7
Supply and Development, Department of, 177
'Swan Diagram', 56
Swan, Trevor, 55–7, 128n32, 223

Tange, A. H., 210
Tasmania, 5–6, 31–2, 150, 151, 153–7, 158
Tasmanian University Council, 32, 34, 35
Taussig, Frank, 56, 70, 91
taxation, 155–6, 159
   during the Second World War, 184–6, 188, 189, 190–2, 193, 224
terms-of-trade argument, 64, 70
'Theodore Plan', 119, 120
Theodore, Edward Granville, 119, 126
Tichborne Claimant, 42
Tinbergen, Jan, 102
Tract on monetary reform (Keynes), 50
trade preference, 176
Treasury, 161, 163, 228
Treatise on money (Keynes), 48, 85n2, 97–8, 116n14, 136

UAP Government, 136, 158, 165
underconsumptionism, 86, 95
unemployment, 122–3, 130, 135, 137n14, 173, 183–85, 187. See also full employment
   in 1930, 111, 115, 126
United Australia Party (UAP), 121, 183. See also UAP Government

United Kingdom. See Britain
United Nations Charter, 202–5
United States, 199, 200–5. See also International Monetary Fund
   and Copland, 48, 200
   and international economic aid, 198
   and Wilson, 46–7
University Association of Canberra, 161
University of Cambridge, 7–9
   and Copland, 107, 128
   and the multiplier, 93–4
University of Chicago, 46
University of Harvard, 57, 107
University of London, 6, 8
University of Melbourne, 217
   Copland at, 59, 60–3, 66, 90–2, 213–16
   and Giblin, 90, 100, 121
University of Oxford, 42, 45–6
University of Tasmania, 27, 28, 31, 59
   and Brigden, 37
   and Copland, 32–5
   Wilson at, 38, 58
Unwin, Paul, 147–8

vested interests, 136
Victoria, 159
Viner, Jacob, 46–7, 53, 56, 57, 58, 69, 91

wage cuts, 125–6, 134–5, 182
wage maximisation, 65
Walker, E. Ronald, 56, 94n21, 98, 99, 117, 128
Wallace Bruce report, 123, 122–4
Wallace, Alfred, 15
Wallace, R. S., 217
war expenditure, 184, 186, 188, 189, 190, 193
war finance, 103, 185, 187, 189, 192, 193, 194
Ward, Eddie, 208
Warming, Jens, 85n2, 94
Wedd, Nathanial, 32, 148
Western Australia, 152, 158
Wheeler, F. H., 210
White Australia policy, 15, 75
White Paper on Full Employment in Australia, 225

White, Harry Dexter, 209, 210
White, Sir Thomas, 141, 142
Wickens, C. H., 66, 120
Wilkinson, Patrick, 103
Wilson, Roland, 28, 136, 139n16, 228n30
  and the ANU, 221–3
  and Brigden, 38
  Capital imports and the terms of trade, 53–7
  and central bank borrowing, 186
  and 'child endowment', 78
  and Copland, 38, 41, 238
  as debator, 42
  and relief for deficits, 153
  and the F&E Committee, 178
  and Giblin, 38–41, 188, 233, 236, 238
  and the Commonwealth Bank, 161, 228
  and the IMF, 209, 213
  and Isles, 52
  and Oxford University, 42, 45–6
  personal attributes, 38, 47, 205
  at post-war planning conference, 201
  and public administration, 163
  and the Second World War, 177–8, 190, 191, 197–8
  at the University of Tasmania, 38, 58
  at the UN, 212
  and the UN Charter, 202–5
  in the US, 46–7, 202–5
Wilson, Valeska (née Thompson), 47
women, 75, 95, 162n16, 164, 181
Women's Non-Party League of Tasmania, 151
Workers' Education Association (WEA), 25–6, 35
World War, First
  Brigden in, 24–5
  and Copland, 27
  Giblin in, 16–19, 145
  influence of, 45
World War, Second
  1942, 195–8
  arming for, 179–82
  financing of, 183–94
Wright, A. L., 94n21

Yukio Tani, 11–13

www.ingramcontent.com/pod-product-compliance
Lightning Source LLC
Chambersburg PA
CBHW040933240426
43668CB00029B/2445